DATE DUE

GAYLORD			PRINTED IN U.S.A.

Brief Tests of
Collection Strength

Brief Tests of Collection Strength

A Methodology for All Types of Libraries

Howard D. White

Contributions in Librarianship and Information Science,
Number 88

Greenwood Press
Westport, Connecticut • London

Library of Congress Cataloging-in-Publication Data

White, Howard D.
   Brief tests of collection strength : a methodology for all types
of libraries / Howard D. White.
      p.   cm.—(Contributions in librarianship and information
science, ISSN 0084–9243 ; no. 88)
   Includes bibliographical references and index.
   ISBN 0–313–29753–3 (alk. paper)
   1. Collection development (Libraries)—United States—Evaluation.
I. Title.   II. Series: Contributions in librarianship and
information science ; no. 88.
Z687.2.U6W48   1995
025.2'1'0973—dc20   95–2904

British Library Cataloguing in Publication Data is available.

Library of Congress Catalog Card Number: 95–2904
ISBN: 0–313–29753–3
ISSN: 0084–9243

First published in 1995

Greenwood Press, 88 Post Road West, Westport, CT 06881
An imprint of Greenwood Publishing Group, Inc.

Printed in the United States of America

The paper used in this book complies with the
Permanent Paper Standard issued by the National
Information Standards Organization (Z39.48–1984).

10 9 8 7 6 5 4 3

for Maryellen McDonald

Contents

Tables and Figures   i x
Acknowledgments   x i

Part One: The Methodology

1 A Collection-Centered Measure for All Types of Libraries   3
2 Problems of the Past   15
3 The Logic of the Test   33

Part Two: Results

4 Setting Levels   55
5 Verifying Levels   73
6 Gains in Strength through a Consortium   89
7 The French Literature Test   107

Part Three: The OCLC Database and Holdings Counts

8 Creating New Tests   123

Appendix A: Eight Specimen Brief Tests   153

American History   153
American Studies   159
Classical Music   161
Cultural Anthropology   165
French Literature   169
Genetics   172
Mathematics   175
Policy Studies   179

Appendix B: Additional Brief Tests   183
Bibliography   185
Index   189

Tables and Figures

Table 1.1   RLG Definitions of Collecting Levels   5
Table 1.2   Titles by Number of 'Consortium' Libraries Holding Them   8
Table 1.3   Titles in One Library by 'Consortium' Scale   9
Table 1.4   Titles in Individual Libraries by 'Consortium' Scale   9
Table 1.5   Titles in Individual Libraries by RLG Libraries Holding Them   10

Table 2.1   Results of French Literature Verification Study, 1983   16
Table 2.2   Sample Items from RLG Verification Study in Genetics   18
Table 2.3   RLG Verification Studies Completed   19
Table 2.4   Four Hypothetical Schemes for Converting Coverage to Levels   21
Table 2.5   Hypothetical Scheme for Collection Sizes at Four RLG Levels   23
Table 2.6   WLN or Pacific Northwest Conspectus Guidelines for Interpreting Finer-Grained Collection Levels   24
Table 2.7   Sample Form from Consortium X Collection Inventory Project   26

Table 3.1   Hypothetical Outcome of Brief Test   37
Table 3.2   Counterhypothetical Outcome of Brief Test   38
Table 3.3   Ideal Guttman Scale   39
Table 3.4   Titles in Byzantine Studies: Assignment to RLG Levels by OCLC Counts and by Selector   45
Figure 3.1   Two Hypothetical Tests with Different Ranges of Difficulty   46

Table 4.1   Percentage Patterns in 268 Brief-Test Trials   59
Table 4.2   RLG Levels Attained with Brief Tests   64
Table 4.3   Validation Trials in Setting Levels with Brief Tests   70

Table 5.1   Librarians' Ratings and Brief-Test Ratings of RLG Levels at Two Universities   76
Figure 5.1   Comparison of Levels Subjectively Claimed and Set by Brief Tests at Two Universities   77
Table 5.2   WLN Collection Level Indicators   79

Table 5.3	Special Rules for Using Brief Tests with WLN Scale	80
Table 5.4	Hypothetical Relationship between WLN and RLG Scales	81
Table 5.5	Comparisons of Librarians' Ratings and Brief-Test Ratings of RLG Levels at Three Virginia Libraries	83
Figure 5.2	Claimed Collection Level by Brief-Test Level	85
Figure 5.3	Claimed Acquisition Commitment Level by Brief-Test Level	85
Table 6.1	Collection Levels Achieved by Tri-College Consortium	91
Table 6.2	Detailed Scores across Levels for Colleges Singly and Jointly	92
Table 6.3	Number and Magnitude of Gains per College	94
Figure 6.1	Actual Tests with Different Ranges of Difficulty	95
Figure 6.2	American History	97
Figure 6.3	American Studies	98
Figure 6.4	Classical Music	99
Figure 6.5	Cultural Anthropology	100
Figure 6.6	French Literature	101
Figure 6.7	Genetics	102
Figure 6.8	Mathematics	103
Figure 6.9	Policy Studies	104
Figure 6.10	Social Theory	105
Table 7.1	The RLG French Literature Sample	108
Table 7.2	The RLG Sample and the Brief Test in French Literature Compared	110
Figure 7.1	French Literature Test Results for 22 Libraries	112
Figure 7.2	Median Percentages of French Literature Holdings for Two Groups of Libraries across RLG Scale	114
Table 7.3	Percentage Scores and Levels Claimed and Attained in the French Literature Test	115
Table 7.4	Total Counts and Rankings in 1983 Verification Study and 1993 Brief Test in French Literature	116
Figure 7.3	French Literature Test Results as 'Strata'	118
Figure 8.1	Hypothetical Frequency Distribution of Titles Held by Various Numbers of Libraries	125
Figure 8.2	Empirical Frequency Distribution of Titles Held by Various Numbers of Libraries	127
Table 8.1	Levels of RLG Scale Mapped to Ranges on Holdings-Count Scale	127
Figure 8.3	Holdings-Count and RLG Scales Calibrated	130
Figure 8.4	Ranges of Holdings Counts Assigned to RLG Levels before and after Discriminant Analysis of Titles	133
Table 8.2	Joint Prediction of Levels by Mechanical 10s Method and by Discriminant Function	134
Table 8.3	Titles Ranked Highest and Lowest in Eight Brief Tests	140
Table 8.4	Hypotheses on Variation in Characteristics of Titles at RLG Levels 1 through 4	142
Table 8.5	Hypothetical Distribution of In-print Status by RLG Level	143
Table 8.6	Hypothetical Mixes of Libraries Contributing to Holdings Counts at Different Levels	144

Acknowledgments

This book grew out of many opportunities, for all of which I am grateful. The persons and organizations providing them should not, of course, be charged with its errors or infelicities. They, along with the methodological decisions and interpretation of results, are solely mine.

The first major impetus came from OCLC in 1987: a Library School Research Equipment Support Grant of an M-310 workstation to explore the idea of brief tests, then new.

The second was the Drexel Tri-College Research Project, funded by the U.S. Department of Education during 1988–1991, in which the tests were tried at Bryn Mawr, Haverford, and Swarthmore Colleges with the advice of Linda Bills, Robert Kieft, Susan Williamson, Steven Sowards, and Trudy Reed. I thank my colleagues Belver Griffith and Thomas Childers, who led Drexel's participation in the Tri-College project, and especially our coordinator, Cynthia Lopata, now of Syracuse University, for her invaluable efforts in the early trials of my methodology.

I also owe debts to providers of intellectual stimulation in matters of collection assessment before and after the work on brief tests began. I thank the Council of Library Resources for its senior fellows program at the University of California at Los Angeles in 1983; the School of Library and Information Studies, University of California at Berkeley, where I spent a term teaching collection development in 1985; and the Association of Research Libraries, sponsor of the Institute on Research Libraries for Library and Information Science Faculty, held in Chicago in 1988.

Drexel University granted two faculty leaves: one made the visiting professorship at Berkeley possible; the other permitted the writing of parts of this book during 1992–1993.

Several organizations have allowed me to address them on brief tests and to receive informal feedback from their members. I thank the Philadelphia Area Reference Librarians' Information Exchange (1989); the METRO Collection Management Institute of the New York Metropolitan Reference and Research Library

Agency (1989); the American Library Association's Library Research Round Table (1990); the staffs of Temple University's Paley Library and Drexel University's Hagerty Library (1991); the Pennsylvania Library Association (1993); the PALINET Seminar (1994); and Beta Phi Mu's Philadelphia chapter (1994).

Individuals from whose conversations and good offices I have benefitted during my work include Paul Mosher, J. Dennis Hyde, and Stephen Lehmann of the University of Pennsylvania; Frances Hopkins and Cornelia Tucker of Temple University; Jeffrey J. Gardner of the Association of Research Libraries; Michael Buckland, William S. Cooper, and Sheila Dowd of the University of California, Berkeley; Elaine Svenonius of the University of California, Los Angeles; Ross Atkinson of Cornell University; Anthony W. Ferguson of Columbia University; Thomas A. Lucas of the New York Public Library; Jim Coleman of the Research Libraries Group; Larry L. Nesbit of Mansfield University; Jeanne-Elizabeth Combs of PALINET; Collette Mak of OCLC; Helen Hughes of AMIGOS; and Sally Loken of WLN. I have twice been a guest of the Research Libraries Group's Conspectus Subcommittee and received highly useful documents at their meetings.

My honor roll of selectors appears in Appendices A and B. I could not have proceeded without their generosity in both creating and administering tests.

Another major group of contributors were librarians who used brief tests by others to check their holdings. I thank Joyce MacDonald, coordinator of the Piedmont Area Collection Assessment Program, and her team for the data appearing in Chapter 5. Librarians responding to my request for assistance with the brief test for French literature, which helped make Chapter 7 possible, were Russell Clement, Brigham Young University; Dwayne Davies, Brown University; Evelyn Haynes, Colorado State University; Marcia Jebb, Cornell University; Robert D. Jaccaud, Dartmouth College; Charles S. Fineman, Northwestern University; John R. Kaiser, Pennsylvania State University; Lawrence Gorman, University of Iowa; and Yvonne Wulf, University of Michigan.

To my wife, Maryellen McDonald, I owe the greatest debt of all. She has encouraged me in this project since its earliest days and worked with me on it in all its parts. It is truly her project, too. No one could deserve the dedication of a book more.

PART ONE

The Methodology

CHAPTER 1

A Collection-Centered Measure for All Types of Libraries

INTRODUCTION

The two most important determinants of quality in library collections are money, which is everyone's favorite measure, and love, which is unquantifiable. It seems wise to admit their primacy at the outset, because the present work speaks directly to neither. At best it registers effects of their combined power.

What is described here is use of a new, relatively brief test to assign libraries a score for existing collection strength in a subject area. The test draws on both expert human judgment and holdings data from the union catalog of the Online Computer Library Center (OCLC). It can assist in setting or verifying collection levels. These are now set impressionistically and verified only with great labor.

After supplying some background and sketching the problems that make this work timely, I give the reasoning behind the tests and tell how they are created and administered. I then exhibit, in several chapters, the results of hundreds of trials in scores of subjects at dozens of U.S. libraries. The final chapter is devoted to ideas for improving the tests and for extending the lines of inquiry they have opened. Some critical commentary on procedures and terminology now current in collection evaluation will be found along the way.

Very little on brief tests has appeared in the literature to date. After publishing a short account of the earliest trials (White, 1988), I presented further results at public and private meetings. A fair number of attendees found the methodology promising, and two (Lucas, 1990; Coleman, 1992) have mentioned it in print. Other public notices (Schenck, 1990; Siverson, 1992; Coffey, 1992) are based on my 1988 paper.[1] News also seems to have reached various people through professional grapevines. This book, long in progress, is the first full rendering of developmental work and empirical outcomes. It covers the period 1987–1994.

Brief tests emerge from the collection evaluation movement that has influenced American librarianship for more than a decade. In the Research Libraries

Group (RLG), the movement produced the Conspectus for making information on members' subject-collection strengths explicit and nationally available, thereby promoting coordinated acquisitions and resource sharing (Gwinn and Mosher, 1983; Ferguson et al., 1988; Mosher, 1990; Coleman, 1992; Ferguson, 1992; Grant, 1992). The RLG idea was adopted by the Association of Research Libraries in the North American Collections Inventory Project (Miller, 1987). It also was recast for smaller libraries in tools such as the Pacific Northwest Conspectus (Forcier, 1988) and the *WLN Collection Assessment Manual* (Johnson, 1991; Powell and Bushing, 1992).[2] Interest in Conspectus-style evaluation is now international (e.g., Hanger, 1987; Crandlemire and Otto, 1988; Farrell and Reed-Scott, 1989; Henri, 1989; Heaney, 1990; Matheson, 1987, 1990).

Librarians in this movement state publicly at what level they collect in major subject categories (Jakubs, 1989; Wood, 1992). Usually the statements are part of written policies shared in consortia. The levels developed by RLG for that purpose make up an ordinal scale of 0 to 5, as in Table 1.1, which has glosses from Gwinn and Mosher (1983). In the Supplemental Guidelines for broad subject divisions of the Conspectus (such as agriculture or music), the glosses include standard bibliographic tools against which holdings, particularly serials, may be checked (cf. Coleman, 1992; Coffey, 1992; Underwood, 1992).

Within these broad subject divisions, literatures are defined by ranges of the Library of Congress (LC)—or possibly Dewey—classification scheme. These are generally called "Conspectus lines," and they number about 7,000 (Nisonger, 1992, pp. 120–121). The RLG scale is used to rate Conspectus lines, not entire collections. Throughout this book, references to "collections" usually mean subject subcollections, such as those associated with Conspectus lines.

Although the developers of the scale do not always make it explicit, the levels are cumulative in nature.[3] For example, a Level 3 collection would presumably also meet the criteria for Levels 1 and 2. This point is expanded later.

Brief tests produce readings on the RLG scale. (Their use with the version of the scale in the WLN *Manual* is discussed in Chapter 5.) If librarians have not assigned levels to their subcollections, brief tests would be used to assign them. If librarians have already set levels, brief tests would be used to verify their judgments. Given limited time and resources, the tests may be more useful in the latter case, when a preset level is actually in doubt.

In real life, librarians doing Conspectus-style evaluation sit at high-piled desks on rainy afternoons, look at lines naming subject literatures, think about the collection—what they know from the shelflist, user comments, their own browsing—and say things like, "Well, I guess we're a 2 on that one." But they can be construed as responding to RLG scale-items as to questions literally on a questionnaire:

Does your collection meet the requirements of Level 1?	Yes	No
Does it also meet the requirements of Level 2?	Yes	No
Does it also meet the requirements of Level 3?	Yes	No
Does it also meet the requirements of Level 4?	Yes	No
Does it also meet the requirements of Level 5?	Yes	No

TABLE 1.1

RLG Definitions of Collecting Levels

0 *Out of Scope:* The library does not collect in this area.

1 *Minimal Level:* A subject area in which few selections are made beyond very basic works. For foreign law collections, this includes statutes and codes.

2 *Basic Information Level:* A collection of up-to-date general materials that serve to introduce and define a subject and to indicate the varieties of information available elsewhere. It may include dictionaries, encyclopedias, selected editions of important works, historical surveys, bibliographies, handbooks, a few major periodicals, in the minimum number that will serve the purpose. A basic information collection is not sufficiently intensive to support any courses or independent study in the subject area involved. For law collections, this includes selected monographs and loose-leafs in American law and case reports and digests for foreign law.

3 *Instructional Support Level:* A collection that is adequate to support undergraduate and most graduate instruction, or sustained independent study; that is, adequate to maintain knowledge of a subject required for limited or generalized purposes, of less than research intensity. It includes a wide range of basic monographs, complete collections of the works of more important writers, selections from the secondary writers, a selection of representative journals, and the reference tools and fundamental bibliographical apparatus pertaining to the subject. In American law collections, this includes monographs.

4 *Research Level:* A collection that includes the major published source materials required for dissertations and independent research, including materials containing research reporting new findings, scientific experimental results, and other information useful to researchers. It is intended to include all important reference works and a wide selection of specialized monographs, as well as a very extensive collection of journals and major indexing and abstracting services in the field. Older material is retained for historical research. Government documents are included in American and foreign law collections.

5 *Comprehensive Level:* A collection in which a library endeavors, so far as is reasonably possible, to include all significant works of recorded knowledge (publications, manuscripts, other forms), in all applicable languages, for a necessarily defined and limited field. This level of collecting intensity is one that maintains a "special collection"; the aim, if not the achievement, is exhaustiveness. Older material is retained for historical research. In law collections, this includes manuscripts, dissertations, and material on nonlegal aspects.

Language Coverage Codes

E English language material predominates; little or no foreign language material is in the collection.

F Selected foreign language material included in addition to English language material.

W Wide selection of material in all applicable languages. No programmatic decision is made to restrict materials according to language.

Y Material is primarily in one foreign language. The overall focus is on collecting material in the vernacular of the area.

Assuming they respond as expected, their answers would scale cumulatively. But to what do the question-items actually refer? They refer to the possession of works—of titles. The questions about levels are really very coarse-grained inquiries about what titles librarians have. Since brief tests represent the items of the scale with titles, they are grounded in this underlying reality. Indeed, a way of understanding brief tests is to see them as converting a few coarse-grained questions about levels into at least 40 finer-grained questions about titles, in hopes of confirming one's intuitions about a collection.

FOR ALL TYPES OF LIBRARIES

Brief tests have been tried most often in large academic libraries—for example, at the University of Pennsylvania ("Penn"), which has extensive research collections and is an RLG member. But that is merely a contingency of how and where they were developed.[4] The prevalence of such sites in this book should not be taken to imply that brief tests are not potentially useful elsewhere. They have been tried successfully in other types of libraries, and those results, too, though still rather scant, are presented later. Brief tests are, in fact, usable by librarians in any setting as long as they are interested in defining their collections by level on a scale such as the one developed by the RLG.

Despite its provenance, RLG's scale (or the variant found in the WLN *Manual*) is usable by libraries generally. Its use does not entail participation in the elaborate Conspectus project, which most public, special, and school librarians probably see as beyond their capabilities (and which has detractors even in academe—e.g., Henige, 1987). The scale, of course, reflects the capabilities of large libraries that support the creation of new knowledge, and librarians who use the scale (or something similar) for registering subject collections of less than Level 4 will necessarily see their collections in the context of these regional and national powerhouses. But that is all to the good: most librarians support the idea of integrated hierarchies of collections, with strength related to the needs of particular clienteles.

What they may need to reject is the inference that the only collections worth registering are at the high end, where doctoral and postdoctoral research is supported, or in subjects read by only the specialized few, such as Swiss history. Since librarians already know that basic, nonresearch collections are a positive virtue for most clienteles, improvement lies in stating and sharing what they know about *these* collections as a matter of policy. When that is done—and it is being tried in many settings other than the largest research libraries (Oberg, 1988; Bushing, 1992)—then the relevance of brief tests for insight into any collection becomes apparent.

It is fair to add that they seem most useful in library consortia, where comparable estimates of collection strength are desirable. Chapters 5, 6, and 7 address this matter in various ways. For example, Chapter 6 shows how they may be used to assess gains in strength when separate collections in a consortium are pooled for joint use. Again, the examples are from academe, but the methodology could be transferred to a school district library system or a public library system with branches.

COLLECTION-CENTERED

In the current terminology (Hall, 1985), brief tests are a collection-centered, rather than a client-centered, measure. That is, they crudely indicate a collection's strength or depth rather than its serviceability. Ideally, it would be better to measure serviceability, since notions of "strength" or "depth" are idle if the collection fails to respond to customer demands. However, measures of collection usefulness or user satisfaction are even more primitive than those of collection strength. We are far from being able to connect what libraries provide with gains in personal enlightenment, even though we know that such gains occur.

The best measure of collection strength might be the fraction of a literature held, but that has not yet been developed in a form for widespread use. (There is no standard definition of what constitutes a literature.) Libraries now are fortunate if they can give percentage breakdowns of their collections in major LC or Dewey subject areas; not too long ago, almost none could, as Machlup (1978) complained. The main reason for the advance is the National Shelflist Count, but participation in that remains quite limited (Nisonger, 1992, pp. 146–148). Another measure, computerized matching of holdings against a standard list such as *Books for College Libraries* (Kreyche, 1989), is still somewhat avant-garde.

Given this state of affairs, the measure represented by the RLG scale (or some counterpart) is worth keeping for the foreseeable future. It emerged from within the profession as a measure of something over which librarians felt they had some control (Ferguson et al., 1988; Coleman, 1992). It has the merit of relating fairly clearly to intended level of service. It compels librarians to think about how, under the permanent constraint of scarce resources, their subject coverage will support institutional goals. It produces readings that can be made meaningful to nonlibrarians, such as faculty members, administrators, or accreditation teams (Treadwell and Spornick, 1991). Perhaps most important, it allows judgments on collections to be communicated succinctly, like the similarly general A-to-F scale for grading students. (Most of the time we do not want the details on which evaluations rest; we want merely the instant overview: "She's a straight-A performer"; "It's a Level 4 collection.")

Of course, the RLG scale need not bear the full weight of collection evaluation, being merely one of a growing number of measures that have been proposed to inform librarians' decisions.[5] Nevertheless, whenever the RLG scale is used, doubts about the subjective assignment of the level codes may arise, and it is in addressing such doubts that brief tests are likely to be helpful. In general, the tests are a response to what Strauch and Wood (1992, pp. 191–192) identify as major drawbacks in the current Conspectus model: "the lack of benchmarks or guidelines which assure that evaluations between and among libraries are consistent" and the lack of resources (time, money, staff) for making Conspectus-style evaluations as useful as their advocates intend.

ORIGIN OF BRIEF TESTS

A background sketch will explain a key idea behind brief tests, whose origin might otherwise seem mysterious.

In 1983, as a senior fellow in the Council of Library Resources summer program at the University of California, Los Angeles, I volunteered to show participants how the Statistical Package for the Social Sciences (SPSS) could be used to produce tables from library holdings data. My data file, new to me at the time, was obtained from the director of the UCLA program, Robert M. Hayes, who had created it to analyze 300 books in science, engineering, and business in a proprietary study for a publisher. In addition to bibliographic descriptions of the 300 titles, the file had data on whether they were held by individual libraries, the latter a judgment sample of 72 nationwide.

By one of the techniques reported in White (1987), I was able to group these real libraries in an imaginary consortium and to look at the distribution of ownership of titles over all 72. That is, each title was assigned a score equal to the number of libraries that held it. These scores ran from 0 (one book was not held by any library) to 60. The average title was held by about 30 libraries, and the rest of the distribution was approximately normal, with a standard deviation of about 10. From this outcome, it was easy to create a six-point scale that ran from titles held by 1–10 libraries to those held by 51–60, as in Table 1.2. Each of the 299 books held by at least one library is in a category on this scale.

TABLE 1.2

Titles by Number of 'Consortium' Libraries Holding Them

Number of Libraries	1-10	11-20	21-30	31-40	41-50	51-60
Titles in Category	7	36	112	98	38	8

In this table, we see the increasing popularity of the 299 titles across the libraries, with the eight top favorites at right. (Those eight, or any other books in the Hayes file, could be retrieved by name if desired.)

Next it was possible to ask: what percentage of titles in these six categories does any *one* library have? Harvard was one of the sites studied, and its percentages, to the base of the numbers in the distribution in Table 1.2, are in Table 1.3.

Harvard holds none of the seven items in the first category; 50 percent (or 18) of the 36 items in the second category, and so on. Just as one might expect, the percentage of titles held increases (with one small irregularity) from left to right. This outcome reflects the fact that, as popularity of titles increases overall—here measured by frequency of holdings in the imaginary consortium—the likelihood of finding those titles in any one library increases as well.

TABLE 1.3

Titles in One Library by 'Consortium' Scale

Harvard University	Number of 'Consortium' Libraries Holding a Title					
	1-10	*11-20*	*21-30*	*31-40*	*41-50*	*51-60*
Held	0%	50%	75%	95%	90%	100%
Not Held	100%	50%	25%	5%	10%	0%
	100%	100%	100%	100%	100%	100%
Titles in Category	7	36	112	98	38	8

This effect is general in the Hayes data. That is, we repeatedly observe a tendency for individual libraries' percentages to rise rightward across the categories of holdings counts, just as the counts themselves rise. Table 1.4 illustrates the tendency for six more of the libraries. Note that this table shows only the percentages of titles held (and omits the complementary percentages not held), to the same numerical bases.

Another way of describing the scale is to say that it measures the "ease"— or, conversely, the "difficulty"—of holding a particular title. Titles that are held

TABLE 1.4

Titles in Individual Libraries by 'Consortium' Scale

Individual Libraries	Number of 'Consortium' Libraries Holding a Title					
	1-10	*11-20*	*21-30*	*31-40*	*41-50*	*51-60*
Boston University	14%	19%	51%	76%	87%	88%
University of Chicago	0%	22%	36%	78%	71%	100%
Rice University	0%	44%	60%	68%	87%	88%
UCLA	0%	53%	79%	94%	100%	100%
New York University	14%	28%	56%	84%	97%	100%
University of Maryland	86%	83%	94%	98%	100%	100%
Titles in Category	7	36	112	98	38	8

by few libraries (like 1–10) are "hard" to hold; titles that are held by many (like 51–60) are "easy" to hold, with the others in between. Analyzed with such scale, the libraries in the Hayes file have lower percentages of the hard items and higher percentages of the easy items. Take, for example, the first library in Table 1.4:

	1-10	*11-20*	*21-30*	*31-40*	*41-50*	*51-60*	<–Scale
Boston U	14%	19%	51%	76%	87%	88%	<–Effect

This "difficulty effect" is the origin of my use of titles as test items. (It is, of course, quite distinct from whatever difficulties of *content* the books may pose.)

Paul Mosher, one of the architects of the Conspectus, was also a senior fellow at UCLA in 1983, and through him I became acquainted with some of the problems of Conspectus management, such as verification of the subjectively set levels (Mosher, 1984). However, I did not pay much attention to the difficulty effect until it reappeared in an unpublished table I obtained on a visit to RLG headquarters in 1985. The data are a by-product of the verification study for French literature (Larson, 1984), in which 20 RLG libraries participated. I reproduce the lines for six of them in Table 1.5. It is read exactly like Table 1.4, except that here the "consortium" comprises the 20 RLG participants, and the scale (italicized) is grouped in increments of five.

Reading rightward, one sees again that the more likely the 20 consortium members are to hold a title, the more likely individual libraries are to hold it. This result independently confirmed the effect in the Hayes data and led to the idea that the different levels of difficulty in holding titles might be exploited to put the

TABLE 1.5

Titles in Individual Libraries by RLG Libraries Holding Them

Individual Libraries	Number of RLG Libraries Holding a Title			
	1-5	*6-10*	*11-15*	*16-20*
UC Berkeley	31%	72%	91%	97%
Brigham Young University	7%	15%	38%	80%
University of Michigan	18%	56%	80%	91%
Penn State University	4%	21%	42%	75%
Cornell University	13%	58%	90%	99%
Yale University	32%	69%	89%	98%
Titles in Category	272	164	207	235

levels of the RLG scale on a somewhat more objective basis. As explained in Chapter 3, this is done by creating four levels of difficulty in a set of titles that define a subject and equating them with Levels 1 through 4. Level 0, at which the library collects nothing, and Level 5, at which the library attempts to collect everything, are not considered problematical.

As the foundation of brief tests, the difficulty effect reappears often in later chapters. One point must be explained, however. In the preceding tables, the ascending count of holding libraries puts the "hardest" test items on the left and the "easiest" on the right. In the Hayes study:

Hardest *1-10* *11-20* *21-30* *31-40* *41-50* *51-60* Easiest

And in the French Literature verification study:

Hardest *1-5* *6-10* *11-15* *16-20* Easiest

If the RLG scale is made to run in the same way, its numbers are reversed:

Hardest 4 3 2 1 Easiest

That is because the relationship between the RLG scale and any scale of holdings counts is inverse—low values on one scale go with high values on the other, and vice versa. In the chapters to come, presentation of the RLG numbers in conventional left-to-right order makes the underlying order of difficulty run as follows:

Easiest 1 2 3 4 Hardest

DIFFICULTY AND CUMULATIVENESS

What produces the difficulty effect? A commonsensical explanation is that, in any sizable literature, certain titles are "must buys"; they are the sorts of things that most librarians want to have if they buy in a given literature at all. Thus, if it is highly probable that many libraries will buy an item, it is highly probable that any one library, examined singly, will buy it.

One would expect reviewing sources popular with librarians, such as *Choice, Magazines for Libraries,* or the *New York Times Book Review,* to reinforce the notion that some things must be purchased, but the tendency would very likely exist even without them. An issue of the RLG (1987) *Operations Update,* for example, shows that members' most-cataloged books in mid-1987 were led by the 13th edition of *The Chicago Manual of Style* and the 3d edition of *The Elements of Style* by Strunk and White. These are the sorts of titles that libraries everywhere in the United States simply *get.* Naturally, they are also the sorts of titles that reappear below as Level 1 Minimal items. At the opposite extreme are items about which librarians are distinctly choosy, depending on their clienteles. They may have them, particularly if they work in large libraries with a history of strong collections in certain subjects, but it is more likely that they will not. These, of course, are potential Level 4 Research items. In between are the titles whose probability of being held in any one library varies with their probability of being held in an appropriate reference group of libraries.

This explanation has the merit of suggesting why the levels, as measured in any one library, should be cumulative. In a cumulative scale, attainment of a level implies attainment of all lower levels. In brief tests, the levels are defined by sets of titles, and all the titles can be ranked so as to be increasingly probable as holdings. For example, if we take any four titles with markedly different probabilities of being held and make them stand for the four levels, thus:

Level 4 title	.04
Level 3 title	.21
Level 2 title	.46
Level 1 title	.80

it is clear that any library has an increased chance of holding an item as we move down the levels from 4 to 1. If we move up the levels, it is clear that any library has an increased chance of holding an item at all *lower* levels. This supports the expectation of cumulativeness. Chapter 4 tells how this expectation is borne out by data from real libraries. In general, the best estimate that a title is in one's own collection is the probability that it is in everyone's collection. "Everyone's" may be defined as the largest appropriate reference group about which one has holdings data. In Tables 1.2 to 1.5, the reference groups are artificial and small, created from the very libraries whose collections are being studied. However, a group both real and enormous now provides such data—the membership of OCLC. It is counts of their holdings that are used to create brief tests.

WHY OCLC?

One of the main problems in devising tests of human abilities is creating the pool of questions that will be used. From this standpoint, the *Oxford English Dictionary* might be seen as an admirably large supplier of words for spelling tests. In like fashion, the OCLC online union catalog is an incomparable pool of items for testing libraries. At this writing it contains bibliographic data on more than 29 million titles (OCLC, 1994), and every one of them can be scored as held or not held in collection evaluations, just as one's spelling of any word in the dictionary can be scored as right or wrong in spelling tests. Moreover, OCLC records come with data that can be used like the teacher's sense, in spelling tests, of the relative difficulty of items.

In brief tests, the difficulty of any title as a test item is fixed by the number of OCLC libraries holding it: the more holders, the easier the item; the fewer, the harder. Because the counts reflect the acquisitions of more than 6,700 member libraries (OCLC, 1994), they are highly informative as to a work's reception over time. Ranging from one to several thousand, the counts are generally too large to be much affected by the holdings of any one library and so provide a standard that is virtually independent of whatever collection is being tested. Also, since libraries reporting holdings are of various types (not merely academic), OCLC offers a rich diversity of literatures from which to choose items. For example, if one wants to include in a test such titles as *Baby and Child Care, Gone with the Wind,* or *Green Eggs and Ham,* one can obtain holdings counts that convey their importance in American popular culture.

As used here, titles refer to editions of works. (An edition comprises all copies made from a particular master.) The bibliographic descriptions found in OCLC and other databases identify editions. Beyond their other uses, such descriptions make it possible to select counts for different editions of a work (e.g., *Beowulf*) or to aggregate counts over editions to measure the reception of the work as a whole.

Of course, it takes time for titles to accumulate counts, and only titles that have done so make satisfactory test items. Brief tests are not designed to reveal the currency of a library's acquisitions or how up-to-date its collection is. (There are other tests for doing that.) Still less are they designed to indicate where developmental efforts should be placed in the future. (Those are political decisions arising out of a total milieu.) They are intended for assessing the collection-building activity of the past—perhaps the entire past of the collection. If that is remembered, then they should work well enough in any setting.

Researchers (e.g., Wallace and Boyce, 1989) have just begun to use holdings counts in innovative ways, as something more than a by-product of file creation. The OCLC/AMIGOS Collection Analysis Compact Disc intriguingly suggests the new possibilities. With it, titles in selected library groups can now be ranked by their counts so as to provide a standard for evaluating one's own titles—a development in the same general vein as the brief-test methodology.[6] While the view of the counts presented here is not yet widely shared, it has potential for acceptance by practitioners as well as researchers. This book demonstrates that the OCLC counts are a national resource for practical bibliometrics (Bensman, 1982; Metz, 1990). My hope is that, if a useful application can be devised "manually," software developers will eventually make much of it algorithmic and performable by computer. Successful demonstrations of this sort could lead practitioners to view OCLC as providing data not just for cataloging and bibliographic retrieval but for a collection management information system of unparalleled scope.

NOTES

1. Coffey gets my affiliation right—Drexel University—but calls me Herbert White, confusing me with the well-known former dean of the School of Library and Information Science, Indiana University.

2. WLN used to stand for Washington Library Network, but the customer base has long since extended beyond libraries in Washington state. The letters now

simply identify the organization, which took over management of the Pacific Northwest Conspectus in 1991.

3. RLG distributes a version of its scale for nonresearch libraries that is very like the one in the *WLN Collection Assessment Manual.* In the accompanying guidelines, both say the scale is cumulative. As RLG (n.d., p. 1) puts it, "Each succeeding collection level is presumed to be inclusive of those which precede it." The absence of a similar guideline for the "main" RLG scale in Table 1.1 is probably an oversight, not an implicit indication of difference in kind.

4. Once the methodology was worked out, the tests were tried frequently at Penn and other Philadelphia-area academic libraries by Drexel students in my Research Collection Development course, many of whom are interested in the type of library that employs subject-specialist bibliographers. Penn's library is also very close to the Drexel campus in Philadelphia's University City.

5. Since Nisonger (1992) is a book-length guide, I have not attempted to review other collection evaluation measures here. See also Christiansen et al. (1983), Mosher (1984), Wiemers et al. (1984), Futas and Intner (1985), Farrell and Reed-Scott (1989), Kaag (1991), Baker and Lancaster (1991), and MacEwan (1993). Seay (1992) is an annotated bibliography specifically on collection evaluation with the Conspectus, as is chapter 9 of Nisonger (1992). Wood and Strauch (1993) is the hardcover edition of a 1992 issue of the *Acquisitions Librarian* entirely devoted to the Conspectus.

6. See the discussions of the subcollection metric "Holdings Distribution" in the *OCLC/AMIGOS Collection Analysis CD User Guide* (OCLC, 1989). The titles in each holdings distribution are presented in deciles: those held by 90–100 percent of the peer group, those held by 80–89 percent, and so on, down to titles held by only 1–9 percent and the remainder that are uniquely held.

CHAPTER 2

Problems of the Past

VERIFICATION STUDIES

Brief tests were designed as an alternative to another methodology for assessing collections—that of past RLG "verification studies" (Mosher, 1985; Coleman, 1985). A sketch of the latter's drawbacks helps to understand why the tests are constructed as they are.

RLG collection-level codes are used by librarians to convey their subjective estimates of how they have built a subject in the past (*existing collection strength*, ECS) and how they are presently budgeting for it (*current collection intensity*, CCI). The Conspectus calls for judgments in thousands of subjects made up of LC class ranges. Such judgments have, in fact, been made in many libraries since the 1980s.

Naturally, doubts have arisen over time as to the goodness and impartiality of these assessments (Abell, 1987; Lucas, 1990; McGrath and Nuzzo, 1991; Coleman, 1992). The criteria for assigning levels, particularly for monographic collections as opposed to serials, are vague and leave much to impression (Siverson, 1992). As a result, in the real world of library politics, the ratings may be set as part of a numbers game. One hears, for example, that academic librarians supporting a graduate program in a field will not give their collection in that field a rating of less than 4, whatever its contents, because (implicitly) a Level 4 is needed to support distinguished graduate research. Conversely, a rating could be understated to imply that more money is needed to bring the collection up to the desired level in that area (cf. Jakubs, 1989; Benaud and Bordeianu, 1992). Thus, the numbers may say more about librarians' political intentions than they do about their holdings. Perhaps even more likely is that librarians err simply because they lack detailed statistics on collections other than their own that would allow them to make better judgments.

In an attempt to gain insight into how good their judgments are, the RLG and other academic libraries have sponsored verification studies. In these, a sample is drawn from some sampling frame, usually one or more bibliographies taken to represent a total literature. Participants check their holdings against the sample, which may be quite large (e.g., 1,000 items). Percentages of items held are com-

TABLE 2.1

Results of French Literature Verification Study, 1983

Library	Titles Held / 1000	Percent Held	Level Originally Claimed
Library of Congress	620	62.0%	4
UC Berkeley	619	61.9%	4
Yale	616	61.6%	4
Princeton	603	60.3%	4
New York Public	597	59.7%	4
Columbia	555	55.5%	4
Cornell	549	54.9%	4
Michigan	523	52.3%	4
Iowa	502	50.2%	4
Stanford	479	47.9%	4
Pennsylvania	476	47.6%	4
Northwestern	457	45.7%	4
Johns Hopkins	416	41.6%	3
Brown	400	40.0%	4
Dartmouth	374	37.4%	3
UC Davis	365	36.5%	4
Temple	346	34.6%	3
New York University	338	33.8%	3
Brigham Young	308	30.8%	3
Penn State	307	30.7%	4
Colorado State	163	16.3%	3

puted. This percentage from the sample is an estimate of the true percentage of the literature the library holds—its coverage. The RLG then matches the percentaged coverage scores against previously claimed ratings.

Table 2.1 shows the outcome of the verification study for French literature, conducted with a checklist of 1,000 items in 1983.[1] Not too surprisingly, libraries with very different coverage scores have been found to claim equal ratings—often a 4. Sometimes scores suggest that ratings should actually be reversed; a library with a claimed 3, for example, may have better coverage than one claiming a 4. Verification studies often uncover such discrepancies. As a result, it is easy to be skeptical of the levels as set.

If there were a way of resolving these matters, all might be well. Unfortunately, Table 2.1 and others like it are the final product.

The essence of my argument can be inferred from the question that Table 2.1 leaves hanging: what do the percentages mean? Verification studies, so costly in time and effort, may end up verifying nothing. Let us look further at some of the difficulties.

Compiling the List

The compilation of a checklist of several hundred to a thousand items requires a major commitment of effort from a subject expert. Such a checklist may take months to prepare before its use can begin. (Among the necessary decisions is whether one should represent a subject with works clearly on it or with the broader range of works cited as relevant to it. Both approaches can be found in the collection evaluation literature.) The mere job of compiling the references (from bibliographies, card catalogs, and so on) and making worksheets for all the participants is a major undertaking, creating a small book.

Differences in Levels

For all the effort that goes into them, the checklists inadequately reflect the differences in the levels suggested by the definitions in Table 1.1. For example, there may be no attempt to pick very basic works to reflect the Minimal level. Instead, systematic random or judgment samples are taken from comprehensive scholarly bibliographies, and almost all of the items reflect the higher levels. Table 2.2 shows some typically advanced titles from the RLG checklist for genetics. Or again, in the French literature checklist, 125 items are articles drawn from a very thorough bibliography on Zola. To hold them, American libraries must have vernacular-language serials from places and times like Warsaw, 1882; Sarajevo, 1927; and Tokyo, 1931.

As far as I can tell, no one in the RLG has really confronted the problem of matching the levels of the scale with bibliographies from which checklist items are drawn. At most, one finds more than one kind of bibliography named as sampling frames (e.g., *The Reader's Adviser*, H. W. Wilson indexes, specialized scholarly instruments). But one does not find a plan for characterizing each level

TABLE 2.2

Sample Items from RLG Verification Study in Genetics

433. Ruhland, Wilhelm (ed.)   Handbuch der Pflanzenphysiologie. 18 v. Berlin,
     Springer, 1955-67
434. Ruzicka, Vladislav (ed.)   Ceskoslovenska eugenicka spolecnost, Prague. Praze,
     Nakladem Fr. Boroveho, 1925
435. Sakaguchi, Kenji (ed.), Okanishi, Masonori (ed.)   Molecular breeding and genet-
     ics of applied microorganisms. Tokyo, Kodansha, 1980
436. Sauer, Helmut W. (ed.)   Progress in developmental biology: Symposium, Mainz,
     March 1980. Stuttgart, G. Fischer, 1981
437. Schonewald-Cox, Christine M. (ed.)   Genetics and conservation: A reference for
     managing wild animal and plant populations. Reading, MA., Benjamin/Cum-
     mings, 1983
438. Sosna, Milan (ed.)   G. Mendel Memorial Symposium, 1865-1965 (1965: Brno,
     Czechoslovakia). Prague, Academia, 1966
439. Vago, C. (ed.)   Invertebrate tissue culture. New York, Academic Press, 1971-
440. Vogel, Henry J. (ed.), Bryson, Vernon (ed.), Lampen, J. Oliver (ed.)   Symposium
     on Informational Macromolecules, Rutgers University, 1962. New York,
     Academic Press, 1963

in terms of bibliographies, sampling from them an appropriate number of titles
per level, and stating the fraction of titles that must be held for a level to be
claimed. The project reported in Underwood (1992) perhaps comes closest to this
ideal, but it was done outside RLG for a single Conspectus division, music.

Cumulativeness of Levels

Existing checklists also do not test the cumulativeness of the levels. It is
apparently assumed that if a library has extensive holdings of, say, Level 4 items,
then its holdings at the lower levels are also extensive. Thus, a verification study
may suggest that a library should claim a Level 1 or 2 because it has a relatively
low percentage of items suitable for Level 4. This seems a needlessly indirect
way of establishing a level, and it raises questions about the validity of the study.

Checking the List

Participants must check the list against their holdings. Whether they do this
manually or by computer (in the Research Library Information Network, OCLC,
or a local online public access catalog), the task is formidable and onerous. Not
surprisingly, RLG members and other academic libraries have not done many
verification studies. Table 2.3 gives a list as of this writing (cf. Coleman, 1992).

Yet there is a need for them in every LC class range, including many not yet touched. And since collections are dynamic, there is also a need for the occasional repetition of studies within a class if estimates are to be believed. All of this makes verification a daunting prospect. It might be faced a few times, but the idea of long checklists across many subjects is demoralizing and provokes resistance.

Appropriate Sample Size

Why are the checklists so long? It may be simply that the developers of the first verification studies did not know how to choose an appropriate sample size. At first glance, the studies look as if they were intended to estimate population parameters, such as percentage of a total literature held, from sample statistics. But if so, the sample sizes are arguably too large—for example, French literature with 1,000 items.

Common misconceptions are that sample size is some standard fraction of the population size (like 10 percent), that this fraction depends solely on how big the population is, and that, if one does not know how to pick the fraction, a large round number like 1,000 is a satisfactory alternative. In fact, sample size depends chiefly on the margin of error that one will tolerate in estimating the true but unknown percentages in the population and on how confident one wants to be that the true percentage falls within the margin of error. Generally, one is more confident of estimating the interval in which the true value lies than of estimating the true value exactly. For example, one might say, "According to our sample data, we hold 58 percent of this literature with a margin of error of ± 4 percent and a confidence level of 95 percent. Thus, the true percentage of the literature we hold

TABLE 2.3

RLG Verification Studies Completed

Agricultural Economics
Chemistry
English and American Literature
French Literature
Genetics
Mathematical Journals
Music Ensemble
Neurology
Renaissance/Baroque Art I and II
Romanesque Sculpture
Russian History
Russian Literature
Swiss History
Zola

will lie somewhere between 54 percent and 62 percent in 95 draws out of 100."

In nonfateful verification studies of the present sort, one might tolerate an estimate within ±5 percent of the true population percentage, with a 95 percent confidence level. If so, one would need at most a sample of 384 randomly drawn titles even if the population from which it was drawn—the literature—were infinitely large. Of course, the literatures from which samples are actually drawn are not only finite but small enough (relative to the sample) that a "finite population correction factor" can be used to reduce a number like 384 even further.

Since there are many ways of finding this out, the 1,000-item samples of the early verification studies look ingenuous; they are probably larger than necessary for the job intended. (When split as 500 books and 500 serials, they also look very unbalanced: whereas many monographic literatures comprise far more than 500 books, there are fewer than 500 serials in all but the most broadly defined fields.) Samples in more recent studies have been reduced to about 400 items.

The Conversion Problem

Here we reach the main difficulty. Even if a sample size is knowledgeably chosen, the sample survey methodology of the initial studies is not related to what the studies were supposed to accomplish: the verification of levels. The typical survey produces an estimate of what librarians have long called coverage. Unfortunately, not coverage but *level* is wanted, and no one has decided how to convert the percentages of coverage into numbers denoting collection strength. There is no formula for equating a given percentage with levels 0 through 5. Yet only with the latter can librarians "verify"—confirm or disconfirm—the levels they have subjectively set.

The most the RLG has said is that strength is supposed to be absolute rather than relative. That is, if a library has, say, 15 percent coverage of a checklist, and all other libraries have less than that, the top-ranked library should not be able to claim Level 4 simply because it is high relative to all the others. However, without further guidelines, this leads only to quandaries; for example, if one library has 80 percent of a checklist and the next highest has 58 percent, can they both claim Level 4? What, indeed, does "58 percent coverage" mean in terms of the Levels 1 to 5? It is easy enough to devise schemes for converting percentages to levels; for example, since 58 percent falls in the third quintile (between 41 percent and 60 percent), one could simply say it represents a Level 3 collection. But more than one conversion scheme is possible, and the RLG has been silent as to preference.

The problems are not just intellectual. Librarianship in its upper reaches is a political activity, and to choose among the conversion schemes involves political considerations. Whatever scheme is chosen, it may yield numbers that some librarians find too low or too high. The likely result is that they will resist replacing their claims with these numbers in public reports. (Whose ox is being gored?) Thus, a hard-and-fast conversion scheme may have seemed controversial enough that no one wanted to chance it (much less enforce it), and there the matter rests.

Several schemes are represented in Table 2.4. Before examining their particu-

TABLE 2.4

Four Hypothetical Schemes for Converting Coverage to Levels

Level	Fraction of Checklist Covered			
	Quartiles	*Quintiles*	*Gwinn-Mosher*	*"Curve"*
5 Comprehensive	ca. 100%	81-100%	85-100%	> +2 SD
4 Research	76-99%	61-80%	70-85%	+1 to +2 SD
3 Instructional	51-75%	41-60%	55-70%	Mean to +1 SD
2 Basic	26-50%	21-40%	40-55%	-1 SD to Mean
1 Minimal	1-25%	1-20%	25-40%	-2 to -1 SD
0 Out of scope	ca. 0%	ca. 0%	below 25%	< -2 SD

lars, I must raise a matter that has clouded the conversion problem from the beginning: the very names of the levels of the scale. They do not lie along one semantic continuum. "Out of scope," "Minimal," and "Comprehensive" refer to levels of acquisition, while "Basic," "Instructional," and "Research" refer to levels of inquiry being supported. Moreover, the first three bracket the second three. As long as the terms are mere labels, as in Table 1.1, the discontinuity matters little, but when one tries to convert them to percentage equivalents, there are awkward implications. The "Minimal" fraction of the literature seems to include works more basic than those in "Basic," and the "Comprehensive" fraction seems to include works more advanced than those in "Research." Thus, puzzles develop. For example, if a collection consisted of 80 percent of the titles in a literature, would the remaining 20 percent be gaps across Levels 1 through 4, or would they be a wholly different set of titles suitable only for Level 5?

For this reason, the *quartile* scheme, which is the simplest in Table 2.4, also seems best. It is absolute rather than relative. Its zero point is meaningful for "Out of scope." Its four divisions correspond to the four problematical levels of the RLG scale.[2] It compels a library to hold very nearly 100 percent of a literature in order to claim Level 5. The latter is desirable because, according to Table 1.1, a Comprehensive collection is supposed to have "all significant works of recorded knowledge...in all applicable languages"; it is a "special collection" for a "defined and limited field" in which "the aim, if not the achievement, is exhaustiveness." In the quartile scheme, a Comprehensive collection would be one that had largely filled the gaps across Levels 1 through 4, rather than a separate, fifth level in its own right. That solves the puzzle above.

By extending the label "Comprehensive" to a collection with as little as 81 perecnt coverage, the otherwise acceptable *quintile* scheme leaves the puzzle unsolved. So does the scheme inferred from Gwinn and Mosher (1983). They write (p. 137), "If one were to distribute the five levels of the scale evenly by percentage of holdings, an institution reporting a level 4 collection should be expected to hold between 70 and 85 percent of the titles considered important." That would make the five "bins" of their distribution only about 15 points wide, and their "Comprehensive" level would be ambiguous as to content. (Would it contain some identifiable block of literature *beyond* Research level—that is, the same block of titles for all libraries? Or would it simply contain items of any sort that happened to take a particular library above the 85 percent mark?) The Gwinn and Mosher scheme has the additional drawback of creating an anomalous zero point; apparently, a library could have over 20 percent coverage of a checklist in some field and still find its holdings mapped to "Out of scope."

The final scheme in Table 2.4 would tabulate the holdings for a group of libraries and use the mean and standard deviation (SD) of the distribution for "grading them on the curve," like students. (The RLG reports such statistics for its verification studies, but it does not actually convert them into levels.) I have shown a plausible way in which the levels might be assigned to standard deviation units of the distribution. But while superficially inviting, this method has the undesirable property of making level relative rather than absolute. By its logic, a group of libraries could all have undistinguished coverage in absolute terms, yet those scoring at the top of the distribution would necessarily be Level 4s, if not 5s. Also, the way it assigns Levels 0 and 5 (on the basis of coverage being ± two standard deviations beyond the mean) does not square with the RLG definitions of these levels. Level 0 really means that nothing is held; Level 5, that virtually everything is held; and that is not what these levels would correspond to if mechanically assigned by the "curve."

An objection to *all* the conversion schemes in Table 2.4 is that they are blind to the qualitative differences of the RLG levels. Despite their convenience, they ignore the goal of representing the levels with appropriate works—for example, very basic works for Minimal-level collections. So once again we have a less than satisfactory situation. The argument that brief tests are more sensitive to qualitative differences than the schemes in Table 2.4 will be developed in later chapters.

HOW MINIMAL IS MINIMAL?

A question remains as to the size of the Minimal level. The quartile scheme just advocated makes it a full fourth of any literature, which is very likely not what the drafters of the RLG scale had in mind. However, the drafters did not establish a cutoff point for this level that makes sense in terms of full literatures. (That is part of their larger problem of not being able to define any levels with percentages of coverage.) If we imagine they thought that, say, up to a dozen titles would constitute a typical Minimal collection, then, in big fields like nineteenth-century British literature or U.S. Civil War history, hugely disproportionate numbers of titles would be left to be assigned to the next higher Basic level—

TABLE 2.5

Hypothetical Scheme for Collection Sizes at Four RLG Levels

Collection Size	Powers of 10	Levels	Labels
Up to 10 titles	10^1	1	Minimal
Up to 100 titles	10^2	2	Basic
Up to 1,000 titles	10^3	3	Instructional
Up to 10,000 titles	10^4	4	Research

or at least somewhere higher up. On the other hand, to many librarians "Minimal" would not connote fully 25 percent of the titles in a field.

In part, the problem lies with the uncertainty of what is being minimized. "Minimal" can be interpreted as "indispensable or irreducible, the sine qua non if studies are to be pursued," which does not necessarily imply that the items are few. But it can also be interpreted as "few in number, scant"—perhaps no more than 10. The latter would be consistent with a scale to powers of 10, and it is possible to wonder whether the drafters might have intended something like the scheme in Table 2.5. Very probably not—had they wanted to wrest actual numbers from their definitions, they would have done so—but the scheme has a certain plausibility, especially for the lower two levels. At the upper levels, there are probably many literatures it will not fit.

My guess is that, for the lower two levels, they envisioned coverage of relatively small core bibliographies or "best books" lists (e.g., items in the *Reader's Adviser*) and then, for the upper levels, switched to coverage of the literature in its entirety without noticing the change in scale. That would produce a set of definitions like those in Table 1.1, with their vague "powers-of-10" aspect. If, instead, they had worked with a consistent model of a literature, such as one defined by Conspectus lines and rank-ordered holdings counts (as explained in Chapter 8), they might have gradated the RLG scale clearly in terms of coverage. That, in turn, might have led to a more coherent progression of labels than "Minimal–Basic–Instructional–Research–Comprehensive," which, conceptually, shift among coverage, collectors' intentions, and the qualitative nature of what is held.

Ideally, the names of the RLG levels should suggest the functions that collections of different sizes are supposed to perform. Thus, the category containing the most widely held titles in a literature needs to be called something more evocative than "Level 1." Either "Essential" or "Core" is all right by itself, but neither goes especially well with "Basic" on the next level up. "Fundamental," "Foundational," or "Minimum" (as in "minimum wage") might be better, because they imply infrastructural holdings, not necessarily few in number, without which a collection is hardly worth the name. Speaking architecturally, they would be the plinth under the base of "Basic." If "Minimal" is to be retained for Level 1, it makes sense to gloss it in this sine qua non sense and to subdivide it as necessary, in the manner of the WLN Conspectus.

The scale from the *WLN Collection Assessment Manual* is annotated in Chapter 5. Here let me merely note that, according to guidelines from it reproduced in Table 2.6, the Basic level would begin at 2,500 titles, which implies that any smaller collection would be Minimal. This is very different from what Minimal implies in Table 1.1. Granted, 2,500 is supposed to be a cutpoint within a *division,* the highest aggregation of subject literatures. (Education, music, and mathematics exemplify divisions, of which there are now 24 overall.) But, clearly, an interpretation of a Minimal collection as having no more than 10 titles is wholly inconsistent with a Basic level starting at 2,500.

Within divisions, categories are the next lower step. Assuming that all Min-

TABLE 2.6

WLN or Pacific Northwest Conspectus Guidelines for Interpreting Finer-Grained Collection Levels

Levels	Number of Titles	Coverage, Major Bibliographies	Coverage, Wilson Indexes
0 Out of scope			
1a Minimal--uneven coverage			
1b Minimal--even coverage			
2a Basic information--introductory	2,500 - 5,000	Less than 10%	
2b Basic information--advanced	5,000 - 8,000	Less than 15%	30%
3a Lower division undergraduate	8,000 - 12,000	15 - 20%	50%
3b Advanced undergraduate	More than 12,000	30 - 40%	75%
3c Master's programs		50 - 70%	90%
4 Research		75 - 80%	
5 Comprehensive			

imal collections corresponding to categories are combined in a division, it would take 250 categories with 10 titles each to bring the collection to 2,500, and the largest division, medical and health sciences, has only 50. On the other hand, according to Table 2.6, a division with only one category, such as auxiliary sciences of history, would need 2,500 titles, presumably all foundational, just to make it to the threshold of Basic level. A requirement of 2,500 Minimal-level titles seems far too large for the auxiliary sciences of history (which include archival science, numismatics, diplomatics, sigillography, and genealogy), but may be too small for divisions like history proper or medical and health sciences, whose associated literatures are truly vast.

One can only conclude that the numerical guidelines in Table 2.6 were not thought through for all literatures. They will work with some but not others. It is simply not clear, by any existing formula, how big a Minimal-level collection is supposed to be. Tellingly, the WLN guidelines do not propose a size—for monographs, they say "few selections but basic authors, or core works, or a spectrum"—and that is why nothing is listed for Minimal level in Table 2.6.

The alternative, obviously, is to refrain from setting cutpoints in terms of absolute numbers of titles (such as 2,500) that are not universally appropriate. One might, instead, base the cutpoints on preset percentages (such as quartiles) that would yield numbers of titles relative to the size of the literature being examined. But even better is the scheme outlined in Chapter 8, in which the RLG levels are redefined in terms of a scale of OCLC holdings counts. The advantages of that approach are taken up there.

THE CONSORTIUM X EXAMPLE

To sum up past problems, let me conclude with a cautionary example from the Consortium X Collection Inventory Project. Consortium X, a real organization whose identity is masked here, provided copies of its "validation forms" (i.e., verification study forms) at a conference for project participants in 1989. The forms corresponded to 10 main divisions of the Pacific Northwest Conspectus, such as art and architecture, natural history and biology, English language and literature, mathematics, and religion. According to instructions distributed with them, they were intended to help participants who, having rated their subject subcollections with the extended version of the RLG scale, "see the need to further test their Conspectus data." It was further noted that the forms "will provide comparative, quantitative data on various libraries, and will enable the [Collection Inventory Project] Task Force to insure the accuracy of the Conspectus."

Each of the forms has a unique mix of questions, which immediately poses difficulties in relating them consistently to the verification of levels. Setting that temporarily aside, I reproduce the more-or-less typical form for the education division as Table 2.7.

Note that it asks for counts of both serial and monographic titles held, which many libraries, particularly those that have not yet computerized their bibliographic records, would find laborious to supply. But that is only the beginning. The total number of titles listed in various large bibliographic tools must then be

TABLE 2.7

**Sample Form from
Consortium X Collection Inventory Project**

VALIDATION FORM FOR EDUCATION DIVISION CONSPECTUS

INSTITUTION_____

LIBRARY_____

HIGHEST DEGREE GRANTED IN EDUCATION _____

ASSESSMENT LEVEL _____

Please give all available figures for the following:

Number of **serial titles** _____

Current subscriptions to titles listed in:	No. of titles	%
Education Index	_____	_____
CIJE	_____	_____
SSCI	_____	_____
Katz	_____	_____

Percentage of titles for which holdings are complete or nearly complete _____

Do you subscribe to the full ERIC? Yes/No

Number of **monographic titles** _____ and/or volumes _____

Holdings of titles listed in:	No. of titles	%
A Guide to Sources of Educational Information	_____	_____
Encyclopedia of Educational Research	_____	_____

Number of titles _____ and/or volumes _____ held in audiovisual and other
media

Do you provide online or CD-ROM access to ERIC? Yes/No

TABLE 2.7 *(continued)*

Percentage of the collection in foreign language _____%

Percentage of the collection with copyright in the last ten years _____%

Funds allocated during last and current budget years for:

	Last	Current
Serials	$_____	$_____
Monographs	$_____	$_____
Audiovisual and other media	$_____	$_____
Database searching	$_____	$_____

Number of titles added to the collection in last budget year _____

What selection tools/methods do you use regularly?

Do you use an approval plan for education? Yes/No
(If so, describe your profile.)

List any special collections.

Compiled by _____   Date_____

obtained, so that the fractions held by a library may be computed and percentaged. For serials, the checkers must learn the number of titles indexed in the *Education Index,* the *Current Index to Journals in Education,* and the education sections of *Social Sciences Citation Index* and Katz's *Magazines for Libraries.* Jointly, these cover many hundreds of serial titles. Next, the current subscriptions of the library must be checked—not, as in RLG verification studies, against a sample from them, but against all four in their entirety. Perhaps the most discouraging feature is the unnecessary repetition of the checking: since the four bibliographies have considerable overlap in titles, in many cases the same title would be inventoried two, three, or even four times. For books a similar process must be carried out. One must find the number of monographic titles in two large bibliographies, Woodbury's *Guide to Sources of Educational Information* and the *Encyclopedia of Educational Research,* and proceed to hundreds of lookups with them as check-lists. (Would whoever listed Woodbury's *Guide* be willing personally to look up every one of its titles in a university library catalog and then go on to do the same thing with the *Encyclopedia?*) Still one is not finished: there are further questions on holdings in audiovisual and other media, percentage of the collection in foreign languages, percentage of the collection with imprint dates in the last 10 years, budgetary allocations across form classes, and so on, all for a single division of the Conspectus, with a prospect of many more divisions to go.

Nor is the validation form for education the most demanding of the lot. The form for library and information science asks librarians to check their journal subscriptions against four big bibliographies and their books against no fewer than 17, including such heavyweights as the *Children's Catalog* and Sheehy's *Guide to Reference Books*. There are also questions about serial titles for which holdings are largely complete, manuscripts, and other matters.

In the real world, of course, no library manager is going to commit staff to data gathering on such a scale. The instructions with the form admit as much:

> It will not be necessary for every project participant to complete all the Validation Forms, or to complete every part of each form. For example, some libraries participating in the project may not have the staff resources to search all the titles listed in the recommended bibliographies, but may be able to search a representative sample of titles from several sources—here the participant could fill in the approximate percentage of holdings, but leave out the total number of titles held. Other libraries may want to search only one or two of the bibliographies, but to search every title. Of course, the more participants who fill out the forms and the more fully they are completed, the more helpful they will be for the Collection Inventory Project Task Force.

While these concessions move in the direction of reason, they are halfway measures, and a bit of imagination projects the result: respondents struggling with sampling techniques, inconsistent procedures, noncomparable answers, "guestimates" predominating over firm counts, and lots of missing data. It is significant that a validation form for education that Consortium X distributed as a handout was filled out with fictional data from a fictional institution—the "McIntosh Library of Applevalley State College"—rather than with real data from Consortium X librarians who had actually grappled with the tasks imposed.

Imagine now the situation at the other end: the filled-out forms pouring in, possibly by the hundreds, and still the problem of how to relate these products of toil and tears to collection levels has not been solved, perhaps not even addressed; it has simply been assumed that if someone looks at the data long enough, levels will emerge. Multiply the 10 Conspectus divisions by the dozens of libraries in Consortium X by roughly the number and variety of questions appearing in Table 2.7, and, even with a large number of answers predictably left blank, one can see that the amount of raw data to be made sense of is potentially enormous. Moreover, it is not this amount, but the far greater *combination* of data elements that is crucial, given the way this verification study is designed. Every element factored in—straight holdings counts, serial literature coverage, monographic literature coverage, audiovisual percentages, budgetary figures, and so on—makes the reading as to level more complex. Recall, too, that the elements differ across forms, so that each subject division poses separate interpretation problems. Yet if large-scale validation of claimed levels is to be done at all, it must be fast and straightforward—virtually algorithmic—and not a matter of many judgment calls over complex data. Judgment has its place, but a good algorithm is needed first.

It is easy enough to see what has gone wrong: librarians have mistaken something they know well—appropriate bibliographies to use as checklists—for a complete study design. The instruction sheet notes that "several of the bibliographies recommended come from the Supplemental Guidelines prepared by the Research Libraries Group." This is commendable linkage, but not a substitute for thinking through the full implications of the data-gathering instrument (cf. Bushing, 1992, on "Statistics"). Questions like the following should have been asked by everyone concerned.

1. How long will it take to fill out the forms? Although they may look short, the forms are, in effect, bibliographies of bibliographies, and each bibliography listed is the equivalent of scores, hundreds, or thousands of questions on a questionnaire. Is it reasonable to expect library staff to take time from other duties to gather data on this scale? Some of the nonbibliographic data requested are time-consuming to gather as well. Will they also be used to validate levels? If not, why are they on the form?

2. Exactly what tables will be generated from these data? The surest way to learn whether a quantitative study is well designed is to require, in advance of approval, mock-ups of the final tables and a statement on how they will be generated. Lacking backgrounds in quantitative analysis, many librarians will consent to survey research projects (which would include verification studies) because someone in their ranks has drafted a questionnaire, rather than because they can clearly envision the tables that will result. The experienced researcher can envision these tables, to which the items on the questionnaire are merely stepping-stones. The inexperienced practitioner should ask for elucidation, because it may turn out that the study designers, too, have only a hazy idea of what will become of the data once they are in—a definite danger sign. Without necessarily understanding all the computational or statistical details, one should be able to tell whether the means of the study have been adjusted to the ends.

Suppose one is the Applevalley State librarian who, in the handout, assessed the education collection as "3b E" (English-language works supporting advanced undergraduate study). One might then examine the items in the verification form and ask, "Which of these, or which combination of these, will actually validate the '3b E' I've claimed? If we're going to do all this work, how will the percentages on the form be converted to a reading on level? And how will the data speak not just to my collection but to everyone's, in all their variety?" Such questions would compel study designers to address matters of the sort discussed in this chapter, including the conversion problem.

Ironically, the problem of converting raw data to levels would remain even if all the tasks of bibliographic checking and computation were lifted from librarians and given to a computer. One can imagine something like present-day OCLC/AMIGOS or WLN collection evaluation software matching library holdings tapes against machine-readable bibliographies and producing the percentaged coverage scores called for on Consortium X's forms. But one would still require an algorithmic scheme on the lines of those in Table 2.4 to make the final statement of levels.

Consortium X, of course, did not begin the practice of recommending that huge bibliographic checklists be used to verify collection ratings. It merely participated in the collection evaluation culture of the 1980s, in particular, the culture of the Research Libraries Group as filtered through the Conspectus Supplemental Guidelines and the *Pacific Northwest Collection Evaluation Manual.* The latter may be the source of the assumption in Table 2.6 that libraries will set or verify levels by checking monographic coverage against "major bibliographies" and serials coverage against H. W. Wilson indexes, then matching those figures against the percentage standards given in the table. That assumption has been carried over into the *WLN Collection Assessment Manual.* The Wilson index checking might be tolerable, since each index covers only several hundred serials. (Counts for each index are now supplied in the *Manual.*) But the monographic titles in major bibliographies can run easily into the thousands, and it is hard to imagine staff members having the time or inclination to undertake checking on this scale in single subjects, much less across entire collections.

A publicist for project LIRN (Library and Information Resources for the Northwest), which was part of the same movement, wrote in a prospectus:

The experience of a number of libraries suggests that from 25 to 75 hours of staff time per *DIVISION* will be needed for those assessing larger collections at the most detailed level. Alaska's experience suggests that for smaller libraries assessing 20 *DIVISIONS* or even 200 *SUBJECTS,* a few hours are sufficient for each *DIVISION* once a library representative—already familiar with the collection—is trained in the assessment process.

It would be nice to know how many libraries have actually undertaken such evaluations across their subject collections in full and, if so, how realistic these estimates are. What, moreover, was the final judgment on the experience by those concerned? [3]

CONCLUSION

For an idea of the labor that can go into developing Supplemental Guidelines for a single Conspectus division—music—and the awesome amount of bibliographic checking that Guideline writers can contemplate, see Underwood (1992). Aside from mainstream RLG- or WLN-style proposals of this sort, there are papers on locally devised methodologies—for example, Stielow and Tibbo (1989), Newby and Promis (1990), and Siverson (1992)—that, once again, involve elaborate instrument building and extensive checking of holdings in order to set or verify levels. The papers cited apply their methodologies to subject literatures ranging in number from none to two. And that is the very point: those numbers are not likely to climb, because the amount of labor required is too great for the task at hand. A minimal requirement for any proposed methodology is that it must be able to generate results quickly across many subject literatures in many settings. Otherwise, as in the RLG verification studies, it simply does not scale up to national needs, however informative it may be locally.

This brings us to the present study and a key distinction. Verification studies to date are tests of what the library *has* collected on a given level, as evidenced by many trials of its past performance. It is rather hard to tell what the designers of these studies wanted to measure, but they identified it with coverage of literatures, and that has produced very cumbersome designs for all concerned. They combine the gathering of massive amounts of evidence with marked confusion as to what to make of it once it is gathered.

In contrast, the brief tests described in the next chapter are essentially tests of whether a library *can* collect on a given level, as evidenced by a few trials of its past performance. It is much easier to show that a library can and does collect on a given level than to show the extent to which it has covered a literature. Moreover, while brief tests do not solve all the problems this chapter has raised, they solve or avoid most, and their own problems are frankly examined. If they represent a sufficient advance over studies of the past, as I think they do, they may gain wider acceptance than those studies, which, at best, were not very helpful and, at worst, lie uncompleted in file drawers, too flawed to be taken up again.

NOTES

1. I am indebted to Jim Coleman of RLG for the data in this table, which also appears in a somewhat different form in Larson (1984).

2. The Level 1 label should be something like "Foundational" rather than "Minimal" to make it consistent with the others as a level of inquiry, not of acquisition.

3. Stephens (1992) is a generally positive account of Alaskan librarians' experience with the Conspectus, but it does not minimize the many difficulties they have had to face in adapting it to their needs. Other comments on difficulties may be found in the reports from American and Canadian academic libraries in Jakubs (1989).

CHAPTER 3

The Logic of the Test

A SINGLE WORK

The logic of the brief test may be surmised from the following example. Suppose a bibliographer had to name a single work that would test the strength of a collection in any field—say, library science. He or she might reason like this: "A strong collection in library science supports doctoral and postdoctoral research. It has a large number of specialized works, such as annual reports of particular libraries, conference proceedings, mathematical and statistical studies, extensive serial runs, items from foreign countries, items not in English, old and rare books, theses on microfilm, and so on. As my test work, I might pick something like Michael Bommer's 1971 dissertation or a directory like *Who's Who in Finnish Librarianship, 1967.*[1] Any library that had either of those would probably have a rich collection in library science overall."

In contrast, the bibliographer would very likely not pick Eugene Sheehy's *Guide to Reference Books* or William A. Katz's *Introduction to Reference Work,* on the ground that libraries of all kinds and sizes—for example, small public libraries—are likely to have well-known works such as these, even if they have very little else in library science. Sheehy or Katz would therefore be too easy a test; holding them would not indicate a strong library science collection at all.

However, while one would not expect the presence of Sheehy and Katz to imply the presence of the dissertation and the Finnish directory, one *would* expect the reverse: holding Bommer and the directory would strongly imply a collection in which Sheehy and Katz were also held. In other words, one infers a cumulative scale in which performance at the higher, more demanding level presupposes the ability to perform at all lower levels. (In social science, the well-known Guttman scale has this property of cumulativeness.) Such logic can, of course, be applied to any subject area and in any type of library.

BRIEF TESTS IN GENERAL

In contrast to the huge checklist surveys described in Chapter 2, brief tests have perhaps 40 titles per subject category. The titles are chosen by a subject specialist, here called a selector, and then ranked by how many member libraries of OCLC hold them. These tests can be compiled in a day or two and self-administered by a staff member in one or two hours, particularly if the checking is done online. Experience gained since 1988 shows that brief tests work quite well to help one set or verify collection levels without undue effort. In addition to their relative convenience, their scores translate directly into readings on level.

The 40-title list is not a sample in the usual sense. That is, it is not used to estimate, within known margins of error, what percentage of the bibliography of a literature some library holds (its coverage). The 40 items are, indeed, a test, resembling ability tests for human beings. They are like a math or spelling test for students in which the teacher has tried to include 10 easy questions (Level 1), 10 that are somewhat tougher (Level 2), 10 that are more demanding still (Level 3), and 10 that are quite hard (Level 4).

In a way, they resemble short tests for aptitude, as opposed to longer tests of achievement, in a given area. "Aptitude" in one of its senses means a natural ability or gift, and ability to buy at a certain level is obviously not a gift but simply a matter of intent and funding. It is used here in the sense of "tendency" or "inclination." "Achievement" in collecting could presumably be measured by a long checklist study, especially if it showed the fraction of a subject literature that a library held.

DISTINGUISHING LEVELS

The purpose of the test is to distinguish among libraries at Levels 1 through 4, on the basis of their "past ability" or "aptitude" in collecting at these levels. Level 1 items are the most likely for a library to hold; Level 4 items, the least likely, with the other two levels in between.

The RLG scale, as noted, actually has Levels 0 through 5. The outer levels are less of a problem to set and verify than the inner. Level 5, which aims at exhaustiveness, can be tested by comparing the collection with the complete list of titles within a Conspectus line: if any title is not held, exhaustiveness has not been achieved. Level 0 can be tested by reversing this logic: if any title *is* held, its subject matter is not out of scope.

RLG has stated that raters of collections should be particularly concerned with distinguishing Level 3, which supports local needs, from Level 4, at which point the collection becomes a regional or even national resource. So any test should do this reasonably well.

The premise here is that librarians can make this (or any other) distinction between levels on the basis of not very many test items. To invoke the model of testing students again: how many problems must examiners set to know whether students are proficient in, say, spelling or calculus or reading a foreign language?

Not very many. Demonstration that the student can solve *enough* of the problems in an hour or two is taken as evidence that he or she can solve infinitely more at that level and so should pass. The logic of brief tests of collection strength is exactly similar.

The logic also rests on the notion of cumulativeness. If, for example, one can correctly do at least half of 10 problems on a test in calculus, it is likely that one will also get right most or all of similar sets of problems in geometry, algebra, and arithmetic. If one can correctly define or spell several very difficult words, it is likely that one can also define or spell progressively easier words. Since a teacher does not need to devise tests of hundreds or thousands of items to find this out, neither should it take many demonstrations to convince us that if a library is collecting at the most difficult level, it can also collect at simpler levels and probably has.

Furthermore, if a teacher tried to foist a test of 1,000 items on us, we would rebel. We would likewise rebel if a driving test required not a brief spin but several days on the road. We know that, for practical purposes, the requisite abilities can be shown with much less expenditure of effort. Similar doubts have kept verification studies thus far to a relative few and account for the interest the brief-test proposal generates when collection developers hear it at meetings.

This is not to deny the value of large-scale surveys of library coverage of subject literatures. It is merely to claim that if a brief test can give clear information as to collection level with less effort, the brief test is to be preferred. This seems especially evident given the nonfatefulness—the unimportance, to be blunt—of measuring collection levels precisely in the overall scheme of library service. It is worthwhile to assess them and to publicize one's conclusions for general use, but not at the cost of doing huge surveys across an endless parade of subjects.

Indeed, if the setting and verifying of levels are tied to large-scale surveys of coverage, then one must conclude that the work will never get done—at least not until computerized collection evaluation is much more advanced than it is now. The promise of computer assistance in large-scale coverage studies is slowly being realized—for instance, through the OCLC/AMIGOS Collection Analysis Systems. But at this writing OCLC software is not linked to RLG-style collection levels, and to do so would require political as well as intellectual decisions in what are different, and in some ways rival, organizations.

In the meantime, those who would carry bibliographic checking to extremes might be asked how they would handle a truly fateful task, such as hiring a library director. Almost certainly they would do it on the basis of interviews, in which time limits force the interviewers to settle on a few key questions—in other words, to behave exactly like test makers, who try to devise just those questions that will elicit, in a reasonable period, a representative sample of what examinees know or believe. It seems logical that anyone who can accept interviews as a means for making consequential decisions about people should be able to accept brief tests as a means for making far less consequential decisions about collection levels.

Brief tests could, in fact, be likened to "interviews with the collection"—interviews deliberately kept short so that the task of evaluation has an end in sight. The purpose is to establish, through a relatively small set of questions about titles, the highest level the developers of a subject collection have succeeded in reaching—no more and no less.

The rough equivalent in conversation is to test someone's knowledge of a field by asking whether he or she knows a particular author or work, a tactic we all use often because of its efficiency. Interestingly, Gaughan (1991a, 1991b) shows that some librarians use this very tactic to test collections. Professors do it, too: Guy Garrison, who called Gaughan's note to my attention, uses Christopher Isherwood and Kenkaburo Oe; I sometimes use David Stacton.

However, while fun, these personal hobbyhorses are not brief tests but "too-brief tests." For example, if a small library lacks a test item, the staff can claim they should be allowed to substitute a "comparable item"— a claim that, for just one case, is hard to deny. On the other hand, if the small library has the item, it has it in common with major libraries such as Harvard's or Berkeley's, and the test thus fails to distinguish between collections of vastly different magnitude. Brief tests are intended to contain *just enough* items to get around these two difficulties.

SMALL SETS OF RANKED TITLES

In brief tests, there are at minimum 10 titles per level to check. These are scaled with OCLC holdings data to reflect both the definition of the level (e.g., very basic works at Level 1) and the cumulative nature of the levels.

As noted in Chapter 1, titles ranked by OCLC holdings data have an inverse relationship with the RLG scale of collection strength. Monographs at the lowest level (1, Minimal) are held by many libraries, and monographs at the highest level (4, Research) are held by relatively few libraries, the other two levels being intermediate. Since progressively fewer libraries hold items as the levels increase, the levels form a scale of relative specialization—the degree to which titles appeal only to scholars rather than beginners or the general reader. For example, materials at Level 1 are popular, standard, indispensable, classic; at Level 4 they are advanced, localized, foreign, academic, obscure, or simply old.[2]

However, the notion of specialization is also similar to the notion of difficulty of test items as stimuli. In this sense, the less likely an item is to be acquired, the more difficult it is on a test. A holdings count for each title measures its probability of having been acquired. The actual probability would be the count of OCLC member libraries holding the work, divided by the total OCLC member libraries at a given time. (The counts alone suffice in actual tests.)

In making the test, the titles are ranked high to low by their counts and then grouped as quartiles. The 10 items most frequently held become Level 1 test items; the next 10, Level 2; the next, Level 3; and the 10 least common, Level 4. (A refinement to this procedure is proposed in the final chapter.) Ability-test instruments of this sort, in which items become increasingly difficult as the levels rise, are called "power tests" in the psychometric literature.

CUMULATIVENESS AND LEVELS

If the scale is cumulative, an exemplary library should have a coverage pattern that is strong at all levels. For example, if a library has sufficient titles to support advanced research, it should also have sufficient titles to support instructional and basic reference activities. More particularly, if the library exceeds a threshold at a given level—say, 50 percent or 5 out of 10 items—it should do at least as well at all lower levels. Since levels are scaled to be increasingly difficult to attain, a pattern of diminishing "percent held" should emerge quite often as in, for example, Table 3.1. The similarity of this measure to a Guttman scale is explored in the next section. For now, note merely that the cumulative score on levels depends on *blocks* of 10 (or more) items, rather than on the single items seen in the examples of Guttman scales in textbooks.

TABLE 3.1

Hypothetical Outcome of Brief Test

Level	No. Titles	% Held
1 Minimal	10	100%
2 Basic	10	90%
3 Instructional	10	80%
4 Research	10	30%

It was decided when the tests were first designed that a library must have *at least 50 percent* of the items at a given level in order to claim that level. Thus, a library scoring as in Table 3.1 could claim a Level 3 collection because it scores more than 50 percent on the first three levels, but not on the fourth, where it has only 30 percent.

The 50 percent threshold, although arbitrary, has worked well in practice. Even so, it can be misunderstood. A colleague who read about it in 1989 wrote me: "This may be too severe for Level 4. There must be innumerable items at this level; can a library be expected to have 50 percent of all of them? Try regarding your list as a systematic sample of the universe." His mistake was to confuse a brief test with a sample survey of coverage (which is the reigning mental model). There is a great difference between holding at least half of a research literature and holding at least 5 titles out of 10 in the most difficult part of a test— "getting them right," so to speak. Brief-test theory specifically predicts that some libraries will hold five or more of the Research-level items listed, and that other libraries will not. It further implies that this is a highly efficient way to tell Level 4 collections from lesser ones.

Specifically not predicted, under brief-test theory, is a pattern like that of Table 3.2, in which cumulativeness breaks down, and percentage scores actually increase as levels become more difficult to attain. Such a pattern—little or no buying of basic works; much buying of the advanced and specialized—*could* occur, of course. Another colleague who heard the brief-test proposal thought that it would occur in such places as the research collections of the New York Public Library. Whether he was right is taken up in the next chapter.

TABLE 3.2

Counterhypothetical Outcome of Brief Test

Level	No. Titles	% Held
1 Minimal	10	0%
2 Basic	10	10%
3 Instructional	10	40%
4 Research	10	100%

GUTTMAN SCALING

As Stielow and Tibbo (1989) point out, RLG-type scaling of collections is interpretable as Guttman scaling. The Guttman method is used in the social sciences to build attitude measurement scales that are unidimensional in nature (like scales of temperature or distance), usually by ordering several questions from a questionnaire. If a scale measuring attitudes is unidimensional, a positive answer to a particular question implies positive answers to all preceding questions, and a negative answer implies negative answers to all subsequent questions. (Readings on thermometers and yardsticks can be interpreted in this way.) It is the empirical task of Guttman scaling to discover whether, for a proposed scale of questions, unidimensionality holds.

TABLE 3.3

Ideal Guttman Scale

Libraries	Minimal	Basic	Instructional	Research	Comprehensive	Score: Level
D	1	1	1	1	1	5
F	1	1	1	1	0	4
B	1	1	1	0	0	3
A	1	1	0	0	0	2
E	1	0	0	0	0	1
C	0	0	0	0	0	0
Item total	5	4	3	2	1	

McIver and Carmines (1981, p. 40) write, "Guttman scaling, also known as scalogram analysis and cumulative scaling, is a procedure designed to order *both* items and subjects with respect to some underlying cumulative dimension." (Their "items" are questions, and their "subjects" are human participants in a survey.) Adapting their language to the present context, the items are the RLG scale levels (which could be put as questions, as in the little "questionnaire" in Chapter 1), the subjects are libraries (actually, librarians speaking for libraries), and the underlying dimension is collection strength.

Table 3.3 adapts a common textbook diagram of the ideal Guttman scale, in which librarians have answered cumulatively along a single dimension. Their imaginary libraries are designated with letters on the rows. The named levels of the RLG scale run atop the columns. Librarians claiming a level have a 1 (positive answer) in its column; otherwise, a 0 (negative answer). Their libraries are ordered not alphabetically but by their scores, which are totals of all the 1's they have received. In ideal Guttman scales the triangular patterns of 1s and 0s in the cells are always predictable from the scores column, and neither libraries nor scale levels can be legitimately rearranged. For example, a score of 3 not only fixes Library B's place in the ranking of libraries, but also implies positive answers to the *first* three items, and not some other combination, on the cumulative scale. Library B cannot legitimately score a 3 by, say, getting a point for the first level, skipping the second and third, and then getting two points for the remainder, as it might on a scale other than Guttman's.

The Conspectus manual writers imply that any librarian who rates a subject collection with the RLG scale should have in mind (or recognize as relevant) a model like Table 3.3. But to date that is as far as anyone has gone; no one has proposed that the rater actually check the cumulativeness of levels at his or her library with data. That is where brief tests mark an advance. Unlike other forms of collection evaluation, they explicitly show whether levels are cumulative (and Guttman-scalable), in line with expectations of people in the Conspectus movement.

Here, however, we reach matters that must await fuller discussion in the final chapter: the nature of the RLG scale and the way the brief-test methodology operationalizes it. What the scale purports to measure—collection strength—is almost certainly not unidimensional but multidimensional. Its levels are broad and vague, not neat, sharp gradations. The brief-test "items" that operationalize the scale are not questions about levels per se, but titles, scored "held" or "not held"; and it is the library's scores on *blocks* of these titles—do they meet the 50 percent threshold?—that determine whether a level can be claimed. Obviously, we are at some distance from the Guttman scales of the textbooks and moving toward some region of fuzzy set theory.

The development of strict Guttman scales poses well-known problems (Gorden, 1977; McIver and Carmines, 1981). I have taken a heterodox approach because, unlike Guttman, I am not concerned with strict unidimensionality, at this stage at least. Nevertheless, I think theoretical considerations of scale creation such as his, long familiar to social scientists and psychometricians, should inform developmental work. There is a large literature on the preparation of easily taken, pencil-and-paper tests of human abilities that the library field can draw on in creating short tests of "library abilities." The payoff may be a Guttman-influenced instrument that is better and much briefer than anything in the past.

MORE ON TEST SIZES

To return to practical details, the choice of 40 test items, as against some other number, reflects a desire to have at least 10 items for each of the four levels, while at the same time not burdening any selector with too much of a task. (Selectors are busy people from whom one is extracting a volunteer effort.) Clearly, however, with only 10 items per level, the percentages are less stable than one would like, since each item represents fully 10 percent of the total. A single missing or misclassified item could mean the difference between making the threshold at 50 percent and not making it at 40 percent. Thus, longer tests are desirable to keep single items from counting so heavily.

One remedy is to obtain a second test from another expert on the same subject, so as to have a combined instrument of about 80, rather than 40, items. (See Chapter 6.) The ideal would be to have several 40-item tests per subject area so as to be able to combine them modularly. Nevertheless, the results show even the 40-item tests to be performing reasonably well, and so one must decide whether the stabler percentages are worth the extra effort.

The division of the checklist into four equal sets (e.g., of 10) might be revised. One collection development officer objected to having 10 items at the Minimal level because the RLG definition says, "A subject area in which few selections are made beyond very basic works." His reading of this was that, at the

Minimal level, a library would hold literally few works—for example, 3 or 4, rather than 10, as on the test. I think his is a misreading—the "few works" are those *beyond* the very basic ones, and the latter could easily exceed 10. However, one might adapt the test to local goals by altering its proportions—for example, by including only 5 works at the Minimal level, 10 at the Basic level, 15 at the Instructional level, and 20 at the Research level. (There is no experience as yet with weighting in this form.)

CHEATING AND BIAS

With levels dependent on so few items, the possibility of cheating or manipulation may be raised, especially when librarians score their own collections. The suspicion is that testing will be tainted by politics. The previously mentioned collection development officer wrote me, "The paranoid part of me worries that some libraries will corrupt the methodology by buying the items on your time-saving list."

What, indeed, does prevent someone who misses a 50 percent mark by only one or two items from running out and buying them, thereby becoming able to claim a higher level? The answer is: nothing. However, if one insists on a level for political reasons, then why go to the trouble of using brief tests at all? Since they are intended merely to supplement one's judgment, using them and then falsifying what they reveal is as pointless as cheating at solitaire.

Only slightly less egregious would be someone who biases a test by basing it on the collection to be evaluated. This may seem to go without saying, but sometimes hearers of the brief-test proposal assume that a librarian will create the tests and then use them to assess his or her own collection. That is a misunderstanding. The more independent a selector is, the better. Selectors should know the literature and perhaps the bibliographic tools of a subject, but not the specific collection(s) in which their tests will be employed; nor, within reason, should the bibliographic tools used to develop a collection be used as sources of titles for the test.

The misunderstanding may arise because the person who chooses the 40 test items is confused with the person who obtains their OCLC holdings counts. Only persons with an OCLC account can do the latter, and they typically are librarians who may also want their collections assessed. It would not appear to introduce bias if the librarian whose collection was to be evaluated looked up the counts for a test produced by an independent selector, as long as the selector's wishes (as to editions, serial subscriptions, and so on) were scrupulously carried out. The selector in such a case could be a graduate student, a professor, another librarian, or any qualified person, as long as he or she was not associated with the target collection. It is quite possible, too, that a librarian with access to OCLC could both choose 40 titles and obtain their counts if the resulting test were intended for collections elsewhere. Library school students, who often have both knowledge of literatures and access to OCLC, are capable of making excellent tests, as is shown in the next chapter.

INSTRUCTIONS TO SELECTORS

To obtain brief tests, selectors are given the definitions of the RLG levels shown in Table 1.1 and instructed in writing to choose, as best they can, 10 items per level that reflect the definitions. The letter (or, in my course, a hand-out) includes such statements as these:

• Most of the titles should be monographs, but it is all right to include some serials at the various levels as well.

• The list may consist of works in any edition or in specific editions, if you so choose.

• I hope your selecting will go quickly and perhaps even be fun. Don't agonize over the levels; just use your intuition.

A typical response appears in the introduction to a brief test on American constitutional history that Thomas Fasching wrote as a Drexel student in 1991:

> Materials were essentially selected from *American Constitutional Development,* a one-volume bibliography compiled by Alpheus Thomas Mason and D. Grier Stephenson, Jr., and the five-volume *A Comprehensive Bibliography of American Constitutional and Legal History,* which was prepared by Kermit L. Hall. Forty titles were selected reflecting the four "collecting levels" as set forth by the Research Libraries Group. Selection criteria were based for the most part on an intuitive grasp of where materials would most likely be found among the various collecting levels. Those titles considered to be classic works-or very popular in scope were assigned to Level 1. Voluminous primary works and monographs touching upon relatively narrow and specialized topics were placed in Level 4. The only foreign language item, *De l'esprit des lois* by Montesquieu, was also given a Level 4 placement. Broader-based monographic titles were assigned to Levels 2 and 3, with reference materials typically being placed in Level 2.

In other words, a selector consults appropriate bibliographies (or memory or local collections), then assigns 40 chosen titles to levels according to the RLG definitions. It is all quite straightforward.

As originally conceived, selection was somewhat more complex: brief tests would contain only those titles that were assigned to a given level by a selector *and* that were placed in that same level when OCLC holdings counts were ranked. However, since selectors' assignments and OCLC placements often fail to agree, this plan was discarded in 1988 as too wasteful of items. (Agreement is most likely at the extremes, of course: very basic works for Minimal level and very specialized works for Research level are easier to pick than intermediate works.) As experience with the tests was gained, it was decided to let the levels set by the OCLC counts override the selectors' assigned levels, on the ground that the OCLC counts provided a stricter power test, which, in turn, meant more readily interpretable results. Thus, all 40 items of any selector's test could be kept. (It has not been concealed from selectors that their titles might be reassigned to different levels. Many received White (1988), which sketches the whole process.)

Despite the override, it is by no means idle to have selectors initially assign items to different levels. In all tests thus far, this practice has assured that the counts for the items exhibit good variety and range; typically, they are spread over three orders of magnitude. (Counts running from tens through hundreds to thousands may be observed in Appendix A.) In other words, selectors' attention to the levels ensures that a test will not consist only of easy items or only of hard items. (Either is a real possibility in checklists drawn as samples from certain bibliographies.)

Implicit in the instructions to selectors is the notion that all levels from 1 to 4 are equally worthy as collection goals. (A roughly similar notion attempts to make tests "culture-fair" for persons.) If, for example, a library collects only Level 1 works—items of the sort that are always in print and that are found in chain bookstores—the test will reflect that choice without prejudice. Thus, it could be used by a high-school library or by a research library that was deliberately restricting its holdings in some area. There is no presumption that only advanced research items are worth holding, such as can be inferred from the checklists used in some verification studies.

SEARCHING ON OCLC

After selectors' choices have been made, they are searched for holdings counts in the OCLC online union catalog. To date, counts have been obtained in two ways. In 1987 I received an equipment grant (an M310 workstation) from OCLC to explore the brief-test methodology. From then until 1991, counts were rather laboriously made by retrieving a title, downloading the three-letter codes for the libraries that held it (such as "TEU" for Temple and "PAU" for Penn), and then counting the codes with a program supplied by Danny Wallace of Louisiana State University (Wallace and Boyce, 1989). In 1991 the PRISM version of OCLC software became available on the workstation, and since then holdings counts have been routinely supplied with the bibliographic record for every item searched. Brief tests may now be readily compiled by anyone with access to this software.

Even with PRISM, however, one needs conventions to handle, first, the case of multiple catalog records (with different holdings counts) for a single edition of a work and, second, the case of multiple editions of a single work, which may also involve the first problem.

The convention in the first case is to prefer the count attached to a catalog record created by the Library of Congress (the one coded "DLC" on OCLC screens). Since LC cataloging is generally the choice of the great majority of libraries, the counts attached to LC-created records are by far the highest and reflect the acquisitions history of an edition most fully. Counts accompanying other catalog records for the same work may then be added if they affect the total more than negligibly. Also, the latter are used if no LC record has been created.

The convention in the second case is to accept "significant" counts—usually those accompanying LC-created records—for all editions of a work in standard printed form (i.e., excluding editions in microform, Braille, large print, audiotext, and so on). These are simply totaled for a final count. As a result, libraries that have more than one edition of a work get counted more than once, but that is accepted as an indication of the work's prominence. Occasionally, a selector specifies that only a particular version or edition of a work is to be considered (e.g., *Anna Karenina* in Joel Carmichael's translation); if so, that wish is respected.

While brief tests to date have comprised printed monographs and serials almost exclusively, it is foreseeable that nonprint items cataloged through OCLC, such as films, sound recordings, and electronic works, will increasingly be included. In the case of electronically stored works, it would not seem to matter whether an institution actually holds them or simply provides remote access to them, as long as it uses some sort of OCLC catalog record to note their availability to customers. Here, it would be ownership of the catalog record, rather than ownership of the item, that would increment the count.

Librarians sometimes ask whether searches fail because a selector's item is not yet in the OCLC database: it may be too new or, conversely, so old that retrospective conversion of catalog copy has not yet caught up with it. The answer is: hardly ever. If something is prominent enough that the selector knows of it, the chances are excellent that it is in OCLC. This is not to say that the database "cannot be stumped," merely that search failures of this type have not been a problem to date. If they do occur, a count for a substitute can readily be obtained.

A different issue is the dynamism of the counts. It must be recognized that the counts used in any test may increase after the test maker records them. The market for some works, particularly newer ones, may still be active; if they were searched later, their counts would be higher, and they might end up in a different level when rank-ordered.

The dynamism of the counts depends, in some measure, on how recently a work was published, which is just one of the factors affecting where it ends up in a brief test. Without conscious effort, selectors pick some works that have reached their full market penetration and others that have not. Many such factors are apparently randomized over their whole set of choices. Since the usefulness of the tests is not contingent on unchanging counts, their mutability does not seem to matter much in practice. It would matter more if one were using a count to claim definitively that such-and-such a title was at a certain level—for example, "The *Statistical Abstract of the United States* is a quintessential Minimal-level work, as evidenced by the large number of holding libraries." More on this in Chapter 8.

MECHANICAL ASSIGNMENT

Once the counts are known, a "sort" command (such as that in Microsoft Word) is used to rank them and their associated titles in descending order. Assignment to levels is then mechanical; the list is simply divided into quartiles, high to low, as previously described. Table 3.4 illustrates the procedure with the test for Byzantine studies that Lauris Olson created as a Drexel student in 1990.

Two problems with mechanical assignment to levels may be noted. First, for various reasons, titles may not end up in the quartile where one placed them or thinks they belong: compare the "selector's level" with the "OCLC level" for the

TABLE 3.4

Titles in Byzantine Studies:
Assignment to RLG Levels by OCLC Counts and by Selector

OCLC Count	Author and Title	OCLC Level	Selector's Level
1563	P. Veyne, ed. A history of private life, v. 1: From pagan Rome to Byzantium	1	1
1218	P. Sherrard. Byzantium (Time-Life Books)	1	1
1144	G. A. Holmes, ed. Oxford illustrated history of medieval Europe	1	1
1131	C. W. Previte-Orton. Shorter Cambridge medieval history	1	1
954	C. Diehl. Byzantium: greatness and decline	1	1
996	C. Mango. Byzantium: the empire of New Rome	1	2
839	D. T. Rice, ed. The dark ages: The making of European civilization	1	1
754	J. M. Hussey, ed. Cambridge medieval history, v. 4: The Byzantine empire (2d ed.)	1	2
652	G. Ostrogorsky (Hussey, trans.). History of the Byzantine state (2d ed.)	1	2
650	C. McEvedy. Penguin atlas of medieval history	1	1
548	D. J. Geanakoplos, ed., trans. Byzantium: Church, society and civilization...	2	3
538	Procopius (H. B. Dewing, trans.) History of the wars (Loeb)	2	3
467	T. T. Rice. Everyday life in Byzantium	2	1
373	Dumbarton Oaks Papers (Serial)	2	4
371	E. U. Crosby et al. Medieval studies: Bibliographical guide	2	2
345	J. M. Hussey. The Orthodox church in the Byzantine empire	2	2
342	E. Gibbon (J. B. Bury, ed.) The decline and fall of the Roman empire	2	1
341	O. Lancaster. Sailing to Byzantium: An architectural companion	2	1
341	N. G. Wilson. Scholars of Byzantium	2	2
281	P. Schaff & H. Wace, eds. A select library of Nicene and post-Nicene fathers... (2d ser.)	2	3
209	A. Kazhdan & G. Constable. People and power in Byzantium...	3	2
177	M. F. Hendy. Studies in the Byzantine monetary economy, c. 300-1450	3	2
175	R. Browning. Medieval and modern Greek (2d ed.)	3	2
158	R. Krautheimer. Early Christian and Byzantine architecture (4th ed.)	3	3
144	Byzantinische Zeitschrift (Serial)	3	3
125	F. T. Gignac. A grammar of the Greek papyri of the Roman and Byzantine periods	3	3
119	C. D. Du Cange. Glossarium ad scriptores mediae et infimae graecitatis	3	3
100	H. G. Beck. Kirche und theologische literatur im byzantinischen Reiche	3	3
98	A. Bryer & J. Herrin, eds. Iconoclasm: Papers given at the 9th Spring Symposium...	3	4
84	M. M. Mango. Silver from early Byzantium: The Kaper Koraon and related treasures	3	4
80	P. Charanis. Studies on the demography of the Byzantine empire	4	3
41	G. Moravcsik. Byzantinoturcica (2d ed.)	4	3
39	B. G. Niebuhr, ed. Corpus scriptorum historiae byzantinae	4	4
33	Procopius. (J. Haury, ed.) Opera omnia (Teubner)	4	4
31	Dumbarton Oaks. Dictionary catalogue of the Byzantine collection...	4	3
22	J. P. Migne, ed., trans. Patrologiae cursus completus.... series graeca	4	4
13	R. Ratto. Monnaies byzantines...	4	4
11	Bibliographie de l'art byzantin et post-byzantin, 1945-1969	4	4
5	P. P. Kalonaros, ed., trans. Vasileios Digenes Akritas	4	4
1	J. S. Allen, ed. Literature on Byzantine art, 1892-1967. (Bibliography)	4	4

titles in Table 3.4. Some selectors worry that their own assignments erred when they differ from those set by the counts. That is not the case: the OCLC ordering is not the "right" or "official" one; it is simply better, on the whole, for making brief tests into power tests. Other selectors believe that not they but the OCLC counts misplaced certain works, and they may want to know why. If not simply an error, "misplacement" can happen when the count is for a particular edition of a work rather than all editions. In that case it is easy enough to correct by including more editions. Another reason, of a different sort, is that one's intuition in placing titles reflects a sense of subject treatment running from "rudimentary" to "advanced," and the reality captured by the counts is more complex. For example, some very advanced works (e.g., Jacques Derrida's) are widely held by research libraries, and some rudimentary or popular works are not.

The latter could happen with, say, an elementary textbook because academic libraries make a point of *not* buying every textbook that comes along or because the item is foreign (such as a British introduction to librarianship, deemed redundant in an American setting). Although one may scrap the "erring" test item and substitute a new one, it seems more expedient to focus on the *block* of 10 (or more) test items defining a level. Is the block as a whole patterning cumulatively and yielding intelligible results? If so, it may be best to leave well enough alone: "adjusting" the test items until they yield results that fit one's preconceptions is soon likely to defeat the purpose of obtaining quick readings on a collection.

Second, mechanical assignment to levels raises a "rubber yardstick" problem: the relativity of the counts. In the scales shown in Tables 1.2 to 1.5, the counts were grouped in increments of tens or fives—that is, in equal intervals. Assignment by quartiles does not produce neat increments of this kind. The width of the intervals may vary widely, both within a single test and across tests. Because the counts are not tied to the levels in any absolute sense, the four-level scale is not dependably calibrated.

FIGURE 3.1

Two Hypothetical Tests with Different Ranges of Difficulty

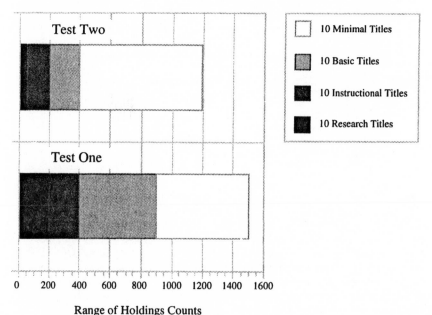

Range of Holdings Counts

The problem is illustrated in Figure 3.1, which diagrams two hypothetical tests as bars. Each band in the bars represents a set of 10 test items. The lower the sets are on the scale of holdings counts, the more difficult they are. Obviously, the two tests differ in difficulty.

Test One has turned out to be easier. For example, only 20 of its items (Research and Instructional) are held by fewer than 400 libraries, whereas 30 of the Test Two items (Research, Instructional, and Basic) are similarly difficult. Note also that fully half of the items in Test Two are below the 200 mark, as against only a quarter of those in Test One.

The visual sign of Test Two's greater difficulty is that its levels look compressed beside those of Test One: both tests have 40 items, but Test Two packs a greater number of hard items into the 40. Diagrams like Figure 3.1 are used later to compare the difficulty of actual tests.

In actual tests, different level-assignments like these do not come about by design; the selectors do not know (or only have hunches about) how the overriding counts will place their titles. Judging from about 75 tests thus far, the most common distribution of ranges resembles that of Test One rather than of Test Two. However, there are some like that of Test Two—for example, in French literature, as discussed in Chapter 6. A research goal for the brief-test methodology is to learn more about controlling the variation of counts over levels so as to produce tests that reflect their creators' intentions as to difficulty. This matter is taken up further in Chapter 8, where an absolute calibration of RLG levels and holdings counts is proposed.

THE RLG SCALE AND BRIEF TESTS

A question may have grown on some readers, namely, what does all this innovation have to do with the original RLG scale? When one rereads the definitions in Table 1.1, they give little hint of what has been presented here; librarians would not operationalize the levels as I have done. In truth, librarians have reworked the definitions of Table 1.1 for various Conspectus subject areas, and while these Supplemental Guidelines may name bibliographies of works appropriate for certain levels, they do not recast the scale in terms of individual titles. I think the best way to characterize the matter is to admit that there are now two ways of measuring Levels 1 to 4: through librarians' estimates, guided by the RLG definitions, and through brief tests. The two ways are not unrelated; selectors draw on the RLG definitions to help them pick titles. But the two are different enough to claim that brief tests are not merely a direct outgrowth of the original RLG scale.

Let us imagine a collection development scale in its earliest state, even before the definitions in Table 1.1 have been written. It simply corresponds to our knowledge that collections differ in the types of interests they support. Now, in fact, this knowledge is multidimensional in nature. We know, for example:

• That some works are appropriate for novices or general readers; others, for initiates or those with specialized interests.

• That works in the first category are relatively few; works in the second, relatively many. (Think of the outpourings, vast in the aggregate, of the nation's specialized presses.)

• That subjects vary in the intellectual demands they place. (Hollywood biographies at their hardest are more approachable than calculus at its simplest.)

• That readers want different form classes—some, mostly journals; others, monographs; still others, technical reports.

And so on. If we had to arrange such knowledge explicitly on a single dimension, almost certainly we would produce something like the RLG scale in Table 1.1, which captures the degree to which collections are specialized toward research, from low to high.

What brief tests provide is an alternative way of measuring the same thing. They are grounded in the claim that ranked OCLC holdings counts capture in a single dimension the same multidimensional knowledge of collections. That is, all the reasons that cause some works to be foundational are reflected in high OCLC counts. All the reasons that cause other works to have increasingly narrow appeal, until they are of interest only to the scholarly few (and perhaps not even to them), are reflected in progressively lower OCLC counts. The reader who ponders why some journals or some ready-reference works or some bibliographies are more widely held than others will grasp what I mean.

This claim about the counts cannot be directly proved. Nonetheless, one can evaluate collections both subjectively, with the RLG definitions, and objectively, with brief tests, and see whether the results converge. The two methods of measurement are intellectually distinct yet have the same goal. If they tend to give the same results, librarians can be more confident in their estimates of collection strength. If they give different results, librarians are prompted to explore why the estimates diverge. This is verification in the strict sense, to be taken up again in Chapter 5.

A CONTROVERSY

The scheme of ranking titles by their counts has already drawn fire, perhaps because it was only minimally explained in White (1988). Siverson (1992, p. 61) objects to it on the ground that it "uses scarcity as a discriminator in the analysis of collection coverage, one that I think completely misrepresents the decisions behind acquiring monographs."

Some confusions here need to be corrected. First, brief tests address not coverage but level. Second, the counts do not reflect "scarcity" unless that is construed as a continuum extending to high degrees of nonscarcity. Brief tests include titles from the whole continuum, not just those that are relatively scarce. Third, I do not claim that "scarcity" underlies decisions to acquire monographs (with the obvious exception of certain rare books). I claim just the reverse, that decisions to acquire monographs underlie the counts, which vary from low to high. These decisions in turn rest on a variety of qualitative considerations, which indirectly inform the counts, thus:

Qualitative considerations –> decisions to buy or not buy –> holdings counts

My contention, developed more fully in Chapter 8, is that when titles in a literature are ranked by their counts and then mapped onto the RLG scale, at least some of these underlying qualitative considerations can be inferred and that generally they will involve the likely usefulness of titles with certain characteristics to various reader markets. Broadly speaking, it is the *perceived audience appeal* of titles, and not primarily their "scarcity," that the counts discriminate. They are correlates of precisely the sorts of qualitative information that, in Siverson's view, checklist studies now wrongly ignore.

Such studies, he argues, assume "that all items of the testing instrument contribute equally to a collection's development" and that this treats "all items as if *collecting levels indicate nothing more than volume thresholds*" (p. 55, italics his). What is missing, he says, is information about type of items owned: "[T]he items within each level must be ordered according to some hierarchy of value. In practice, this means that certain items are collected before others" (p. 54).

He is right about the limitations of past checklist studies, with their single-percentage outcomes. However, brief tests are aimed directly at the very goal he seeks, the prioritization of items across levels. For any literature, brief tests provide an estimate of a library's *individual* hierarchy of values with titles scaled on the basis of a *national* hierarchy of values, as revealed by OCLC-member libraries. Formulaically:

Ranked counts = hierarchy of values =
likelihood of collecting some items before others

If librarians want to make their collection evaluations more consistent, their best alternative lies in test instruments that reflect the national values placed on titles—the OCLC consensus. Siverson (1992) proposes a time-consuming test that goes in the opposite direction, toward local idiosyncrasy. It would make the setting of RLG levels depend on each library's own weighting of titles and interpretation of percentages—a recipe ensuring that tests could not be used unmodified, nor results readily compared, at any two places.

CHECKLISTS AGAIN

With the rationale for brief tests now in place, the contrast with long checklist surveys can be explored a bit further. As Chapter 2 noted, the latter style of verification has never really been thought through. Still, one meets librarians who believe that *someone* has warranted it—some statistician, perhaps, whom the nonstatistical must forever labor to please. Thus, when they hear about brief tests, they worry that a naively small sample is being proposed and suggest that the tests be validated against surveys with much larger samples, which they think produce more accurate results. If pressed, they cannot say what "more accurate" means, but remain convinced that several hundred or a thousand items *must* be better than 40 for measuring—well, whatever is being measured. (This may be the comprehensive bibliographer in them, whispering that a strenuously large bibliography is always better than a short one.) "More accurate" really means "less dubious to me."

Chapter 2 argued that, on the contrary, the large-sample checklist studies to date are ill designed to verify anything because they fail to produce levels with which those from brief tests may be compared. But, with some labor, one may also discover proposals for verification studies that combine large samples with more definite criteria for claiming levels. (For example, to claim Level 1, a certain percentage of titles listed in *The Reader's Adviser* is needed.) It is probably something like the latter that skeptics wish to see used as points of comparison.

It is true that one might carry out large-sample studies that would require more effort than brief tests; it is also true that they could be designed to yield levels rather than coverage figures. Nevertheless, the problem of which to trust would remain. Suppose the levels from a brief test and a large-sample study failed to agree, as well they might. One would face the same task of reconciliation that one faces now when brief tests fail to agree with bibliographers' estimates, with the added annoyance that long checklist studies are much more labor-intensive.

The proposed large-sample studies substitute effort for clarity of purpose. Any level they might provide would not be more accurate, for all the work that went into them, than what brief tests provide. While accuracy in estimating a percentage, such as fraction of a literature held, could indeed be improved by enlarging the sample from a well-chosen sampling frame, that is quite different from improving the estimate of a level on the RLG scale. As yet, there is no articulation between these ideas; they are simply confused.

It will be an important advance when the measure "fraction of a literature held" is operationalized and formally linked to collection level as part of library science. Until then, our measures are limited to librarians' judgments and whatever aids to judgment we can devise. Both brief tests and surveys are aids to judgment, not substitutes for it. The insights they give are not, in any absolute sense, definitive.

Meanwhile, there is no cause to assume that large-sample checklist surveys are better than, or needed to validate, brief tests. What skeptics often miss about the latter on first hearing is their power-test aspect. The reason so few titles can indicate level is structural: the ranked OCLC counts add information that an ordinary random sample lacks. The effect of this ordering can be appreciated only by looking at actual test results, to which we shall soon turn.

ADMINISTRATION

Once a brief test is drawn up, it is usually administered by visiting libraries and checking holdings on-site. This is the fairest method, since it allows one to check not only the online catalog (where possible) but also the card catalog for older materials. Alternatively, at the risk of missing the latter, one may be able to check titles by calling up an online catalog through the Internet. Finally, if libraries belong to OCLC and report their holdings, one can look for their three-letter codes after records corresponding to test items, although this risks missing titles not yet reported to OCLC. (It is also very tedious.)

When trying a brief test, it is obviously desirable to have checkers who are both expert and painstaking in searching the appropriate catalogs. All preliminary effort will be wasted if, for example, a checker misses local holdings through ignorance of how to find them or indifference to the task.

Scoring the test is a simple matter of percentaging to the base of however many items represent each level—10, 20, and so on—and then claiming the highest level possible, using the 50 percent threshold.

The resulting levels, varying from 1 through 4, should seem intelligible and sensible. The next section shows how well the patterns produced by actual brief tests attain these goals.

NOTES

1. Bommer's dissertation, titled "The Development of a Management System for Effective Decision Making and Planning in a University Library," applies operations research techniques to libraries at Penn. The directory is actually titled *Suomen kirjastonhoitajat; Finlands bibliotekarier, 1967.*

2. Of course, these terms taken singly also admit of degrees. For example, people differ greatly in their sense of what is academically advanced. To most people something like the *Corpus scriptorium historiae byzantinae,* a 50-volume, nineteenth-century German edition of Byzantine literature in the original texts, would seem abstruse in the extreme; but to a librarian I met, himself trained as a classicist, it was simply "Niebuhr" (after the editor), so basic that hardly any library could be without it; the fact that it appeared on someone's test as a Level 4 item was occasion for raised eyebrows and a sigh.

PART TWO

Results

CHAPTER 4

Setting Levels

INTRODUCTION

This chapter gives results from 268 trials of brief tests in 76 broad subjects.

Most of these tests were created and administered as term projects by Drexel graduate students in my Research Collection Development course, offered once a year during 1989–1994. The students were allowed to choose their own subjects, titles, and one or more collections to evaluate. They also did their own OCLC searches in order to rank titles.

The libraries whose collections were tested are mostly in or near Philadelphia. More distant ones were evaluated by checking their holdings reports in the OCLC database, by making special trips to visit them, through Internet access to their online catalogs, or through collaborators.

Faculty members or professional librarians with subject expertise created a relative handful of tests during 1988–1990. These persons were recruited as selectors with a letter that included the definitions of RLG levels. For their tests, I obtained OCLC holdings counts, ranked the titles, and performed checks against holdings in arbitrarily chosen libraries (for example, at Penn, Temple, and the University of Chicago).

Selectors chose items from personal knowledge or from bibliographies. The test titles are largely monographs. In many tests, serial titles also appear. (There are numerous serials, for example, in the tests in genetics and Middle Eastern studies.) Some tests in music included musical scores (but not phonorecordings). The test in modern cinema is made up entirely of feature-length films (such as *2001: A Space Odyssey*).

The students responsible for the data are adults beginning professional careers in librarianship. Many have advanced subject degrees or long-standing interests in literatures. Their tests are in no way distinguishable from those created by incumbent librarians or academics (except that, in bibliographic matters, they are usually more careful than academics). Most are detail-oriented and seem to enjoy carrying out trials accurately.

None of the students received special training other than a briefing with handouts (the RLG definitions of levels and, in many cases, a copy of White, 1988). No one needed mathematical or statistical skills beyond ability to do percentages. Brief-test methodology thus seems transferrable to "ordinary people," including clerical staff and librarians in settings other than research universities. The scale of effort required is, moreover, attractive. People at Drexel, working at scattered times during 1989–1994, were able to assess collections in many more subjects than the RLG has been able to do in a decade. (This is not to boast, but to address the concern of librarians who dislike the prospect of evaluation with long checklists.) The tables below suggest how quickly the brief-test methodology can be made to yield results.

Surprisingly, there are almost no brief tests in the fields for which Drexel is locally renowned—engineering and business. This is perhaps attributable to the well-known tastes and backgrounds of library school students. Otherwise, the tests represent a nice diversity of subjects, as will be seen.

A complete list of selectors appears in Appendices A and B.

CRITERIA FOR INTERPRETING RESULTS

It was said at the end of the last chapter that brief-test results should be intelligible and sensible. Before outcomes are discussed, the two notions need to be made more definite.

First, intelligibility. It will be recalled that, by hypothesis, library collection development has a cumulative pattern, in which ability to claim a given level rests on ability to claim all lower levels. Results will be intelligible when they bear out the hypothesis of cumulativeness:

If a collection scores at least 50 percent at a given level, it will score at least 50 percent at any lower level.

This amounts to a prediction that strength rests on strength. A corollary, amounting to the same thing, is that if a collection scores less than 50 percent at a given level, it will score less than 50 percent at any higher level. In other words, nonstrength persists.[1]

The hypothesis of cumulativeness does not entail a prediction that libraries will hold progressively fewer items as the levels rise from 1 to 4. In practice, one would expect to see this power-test outcome quite often, but other outcomes are consistent with a power test—for example, a score of 100 percent (or close to it) on all four levels by a library with a very strong collection. Moreover, outcomes inconsistent with strict power-test scalability (such as 60%–70%–50%–90% across the four levels) do not vitiate brief tests if the hypothesis above is borne out. To the degree that it is borne out, the RLG scale *levels* (not the underlying titles) may be considered cumulative (or Guttman-scalable) on the implicit dimension of collection strength.

The intelligibility requirement has to do with consistency of results in any one library. The second requirement—that results be "sensible"—has to do with comparisons between libraries. There are no specific hypotheses here; we simply ask that results from different libraries on the same test not violate our intuitions of fitness. For example, in most academic subjects, collections of public libraries or community colleges should not outscore those of big universities. In the humanities, a technological university like Drexel should not match (let alone outscore) universities like Chicago, Berkeley, and Penn. Generally, brief-test results should not only discriminate among collections; they should also accord reasonably well with the intuitions of developers and knowledgeable users.

RESULTS

Table 4.1, a summary account of patterns, will be explained shortly. The great majority of results through 1994 appear in Table 4.2, which has 232 trials, and Table 4.3, which has 36 trials. Because of their length, Tables 4.2 and 4.3 are placed at the end of this chapter (before the Notes section) rather than here. Percentages have been recorded just as they appeared in students' reports. Errors of measurement may have occurred in any number of places, but, beyond a few emendations following spot checks, little attempt has been made to correct them; this account hews to the model of naturalistic field trials. Effort has been made to include all data not conforming to hypothesis.[2]

The Global Message

The main message of Tables 4.2 and 4.3 is global rather than particular. The tables show many different subjects chosen by many different test makers, many different trials by diverse hands at diverse sites, and, nevertheless, massive consistency of results. (This may be seen by sampling the tables according to one's interests, rather than reading them as wholes.) Despite some problems, the brief test methodology appears quite sturdy. The outcomes are intelligible and sensible, as required; they help directly in setting or verifying collection levels. Findings in later chapters add credibility to this notion.

The details of Tables 4.2 are as follows. The four-point RLG scale reflects the underlying order of difficulty of test items, as shown in the first chapter:

Easiest   *1*   2   3   4   Hardest

The subject collections of individual libraries are measured as percentages within the four categories of this scale. Percentages are not to be added down the columns or across the rows. Each is to be read in its own right, to the base of 10 titles per level.[3] For example, in Byzantine studies (topmost in Table 4.2) the University of Pennsylvania has all 10 of the 10 titles representing Level 1, 9 of the 10 titles at Level 2, 10 of 10 at Level 3, and 9 of 10 at Level 4. Its percentage scores of 100%–90%–100%–90% yield a Research-level rating. (Recall that a library must hold at least 50 percent of titles at a given level in order to claim it.) Bryn Mawr College has only four, or 40 percent, of the 10 titles at Level 4, and so cannot claim a Research-level collection, although it is close. All percentages for individual libraries are read similarly. The highest level that libraries can claim is boldfaced in the column at right. The problematical cases receive a question mark. When a library holds too few titles to attain even Level 1, but the subject is nevertheless not out of scope, a level of 1a has been awarded, using WLN's scale rather than RLG's and a scoring procedure explained in the next chapter.

Table 4.3 differs from Table 4.2 in layout, to bring together trials on comparable tests at certain libraries, but it has the same conventions for interpreting percentages.

The rightmost column of Table 4.2 may be scanned in context for what have been called "sensible" results. More technically, results may be validated against a criterion, the nature of the holding library, which presumably the reader will be able to judge. Note the varying readings over many different collections. Level 4 collections appear quite frequently, but that is because numerous trials have been conducted at big research libraries. Instances of collections at lower levels are also frequent, and accord well with the nature of the holding institution, such as libraries in community colleges, liberal arts colleges, and nonresearch universities; legal and medical libraries; and public libraries. Drexel University is fairly often matched with universities that have full programs in the social sciences and humanities; its collections are almost always less strong, as common sense would predict. (More on this sort of validation later.)

Evidence for Cumulativeness

Tables 4.2 and 4.3 together show 268 trials. In 258 (or 96.3 percent) of them, the hypothesis of cumulativeness was sustained. It appears conclusively that "strength rests on strength" and that the levels are Guttman-scalable. The probability that such a result occurred by chance is less than one in a thousand by a test for significant difference in proportions.

The previous chapter reported a colleague's conjecture that research institutions such as the New York Public Library might have collections that were produced by ignoring the lower levels and buying only at the higher. (The pattern of the hypothetical example was 0%–10%–40%–100% from Levels 1 through 4.) Such a result, a marked contradiction to cumulativeness, is completely absent in Tables 4.2, which includes trials at the New York Public Library, and 4.3. Even the most irregular patterns do not take this form. In case after case, research collections rest on holdings that are strong at all lower levels.

A finer breakdown of patterns over levels provides the types seen in Table 4.1. The first type simply reflects very strong collections. In the second the percentages fall off rightward as one moves up the levels from 1 to 4. This illustrates the "difficulty effect" of Chapter 1. It is also the clearest indication of the power-test phenomenon, reflecting the decreasing probability of holding titles as they appeal to increasingly narrow and specialized readerships. The third type is simply a variant, and, with the first two, constitutes 69.4 percent of outcomes. The remaining type comprises the irregulars, which show "up-and-down" patterns in the percentages. The third and fourth types are not inconsistent with a power test; they simply show idiosyncratic interactions between tests and collections, and remain interpretable.

A Measure of Behavior

Since libraries and the collections in them are things, it may seem that brief tests yield information about things and not people. In a real sense, however, collections result from librarians' behaviors, and any measure of collections is a behavioral measure. It is useful to recall here the earlier claim that brief tests are like traditional tests of human aptitudes and to see them as yielding information not so much about collections, which have no aptitudes, as about collection developers, who do. Although brief tests are informative even when knowledge of past practices is missing (as when a librarian cannot tap corporate memory about them), it seems especially fruitful to read the various lines of Table 4.2 as if one were a librarian who knows the goals of the past and who now seeks insight into how they have been fulfilled—an external check on his or her sense of what the developers have done.

In some subjects, of course, librarians want to create Level 4 (or even Level 5) collections. The most heartening result, in that case, is confirmation that their efforts have succeeded. For example, both the University of Pennsylvania and the

TABLE 4.1

Percentage Patterns in 268 Brief-Test Trials

Type	Number	Percent
Perfect scores (all 100%)	8	3.0%
Descending scores without ties (e.g., 80% - 70% - 40% - 10%)	64	23.9%
Descending scores with ties (e.g., 100% - 70% - 70% - 25%)	114	42.5%
Irregular patterns (e.g., 70% - 90% - 50% - 80%)	82	30.6%
TOTAL	268	100%

University of Chicago have long had strong programs in medieval history. It is no accident that their respective university presses both publish monographic series in this field. One would also expect many years of strong support from their librarians. So it would be surprising if brief tests showed a lack of aptitude here, and they do not: Penn is 100%–90%–90%–90% and Chicago is 90%–80% –90%–80%.

One sees the same thing in library and information science. Both Columbia and Chicago are known to generations of librarians for their library schools and the doctoral programs associated with them. The schools are now sadly gone; but the collections test out at 100%–100%–100%–100% for Columbia and 100%– 100%–100%–90% for Chicago.

In contrast, one often sees cases in which developers appear to have successfully limited a collection without by any means ignoring a subject. Examples will be found in the trials at Drexel. Librarians there have no mandate to build collections to research depth in the humanities or in most of the social sciences, particularly since strong collections in these areas are next door at Penn and a few miles away at Temple. But neither have they gone to the opposite extreme and declared these areas out of scope, as, given Drexel's technological image, some might expect.

Perhaps surprisingly, brief tests reveal Drexel to have Basic-level collections in such subjects as American women's history, post-impressionist painting, Christianity, even Arthurian literature. (The books probably deal with engineering projects under that ruler, but still...) The larger point is that, in most subjects in most libraries, collections *should* be at less than research strength, and brief tests can show the developers of any collection the degree to which they have struck an appropriate balance between under- and overdevelopment.

Occasionally, we can infer a plausible collection level for a particular library and see whether brief tests bear us out. Thus, it is corroborative to note that, in literature pertaining to the Reformation, the Lutheran Theological Seminary attains Level 4, while the St. Charles Borromeo Seminary (which is Roman Catholic) attains Level 2. In Jewish women's studies, Gratz College is Level 4 like far larger institutions (New York University, Boston University, and Penn), but then Gratz is a Philadelphia center for Jewish studies, with distinguished Judaica and Hebraica collections.

As noted, some of the trials in Table 4.2 were made in nonresearch settings, such as:

Byzantine studies in the Camden County (NJ) Public Library
Primatology in the Abington (PA) Public Library
U.S. Constitutional history in the Lehigh County (PA) Community College Library
Toxicology in the San Francisco (CA) Public Library
Modernist and postmodern American poetry in the Berkeley (CA) Public Library

In each, the collection turns out to be a Level 1, which, to an outsider at least, seems exactly right from a policy standpoint. As with Drexel, important subjects have not been ignored, but neither have collections in them been allowed to grow beyond the likely interests of potential clienteles, thereby inviting criticism. Again, the relevance of brief tests for evaluating collections in libraries of any type would seem obvious.

In this context, an interesting outcome is what might be called the "long, thin collection"—one in which the developers have not built to Minimal or Basic level and then quit, but have stretched holdings feebly across all four levels—see, for example, Drexel's collections in toxicology (under medicine) or primatology (under science) in Table 4.2. The reasons for such outcomes would have to be sought locally, of course, but among them might be that developers wanted a distinguished collection and were underfunded, or that they were coordinating purchases with those for a collection nearby, or that someone was riding a hobbyhorse. Perhaps all three. (An outcome in which developers achieve Level 4 by obtaining 50%–50%–50%–50% across the four levels has not been seen and is not likely, but it is possible.)

The 10 trials that do not conform to the hypothesis are of the irregular type, but perplexing in that collections fail to attain some lower level and then attain a higher one (e.g., 80%–40%–60%–10%). Since such outcomes are relatively few, it may be they arise simply from errors (such as obtaining wrong OCLC counts and misranking one's choices, failing to find titles that are indeed held, or miscomputing the final percentages, all of which have been known to happen in actual trials.) Alternatively, they may happen when a subject matter lends itself to idiosyncratic collecting at particular libraries (as, for example, several of the belletristic literatures might).

If errors are not involved, better outcomes could probably be produced merely by increasing the numbers of items on tests, so that single titles did not each represent fully 10 percent of the score at a given level. There is some evidence for this. Three of the nonconforming outcomes occur at Bryn Mawr and Swarthmore—colleges whose collections I studied in the Tri-College Consortium research project, as reported in Chapter 6. In early trials at these colleges, test instruments had only 40 titles, and similar odd results were sometimes seen. But when test instruments were lengthened to 80 titles, the irregularities disappeared, and the results were those of wholly interpretable power tests.

If tests cannot be lengthened, the nonconforming outcome will require a judgment call, preferably by an insider in the library being tested. For example, the holdings on anarchism in the U.S. at Bates College show 80%–40%–60%–10% across the levels. How does one interpret this? To an outsider the collection seems to lie somewhere between Levels 2 and 3. Ali Munif Seden, the Drexel student who conducted the trial, believes that Bates intends only a Level 1 or 2 collection on anarchism. He thinks the reason for their relatively strong showing at Level 3 is that some of his test authors (e.g., Paul Goodman) are needed for the study of other subjects, or that they have a regional interest for New England (Bates is in Maine). But the chief consideration is how the test squares with local librarians' intentions. They would have to decide whether the ambiguous test results are "close enough" to their goal, or whether action is needed to bring the collection more clearly to a higher level.

No doubt we should also note that this is one of those cases where the nonconformity at Level 2—40 percent instead of 50 percent—turns on the absence of a single book. It would be counterproductive to take the brief test result more seriously than it warrants—certainly not as requiring long indecision and debate. One escape route would be to claim the higher level—here Level 3—but to qualify the claim as somewhat weak. Another would be simply to claim the lower level, conservatively.

Problem cases of this sort necessarily call for discussion; but for readers inclined to focus on them, it is appropriate to restate the main message of the chapter thus far: Table 4.2 shows overwhelmingly that brief tests give useful, unproblematical readings on collections. As we shall see, the results in Table 4.3 extend that pleasant outcome.

CONVERGENT VALIDITY

Because a wealth of brief tests became available during 1989–94, it was possible to explore validity of measurement at certain test sites. By good fortune, some of the students in my course chose comparable subjects for their instruments and administered them on the same collections. These student projects were wholly independent of one another. Usually the students took the course in different terms and, in any case, had no knowledge that their results would be compared with anyone else's. Other comparable data came from instruments created by faculty members and administered by me.

It was not initially planned that results would be compared; the various possibilities emerged only as the present account was being written. So what we have is a naturally occurring opportunity to see how well results converge. Note that this kind of validity check differs from the one above, in which we asked whether the levels produced by brief tests seem "sensible"—that is, appropriate to the nature of the holding institution.

The data are presented in Table 4.3. In some cases the comparison is between a general subject and a more specialized one: mathematics and physics/math, philosophy and philosophy of science, women's studies and Jewish women's studies, modern European Jewish history and the Holocaust. In other cases it is between two different tests on the same subject: genetics, economics, African-American studies, and intellectual property law.[4] Lastly, two subjects only roughly comparable are matched: U.S. history 1760–1860 as against the U.S. history 1861–1865.

The results from 11 different libraries exhibit high convergent validity: different tests yield similar outcomes. In 17 comparisons, 14 produce the same level of collection strength. In the other three, Drexel is one level higher in U.S. history of the Civil War than of the 1760–1860 period, and (barely) one level higher in philosophy than in philosophy of science, while the Free Library of Philadelphia is one level higher in women's studies than in Jewish women's studies. (The latter cases are interpretable; the more specialized collections are somewhat less developed.) The outcomes are never markedly different; we do not see a collection scoring at Level 1 on one test and Level 4 on another. The percentages as one compares them across the four levels are not identical but quite often very similar indeed. While one would like to see the same trials run with longer tests so that percentages would be more stable, these initial results encourage the belief that, with these measures of collection strength, "we are measuring what we think we are measuring"—the classic definition of validity.

In the next chapter we will examine the validity of brief tests from yet another point of view—how well their results agree with librarians' own estimates of their collections on the RLG scale. Almost 100 brief-test trials remain to be presented on aspects of the methodology not yet shown.

TABLE 4.2

RLG Levels Attained with Brief Tests

Percentages per Level

History and Area Studies	1	2	3	4	Level Attained
Byzantine Studies					
Bryn Mawr College	90	90	90	40	3
Camden County (NJ) Library	60	10	0	0	1
Drexel University	90	10	0	0	1
Haverford College	50	40	20	10	1
Stanford University	100	90	100	90	4
University of California, Berkeley	100	90	100	90	4
University of Chicago	90	90	100	100	4
University of Pennsylvania	100	90	100	90	4
Yale University	90	100	100	70	4
Medieval History					
New York Public Library	100	90	100	70	4
Temple University	90	70	80	10	3
University of Chicago	90	80	90	80	4
University of Pennsylvania	100	90	90	90	4
Chinese History					
Drexel University	80	10	10	10	1
Temple University	100	100	40	30	2
University of London	90	50	50	10	3
University of Pennsylvania	80	90	50	70	4
Middle Eastern Studies					
University of Chicago	100	100	82	64	4
20th Century British History					
University of Pennsylvania	100	100	92	67	4
20th Century Russian History					
Free Library of Philadelphia	100	90	60	10	3
University of Pennsylvania	100	100	100	90	4
German Colonial Africa					
Drexel University	50	40	10	0	1
Temple University	100	100	90	30	3
U.S. History 1760-1860 (see also Table 4.3)					
Temple University	90	60	50	10	3
U.S. History 1861-1865 (see Table 4.3)					
U.S. Constitutional History					
Lafayette College	100	90	60	20	3
Lehigh County (PA) Community College	90	40	10	0	1
Lehigh University	100	90	40	20	2
University of Pennsylvania	90	90	70	50	4
University of Pennsylvania Law School	50	60	10	40	2
Psychohistory					
Bryn Mawr College	70	50	50	20	3
Haverford College	50	90	20	10	2
Swarthmore College	100	90	80	30 ·	3
Temple University	100	90	50	30	3
History of Technology					
Bryn Mawr College	60	60	50	0	3
Drexel University	90	90	60	0	3
Haverford College	70	40	10	0	2
Swarthmore College	80	90	90	20	3
Temple University	100	100	50	40	3
Anarchism in the United States					
Bates College	80	40	60	10	?
University of Michigan	100	100	100	80	4
University of Utah	100	100	70	30	3
Williams College	70	80	50	20	3

TABLE 4.2 *(continued)*

Percentages per Level

	1	2	3	4	Level Attained
African-American Studies					
African-American Studies 1 (see also Table 4.3)					
Berkeley (CA) Public Library	100	80	90	20	3
Drexel University	70	60	60	20	3
San Francisco State University	100	100	80	60	4
Yale University	100	100	90	60	4
African-American Studies 2 (see also Table 4.3)					
Lehigh University	100	70	40	50	?
Jewish Studies					
Jewish Law					
Brandeis University	90	100	80	20	3
Harvard University	90	80	80	60	4
Jewish Theological Seminary of America	80	60	50	20	3
Reconstructionist Rabbinical College	100	100	100	100	4
University of California, Los Angeles	100	100	50	30	3
Jewish Holocaust, 1939-1945 (see also Table 4.3)					
University of Pennsylvania	90	70	100	50	4
Modern European Jewish History (see also Table 4.3)					
Jewish Theological Seminary of America	100	100	90	90	4
Women's Studies					
Women's Studies (see Table 4.3)					
American Women's History					
Drexel University	50	60	20	10	2
University of Pennsylvania	100	90	90	80	4
Jewish Women's Studies (see also Table 4.3)					
Beaver College	10	30	0	0	1a
Boston University	100	100	80	50	4
Bucks County (PA) Community College	50	10	0	0	1
Drexel University	50	0	0	0	1
Gratz College	100	80	80	50	4
New York University	90	100	90	50	4
University of Pennsylvania	100	100	90	50	4
Religion					
Biblical Studies					
Drexel University	80	30	10	0	1
Pennsylvania State University	100	90	80	50	4
University of Pennsylvania	100	90	80	100	4
Christian Religion					
Drexel University	90	60	30	0	2
University of Pennsylvania	80	90	70	50	4
The Reformation					
Free Library of Philadelphia	90	90	30	10	2
Lutheran Theological Seminary	100	100	100	60	4
Muhlenberg College	100	80	50	40	3
St. Charles Borromeo Seminary	80	60	30	10	2
Feminist Theology					
Drexel University	50	20	0	0	1
Free Library of Philadelphia	100	90	40	40	2
University of Pennsylvania	100	100	90	60	4
Literature					
Arthurian Literature					
Drexel University	60	70	30	20	2
University of Pennsylvania	100	100	100	100	4
Medieval Literature					
Drexel University	100	50	40	30	2

TABLE 4.2 *(continued)*

Percentages per Level

	1	2	3	4	Level Attained
18th Century English Fiction					
University of Pennsylvania	100	90	100	90	4
Victorian Literature					
University of Chicago	80	100	100	80	4
University of Pennsylvania	60	100	100	60	4
German Literature (Age of Goethe)					
Drexel University	90	50	20	0	2
Pennsylvania State University	100	100	90	90	4
University of Pennsylvania	90	100	100	100	4
19th Century Russian Literature					
Temple University	82	54	27	36	2
University of Pennsylvania	100	73	73	36	3
Modern American Literature					
Bryn Mawr College	50	20	50	40	?
Haverford College	70	60	50	50	4
Swarthmore College	70	40	40	60	?
Modernist and Postmodern American Poetry					
Berkeley (CA) Public Library	90	20	20	0	1
Bryn Mawr College	60	30	50	10	?
Haverford College	90	80	60	0	3
Swarthmore College	90	50	70	40	3
University of California, Berkeley	100	100	100	80	4
Postmodern American Novel					
Bucknell University	80	70	80	20	3
Drexel University	70	30	20	0	1
Native American Literature					
Drexel University	40	50	10	0	?
Temple University	100	90	70	10	3
University of Chicago	90	90	60	70	4
University of Pennsylvania	80	90	80	20	3
Contemporary Mexican Literature					
Bryn Mawr College	100	60	40	10	2
Haverford College	90	30	30	20	1
Stanford University	100	100	100	80	4
Swarthmore College	100	80	70	50	4
University of California (all campuses)	100	100	100	100	4
University of Pennsylvania	100	100	80	40	3
Nigerian Literature					
Drexel University	30	10	0	0	1 a
Free Library of Philadelphia	80	80	10	10	2
University of Pennsylvania	100	100	100	100	4
Philosophy					
Philosophy 1 (see Table 4.3)					
Philosophy 2 (see also Table 4.3)					
Temple University	100	80	80	50	4
Philosophy of Science (see Table 4.3)					
Ethics					
Drexel University	70	0	10	0	1
Swarthmore College	100	100	80	30	3
Medical Ethics					
Free Library of Philadelphia	80	70	20	20	2
Temple University	90	60	40	30	2
Arts					
Art Photography					
Drexel University	80	50	50	0	3
University of California, Berkeley	90	70	80	30	3
University of Pennsylvania	90	80	30	10	2

TABLE 4.2 *(continued)*

	Percentages per Level				Level
	1	**2**	**3**	**4**	**Attained**
Modern Cinema (Films)					
Drexel University	50	30	40	20	1
Free Library of Philadelphia	100	100	100	40	3
Interior Design					
Drexel University	70	70	50	20	3
New York Public Library	100	90	60	30	3
Philadelphia College of Textiles & Science	80	70	60	30	3
Rensselaer Polytechnic University	90	80	50	40	3
Temple University	80	60	40	10	2
University of Pennsylvania	80	60	30	0	2
Architectural History (American Emphasis)					
Temple University	80	90	90	40	3
University of Chicago	100	80	90	30	3
University of Pennsylvania	100	100	90	70	4
Post-Impressionism in Art					
Drexel University	70	50	40	0	2
University of Pennsylvania	100	100	100	40	3
Music					
Musicology (Books)					
University of Pennsylvania	100	100	100	80	4
Classical Music (Scores)					
Free Library of Philadelphia	80	50	40	40	2
Temple University	70	60	60	0	3
University of Pennsylvania	100	80	80	50	4
Opera (Books and Scores)					
Drexel University	80	30	0	0	1
University of the Arts (Philadelphia)	90	80	50	10	3
Popular Music: Rock Era (Books)					
Bryn Mawr College	40	10	0	0	1a
Drexel University	50	40	40	0	1
Haverford College	50	10	0	0	1
Swarthmore College	40	10	0	0	1a
Temple University	90	80	50	50	4
Medicine					
Oncology					
San Francisco Public Library	60	0	0	0	1
Thomas Jefferson University	50	100	80	70	4
University of California, San Francisco	60	80	80	70	4
University of Pennsylvania	60	90	50	60	4
Toxicology					
Drexel University	40	10	10	10	1a
Hahnemann University	70	30	10	0	1
San Francisco Public Library	50	20	0	0	1
University of California, San Francisco	100	100	100	100	4
University of Pennsylvania	80	90	60	20	3
Herbs and Herbal Medicine					
Drexel University	60	10	20	0	1
Florida State University	80	70	60	20	3
University of California, Berkeley	100	70	80	80	4
University of Delaware	70	90	50	10	3
University of Pittsburgh	100	30	60	40	?
Sciences					
Mathematics (see also Table 4.3)					
Temple University	80	100	60	60	4
Physics/Mathematics (see also Table 4.3)					
University of Chicago	90	90	100	80	4
Genetics (see Table 4.3)					

TABLE 4.2 *(continued)*

Percentages per Level

	1	2	3	4	Level Attained
Astronomy					
Franklin and Marshall College	90	70	90	30	3
University of Pennsylvania	90	70	60	60	4
Primatology					
Abington (PA) Public Library	50	30	10	10	1
Drexel University	40	30	10	10	1a
Swarthmore College	80	80	80	10	3
Yale University	100	80	70	70	4
Ecology					
Colorado State University	90	100	80	60	4
Biochemistry					
Drexel University	90	70	50	30	3
Harvard University	100	100	90	60	4
New York Public Library	90	70	70	30	3
Princeton University	90	100	70	90	4
Social Sciences					
Archeology of American Southwest					
Arizona State University	50	80	80	70	4
Drexel University	50	10	0	0	1
Southern Methodist University	80	100	90	70	4
University of Pennsylvania	90	100	90	60	4
Social Theory					
Bates College	100	70	20	20	2
Bowdoin College	90	90	70	20	3
Colby College	90	90	30	20	2
Drexel University	70	40	10	0	1
University of Pennsylvania	100	80	100	70	4
Criminology					
Temple University	89	93	100	52	4
University of California, Berkeley	100	92	83	25	3
University of California, San Francisco	50	17	8	0	1
University of Pennsylvania	89	100	100	62	4
University of Scranton	58	75	33	8	2
Developmental Psychology					
University of Delaware	100	90	80	40	3
Linguistics					
Free Library of Philadelphia	80	90	50	40	3
Sociology of the Deaf					
Free Library of Philadelphia	100	63	63	25	3
University of Pennsylvania	72	45	72	54	?
Cultural Anthropology					
University of Chicago	80	100	90	60	4
University of Pennsylvania	100	90	100	60	4
Economics 1					
Temple University	100	90	80	70	4
Economics 2 (see Table 4.3)					
Law					
Roman Law					
Columbia University	100	100	100	100	4
University of Pennsylvania	90	100	60	50	4
University of Pennsylvania Law School	100	100	100	90	4
Intellectual Property 1 (see also Table 4.3)					
Dickinson School of Law	90	70	40	10	2
Jenkins Law Library (Philadelphia)	70	60	50	0	3
U.S. Court of Appeals (2d Circuit)	70	70	40	10	2
University of Pennsylvania Law School	90	60	60	10	3
Widener School of Law (Delaware)	70	80	50	20	3
Widener School of Law (Harrisburg)	80	70	20	0	2

TABLE 4.2 *(continued)*

Percentages per Level

	1	2	3	4	Level Attained
Intellectual Property 2 (see Table 4.3)					
U.S. Constitutional Law					
Dickinson School of Law	100	70	70	10	3
University of Pennsylvania Law School	100	90	90	70	4
Villanova University Law School	90	60	70	10	3
Widener School of Law	60	60	70	10	3
International Business Law					
Drexel University	70	30	30	0	1
Harvard University	70	70	70	70	4
Jenkins Law Library (Philadelphia)	60	70	40	30	2
Social Law Library (Boston)	40	70	50	30	?
University of Pennsylvania Law School	80	40	70	70	?
Villanova University Law School	60	50	70	60	4
Widener School of Law (Delaware)	60	40	30	40	1
Widener School of Law (Harrisburg)	50	30	20	10	1
Widener School of Law (both campuses)	70	50	40	40	2
Business					
Workplace Democracy					
Cornell University	100	100	100	70	4
State University of New York, Stony Brook	90	90	60	30	3
University of California, Berkeley	100	100	100	60	4
Manufacturing Planning and Production Control					
Drexel University	70	60	30	10	2
University of Delaware	100	70	70	30	3
University of California, Berkeley	100	100	100	70	4
University of Pennsylvania	90	60	40	10	2
Information Sciences					
Computer Science					
Brooklyn College	70	80	70	30	3
Columbia University	100	100	100	100	4
Drexel University	60	50	60	10	3
Penn State University (all campuses)	100	100	100	100	4
Rutgers University	100	70	70	40	3
Library and Information Science					
French Institute (New York City)	30	20	0	0	1 a
Marymount Manhattan	70	50	25	20	2
New York Public Library	100	100	83	70	4
New York University	100	70	67	60	4
St. John's University	100	100	92	90	4
Temple University	90	100	70	30	3
University of Chicago	100	100	100	90	4
University of Pennsylvania	90	90	60	30	3
Yeshiva University	80	70	60	30	3

TABLE 4.3

Validation Trials in Setting Levels with Brief Tests

Percentages per Level

	1	2	3	4	Level Attained
Law					
Stanford University Law School					
Intellectual Property 1	100	90	60	70	4
Intellectual Property 2	80	70	70	70	4
UC Berkeley Law School					
Intellectual Property 1	100	70	50	20	3
Intellectual Property 2	100	60	50	40	3
Villanova University Law School					
Intellectual Property 1	100	80	10	30	2
Intellectual Property 2	100	70	40	0	2
Social Science					
University of Pennsylvania					
Economics 1	100	100	90	50	4
Economics 2	90	90	80	70	4
Science					
University of Chicago					
Genetics 1	100	80	80	80	4
Genetics 2	100	100	90	70	4
University of Pennsylvania					
Mathematics	70	80	80	60	4
Physics / Mathematics	100	60	80	90	4
Philosophy					
Drexel University					
Philosophy 1	100	90	50	10	3
Philosophy 2	100	100	70	10	3
Philosophy of Science	80	90	40	10	2
University of Pennsylvania					
Philosophy 1	100	100	90	90	4
Philosophy 2	100	100	100	90	4
Philosophy of Science	100	100	100	70	4
Widener University					
Philosophy 1	70	60	40	0	2
Philosophy of Science	70	60	40	10	2
Jewish Studies					
Drexel University					
Holocaust 1939-1945	70	50	30	0	2
Modern European Jewish History	90	50	20	0	2
Stanford University					
Holocaust 1939-1945	100	100	100	90	4
Modern European Jewish History	100	100	100	60	4
African-American Studies					
University of Pittsburgh					
African-American Studies 1	100	100	100	80	4
African-American Studies 2	100	90	80	90	4
Women's Studies					
Free Library of Philadelphia					
Women's Studies	100	80	60	10	3
Jewish Women's Studies	100	90	30	20	2
Temple University					
Women's Studies	100	90	70	20	3
Jewish Women's Studies	90	100	70	30	3

TABLE 4.3 *(continued)*

Percentages per Level

	1	2	3	4	Level Attained
History					
Drexel University					
U.S. History 1760-1860	80	60	30	10	2
U.S. History 1861-1865	90	70	50	30	3
University of Pennsylvania					
U.S. History 1760-1860	90	70	50	40	3
U.S. History 1861-1865	90	70	50	30	3
Widener University					
U.S. History 1760-1860	80	50	40	20	2
U.S. History 1861-1865	80	60	20	20	2

NOTES

1. "Nonstrength" is used in preference to "weakness" because collections are often limited by deliberate policy; and it "persists" only through a particular test—not, if librarians wish to upgrade a collection, over time.

2. Because the data here were gathered and summarized by many persons (all of them "outsiders"), no guarantee of their correctness is made. The levels based on them should be taken as illustrations of the methodology, not definitive assessments.

3. Occasionally tests have idiosyncratic numbers of items per level, such as 11 or 12. These are signalled in the results by percentages that are not deciles. See, for example, the results of the test in criminology and of some of the tests in library and information science.

4. The question of overlapping test items naturally arises here. There is no overlap between genetics 1 and 2 or among philosophy 1 and 2 and philosophy of science. Economics 1 and 2 have three overlapping titles. Intellectual property law 1 and 2 have 12; it is difficult to avoid them in this highly specialized subject. The overlaps could be eliminated, of course, but they were not deemed compromising enough to make the results unreportable. None of the other tests in Table 4.3 has any duplicate titles.

Overlaps are most likely to occur in selectors' choices to represent the Minimal level. They tend to be items that pop into every culturally literate head, and there are fewer such works to choose from: for example, two in the Economics tests are Adam Smith's *The Wealth of Nations* and Karl Marx's *Capital*.

CHAPTER 5

Verifying Levels

CAVEATS

Here some test results from the last chapter will be re-presented as checks on collection levels first set by librarians.

Recall that librarians rate their collections within RLG subject categories. On Conspectus worksheets, these categories are lines with identity codes that correspond to class ranges in the Library of Congress classification scheme; for example, "industrial relations" has the line code ECO52, corresponding to LC classes HD6961–HD6976 in economics. Since brief-test creators to date have picked their subjects without reference to the Conspectus, their tests may lack exact equivalents (one-to-one relations) among its lines.[1] Nonetheless, in this chapter, tests that are roughly equivalent to lines in overall subject matter have been used to verify librarians' ratings of levels in two Philadelphia and three Charlottesville libraries. When tests seen earlier are not re-presented, either I could not find a proper match, or the staff of a library where a brief test was tried had not rated their collection in that category.

The less than perfect match between existing brief tests and Conspectus lines extends to the level of individual titles. At present, some titles on a test may have LC class codes other than those assigned to the lines they are used to verify. In the future, it should be possible to create tests for specific lines (or other standard categories) wherever access to the Conspectus scheme can be arranged. This stricter style of test making would involve choosing titles exclusively from the fixed range of LC (or Dewey) classes corresponding to a line, rather than relying on intuition, published bibliographies, or footnote sampling for definition of a subject. For example, titles for a brief test in "industrial relations" would be drawn only from those classified in LC range HD6961–HD6976, despite the fact that many selectors would see "the industrial relations literature" as more extensive.

The cost in effort, however, is that titles could no longer simply be chosen; they would have to be checked for conforming LC codes as well. For selectors unable or unwilling to do this, postediting of tests would be necessary; that is, another person would have to look up the titles and replace those whose LC codes were "out of line." Other selectors presumably would check as they went along, assuring the appropriateness of each title to each subject. But the result in either case would be tests more closely suited to verification of librarians' line-based ratings than those in the tables of this chapter.

While the ratings verified here are real, the intent is to convey an aspect of brief-test methodology, not to report on actual institutions, which appear for reasons of convenience only. The verification trials at Penn and Temple were not commissioned at those places—they are unobtrusive measures made by the author without staff participation. The trials in Virginia were carried out with local participation, but, again, the procedure amounted to unobtrusive measurement. For that reason alone, the emphasis here is on what the tests can reveal about any library, rather than on outcomes peculiar to—and perhaps questionable by—the libraries used as examples.

AGREEMENTS AND DISAGREEMENTS

Despite these caveats, the first verification trials are reassuring. The most common outcome is for tests and librarians' judgments to agree. But there are also times when the tests yield estimates of levels that are either lower or higher than librarians', producing the quandary of which to accept. Hence, the next order of business is to suggest ways of handling discrepant results. When a librarian and a test agree, the matter presumably is no longer in doubt; it would be a rare collection developer who second-guessed the rightness of both estimates.

Earlier it was said that political considerations might cause collection developers to inflate publicly claimed levels. Anecdotal evidence gained during the brief-test project suggests that many librarians would rather err on the conservative side, preferring to deflate, not inflate, ratings. Thus, if a test produces a higher level than subjective judgment, the cautious would decide that the collection is at least as good as claimed, and retain the lower, subjectively set level. Occasionally, especially in a relatively unfamiliar subject area, the collection developer might decide to raise a level to that given by a test, on the ground that the test disclosed unexpectedly strong holdings.

A less pleasant discrepancy occurs when a test produces a lower level than that set by a librarian. A collection found not as good as claimed could be politically embarrassing. However, librarians should treat brief tests as no one's diagnostics but their own, which leaves room for maneuver. In this case the librarian learns merely that another look at the collection is called for. It may well be ignorance, rather than vanity or politics, that causes people to overrate collections—ignorance about comparable collections and the literatures from which they are drawn. The next step would be to reexamine both the test (does it seem fair?) and the collection (was it overrated?), which could trigger a further check of holdings against comparable collections, published bibliographies, or expert opinion. Some collection developers might eventually decide to revise the level downward—the conservative course again—but that is not a foregone conclusion. The important thing is that they have been alerted to reconsider their holdings in a subject area and that their final decision will presumably be more informed.

Comparison with Grading

If all this seems like waffling, the analogy first offered in Chapter 3 gives some perspective. Collection evaluation is like student evaluation. The RLG scale is somewhat like the grading schemes that teachers use for students. (It differs in that fault is not implied when levels less than 4 are assigned.) Teachers use tests to help them grade students; I am proposing that librarians use tests to help them grade collections. But, with their own tests at least, teachers enjoy considerable latitude in interpreting results, and they vary in how they translate test scores into final grades. One teacher might use nothing but the score; another might take other facts into consideration as well. The point is that, since there is no absolute scale for measuring student achievement, utter consistency cannot be expected, whatever guidelines are laid down. The same is true for librarians who use brief tests. It would be unrealistic to pretend they lack the same leeway as teachers, and the preceding account does not.

In teaching, of course, there have long been standardized tests and scoring procedures that make student evaluations more consistent. Brief tests are a step in that direction for the library world, since they are fixed sets of questions that can be identically scored at multiple sites. As yet missing from them (and unlikely to appear) is the massive apparatus we associate with American educational testing: extensive reliability and validity checks, norms based on widespread administration, public comparison of results, and so forth. But librarians who want a firmer basis for grading might try small-scale comparisons of their own. Brief tests allow them to evaluate not only their own collections but those of any criterion library they choose. If they are still in doubt after checking their own subjective estimate with a brief test, they could administer the same test at another, carefully chosen site (possibly via the Internet) and compare outcomes.

For example, if a test puts them at Level 3 when they think they are higher, they could try the same test on any collection they know to be superior to their own. If that collection scores Level 4, they gain further evidence that they are only a Level 3 after all. This is admittedly far from national standardized testing, but it is a move toward objectivity, resembling the case in which, at the end of the term, an A-hungry B student learns from the teacher what an actual A student has done.

VERIFICATION AT TWO RLG LIBRARIES

The first evidence on brief tests as verification instruments is presented for Penn and Temple in Table 5.1. The codes for Conspectus lines are followed by brief-test names. Next over are the levels obtained by brief tests and by librarians' estimates of, respectively, existing collection strength and current collection intensity on the RLG scale.[2] Last shown are my conclusions as to how test readings and librarians' ratings compare. Test results are said to be either the same as, or higher or lower than, librarians' ratings, which are the reference point.

TABLE 5.1

Librarians' Ratings and Brief-Test Ratings of RLG Levels at Two Universities

University of Pennsylvania

Conspectus Line(s)	Topics	Brief-Test Level	Self-Rated Level	Match
	History			
HIS84	Byzantine Studies	4	3F I 3F	Higher
HIS9	Medieval History	4	4F I 4F	Same
HIS23-30	20th Century British History	4	3E I 3E I 4	Higher
HIS140-143	20th Century Russian History	4	3F I 3F I 4F	Higher
HIS529-530	U.S. History 1760-1860	3	3F I 3F I 4	Same
	Religion			
PAR89-99	Biblical Studies	4	3 I 3	Higher
PAR78	Christian Religion	4	4W I 4W	Same
	Literature			
LLL187-191	Arthurian Literature	4	4 I 4	Same
LLL190,190.10	18th Century English Fiction	4	5 I 5	Same
LLL191,191.10	Victorian Literature	4	5 I 5	Same
LLL164-169	German Literature (Age of Goethe)	4	4F I 4F	Same
LLL209	Native American Literature	3	3 I 3	Same
	Social Sciences			
ECO103-107	Criminology	4	4 I 4E	Same
ANT15, 19-20	Cultural Anthropology	4	4F I 4F	Same
ANT52, HIS515-518	Archaeology of American Southwest	4	4F I 4F	Same
ECO26,27	Economic	4	4W I 4W	Same
	Law			
LAW57 (Penn Law)	Intellectual Property	3	4 I 4	Lower
POL10	U.S. Constitutional History	4	4E I 4E	Same
	Sciences			
PHY114,135-140	Physics	4	4 I 4F	Same
PHY72-79	Astronomy	4	4 I 4F	Same
	Medicine			
MED107-114	Oncology	4	4 I 4E	Same
MED217-219	Toxicology	3	3 I 3E	Same

Temple University

Conspectus Line(s)	Topics	Brief-Test Level	Self-Rated Level	Match
	History and Area Studies			
HIS.18	Medieval History	3	3F I 2E	Same
HIS.12	Psychohistory	3	2E I 2E	Higher
TEC3	History of Technology	3	2E I 2E	Higher
	Philosophy			
MED85	Medical Ethics	2	3 I 3E	Lower
	Art and Architecture			
ART292-293	American Architecture	3	3 I 3E	Same
	Literature			
LLL230	19th Century Russian Literature	2	3Y I 2F	Same
LLL209	Native American Literature	3	2 I 3E	Same
	Music			
MUS18	Classical Music (Scores)	3	3 I 3	Same
	Social Sciences			
ECO107	Criminology	4	3 I 4E	Same
ECO26,27	Economics 1	4	3 I 3E	Higher

FIGURE 5.1

Comparison of Levels Subjectively Claimed and Set by Brief Tests at Two Universities

Claimed Level	Brief-Test Level			
	1	2	3	4
4			3	16
3			2	2
2				
1				

University of Pennsylvania

Claimed Level	Brief-Test Level			
	1	2	3	4
4				1
3		1	4	1
2			1	2
1				

Temple University

When librarians have rated existing collection strength and current collection intensity differently, a test result that matches on either has been marked "same," since there is no way of temporally distinguishing the librarians' two ratings. Other levels are compared one-to-one. Level 4, which is the top score possible on a brief test, is held to be the same as either a 4 or a 5 (Comprehensive) in librarians' subjective ratings.

To repeat, subject correspondence between lines and tests may be only rough. For example, the classical music (scores) test is broader than the MUS18 line; the psychohistory test is narrower than the HIS.12 line. Nevertheless, the reader will note fairly high agreement between librarians and tests. Exact matches are by far the most common outcome. They occur in 18/23 or 78 percent of the cases at Penn and in 6/10 or 60 percent of the cases at Temple, a 73 percent rate overall. Moreover, large disagreements are lacking—those in which one method gives 1's, the other 4's, or vice versa. There are, of course, instances in which brief tests put a collection one level higher or lower than librarians do, but presumably this is valuable feedback toward reconsideration and not a sign of instrument failure.

Figure 5.1 cross-tabulates test outcomes and librarians' judgments. Agreements in level are on the shaded diagonal, while disagreements are in unshaded off-diagonal cells.

If overall agreement is this good with tests that are relatively loose-fitting, it should be even better when they are crafted with specific Conspectus lines in mind, in the fashion previously suggested. Closer agreement might also come with a scale that allows fractional levels, like that of WLN. A reexamination of the percentages in Chapter 4 shows that most of the one-level differences in Table 5.1 could be construed as more like "half-level" differences.

The further verification trials in this chapter and those in Chapter 7 reinforce the impression that the brief-test results converge well with subjective judgments. This is fortunate, because for most people the proof of any new categorization scheme lies in how well it confirms their existing opinions. A scheme that consistently goes against what they believe would not fare well over time.

BRIEF TESTS AND THE WLN CONSPECTUS

With an adaptation in scoring, brief tests may be used to verify levels set with the revised version of the RLG scale associated with the WLN Conspectus (formerly the Pacific Northwest Conspectus). This capability is important because the WLN scale is geared to libraries other than those in the Research Libraries Group and the Association of Research Libraries. Results from some trials in Virginia are presented after a discussion of the new way of scoring.

The WLN scale subdivides Levels 1, 2, and 3, so as to better reflect gradations in nonresearch collections, such as those in public libraries, community colleges, or secondary schools. Table 5.2 presents glosses adapted from the *WLN Collection Assessment Manual* (Powell and Bushing, 1992). Codes from this WLN scale are assigned to subject collections defined by LC or Dewey class ranges. The subject classes of the WLN Conspectus are somewhat less elaborated, even at their most detailed level, than those in the RLG Conspectus, in keeping with their intended use by smaller libraries.

It may be recalled that the WLN scale was introduced in Chapter 2's discussion of problems in setting and verifying collection levels. The opinion there was that existing guidelines for verifying the WLN levels are unsatisfactory, both in their fit to different subject collections and in the effort they require to apply. As a practical matter, it is doubtful that libraries using the WLN scale have time to verify their ratings by checking coverage across subjects in "major bibliographies," as the guidelines in Table 2.6 recommend. The present section aims at supplying a more realistic alternative.

Preferred Scoring Method

Two ways of adapting brief-test scoring to the WLN scale were considered, but only one is given in Table 5.3, which shows eight levels from 1a to 4. (Levels 0 and 5—Out of scope and Comprehensive—are again omitted as nonproblematical.) In the way not shown, a brief test is simply divided into eighths to correspond to Levels 1a through 4 and then scored in the usual way; at least 50 percent of items must be held at each level in order to claim it. Thus, in a 40-item test, one would need three of the first five titles, three of the second five, and so on. However, this initially plausible version of the scale does not cumulate well in practice; 40 titles are too few to sustain the fine divisions. It is an open question, moreover, whether 80 (or more) titles would make a better test if scored in this fashion; the requisite trials have not been conducted.

The way shown in Table 5.3 takes a different tack and allows us to make use of 40-item tests as verification tools immediately. As in the past, the test is divided into four blocks of 10 titles each. These are then mapped onto the WLN scale by three simple rules. First, if a library has any titles at all in a subject, it

TABLE 5.2

WLN Collection Level Indicators

0   *Out of Scope*

1a *Minimal Level, Uneven Coverage.* Few selections made; unsystematic representation.

1b *Minimal Level, Even Coverage.* Few selections: basic authors, core works, or a spectrum of ideological views are represented.

2a *Basic Information, Introductory.* Resources that introduce and define a topic. Basic reference tools, textbooks, historical descriptions of the subject's development, general works on major topics and figures in the field. Selected major periodicals.

2b *Basic Information, Advanced.* 2a + more depth and a wider range of topics. Bibliographic databases (online or CD-ROM). Selection of editions of important works. Supports informational and recreational needs of highly educated general public or community college students.

3a *Basic Instructional Support.* Resources adequate for imparting and maintaining knowledge of the subject. The most important primary and secondary literature, selected basic representative serials and indexes, fundamental reference and bibliographic tools. Supports lower-division undergraduate work and needs of the lifelong learner.

3b *Intermediate Instructional Support.* 3a + broad range of basic works in appropriate formats: classic retrospective materials, all key journals on primary topics, selected journals and seminal works on secondary topics, access to machine-readable data files, works by secondary figures; reference tools and fundamental bibliographic apparatus. Supports advanced undergraduate work.

3c *Advanced Instructional Support.* 3b + significant number of works and journals on the primary and secondary topics in the field, significant retrospective materials, substantial collection of works by secondary figures; in-depth discussions of research, techniques, and evaluation. Supports master's degree programs and advanced independent study by subject professionals.

4   *Research.* Major published source materials required for dissertation and independent research: materials containing research reporting, new findings, and scientific experimental results. All important reference works, a wide selection of specialized monographs, a very extensive collection of journals, major abstracting and indexing services, and pertinent foreign language materials. Older material is usually retained for historical research and actively preserved.

5   *Comprehensive.* All significant works of recorded knowledge (publications, manuscripts, etc.) in all applicable languages, for a defined and limited field. The aim is exhaustiveness. Older material is retained for historical research and actively preserved.

TABLE 5.3

Special Rules for Using Brief Tests with WLN Scale

Level	Rules for Scoring Brief Test	WLN Scale
1 Minimal	In scope, but not enough items to claim any level	1a
	At least 50% of items at Level 1	1b
2 Basic	Level 1 attained + any higher-level items	2a
	At least 50% of items at Level 2	2b
3 Instructional	Level 2 attained + any higher-level items	3a
	At least 50% of items at Level 3	3b
	Level 3 attained + any higher-level items	3c
4 Research	At least 50% of items at Level 4	4

can claim Level 1a. (In other words, 1a means that some titles are held, but not enough to claim 1b or any higher level. That is how the notion of "uneven coverage" is operationalized.) Second, if a library could legitimately claim Level 1, 2, 3, or 4 on the RLG scale through the rule of "50 percent or more," it can claim Level 1b, 2b, 3b, or 4 on the WLN scale.

Finally, if the library has at least one title on any level higher than the one it can legitimately claim, it is given credit for aspiration and moved up a half-level: 1b becomes 2a, 2b becomes 3a, and 3b becomes 3c. (For example, a library with scores of 70%–60%–10%–10% across the four levels would legitimately be a 2b but is raised to 3a because of the additional holdings at Levels 3 and 4.) These rules take care of the eight levels and, because of the cumulative structure built into brief tests, produce reasonably good results, as will be seen.

The notion of "giving credit for aspiration" may call to mind teachers who refine grade scales to please students. That impression would not be mistaken. In effect, the WLN scale re-creates the RLG scale with "minus" levels added, as in Table 5.4.

In practice, these "minus" levels function rather like "minus" versions of student grades. The latter allow teachers to give students a slightly higher grade than a starker scale would permit; for example, a student who has not quite made the grade of B can be given a B- instead of a C. Just so, the subdivisions of the WLN scale allow libraries to occupy levels with somewhat lesser collections than they would otherwise need. On that interpretation of the WLN scale, the rule about "giving credit" is put forward.

The fact remains that, because the titles involved in brief tests are relatively few, the presence or absence of a single critically placed title can shift the outcome up or down an entire level. By the rules in Table 5.3, for example, a library with scores of 40%–10%–10%–0% across levels would be only 1a, whereas a library with the same total number of books but with scores of 50%–10%–0%–0% would be 2a. This may make overall ratings seem arbitrary, a problem that besets brief tests however they are scored. It is an instance of a classic problem in grading: at any dividing point, some cases fall in the higher group, and others, perhaps barely different, fall in the lower. Like teachers, librarians may sometimes have to make close calls in deciding a rating.

A broader objection is that, while the WLN verification guidelines seen earlier in Table 2.6 may be difficult to meet, they are by no means wrong in principle. They imply that the serious collector will try to find the actual magnitude of subject collections, as measured by titles held. Brief tests, particularly as scored in Table 5.3, may appear to reduce this concern to game playing: consideration is deflected from the full quantum of works to a mere 40 titles and the little points they score. Obviously, the main thing should not be one's score on a test but having a collection that meets demand.

TABLE 5.4

Hypothetical Relationship between WLN and RLG Scales

Label	WLN Scale	Hypothetical RLG Scale
Minimal level, uneven coverage	1a	1-
Minimal level, even coverage	1b	1
Basic information, introductory	2a	2-
Basic information, advanced	2b	2
Basic instructional support	3a	3-
Intermediate instructional support	3b	3
Advanced instructional support	3c	4-
Research	4	4

Perhaps the best way to deal with such objections is to reinvoke notions of practicality. Brief-test methodology clearly has parallels with the test-based grading of people. As a way of routinely summarizing large amounts of information by small numbers of staff, both of these methodologies work, whereas multiple, large-scale surveys of coverage, at least with present technology, do not. If done manually, they are daunting even to try; better look to computers and the promising software of, for example, OCLC/AMIGOS or WLN. On that count, however, current computer programs do not summarily grade collections in a way commonly understood, like letter grades for students, and it is uncertain whether such software will be written or, if written, will be widely affordable.

Brief tests thus seem a stopgap measure that can be used until computerized evaluation technology is available to libraries everywhere. If brief tests are understood as modest aids to judgment, rather than as ends in themselves, then their return on effort looks quite attractive.

VERIFICATION AT THREE VIRGINIA LIBRARIES

Brief tests on 16 topics were requested in 1991 for the Piedmont Area Collection Assessment Program. The participants were the Jefferson-Madison Regional Library, the Piedmont Virginia Community College, and the University of Virginia. Respectively, these are a large public, a small academic, and a large research library in the Charlottesville area. All had rated their collections using the eight-point scale of the WLN (then Pacific Northwest) Conspectus. Thus, in these trials brief tests were used as verification instruments.

Under the WLN scheme, librarians may rate their subject collections on three separate counts: existing level, current acquisition commitment, and target level (Powell and Bushing, 1992). The Charlottesville libraries had assigned ratings in the first two categories, which appear under "self-rated level" in Table 5.5. If only one level is given, it applies to both categories. Otherwise, two levels appear; for example, in architectural history the Jefferson-Madison Regional Library put its existing collection strength at Level 2a but its acquisition commitment at only Level 1b.

Brief-test results across the 16 topics were converted to levels using the "preferred" scoring method presented earlier.[3] For five of the topics, data from the Piedmont Virginia Community College were not received, and so there are 43, rather than 48, trials in all. Table 5.5 compares the librarians' self-ratings with the brief-test level attained and shows whether the test result is the same as, or higher or lower than, self-ratings. As before, test results that match self-ratings in either category are labeled as "same."

The Conspectus line-codes used by the Charlottesville libraries to define a topic have been reproduced as received. A single brief test was sometimes used to verify several lines that vary in how they were originally rated by librarians, so that a simple match between ratings and test result is not possible. (See, for instance, the lines for American history and the postmodern American novel.)

TABLE 5.5

Comparisons of Librarians' Ratings and Brief-Test Ratings of RLG Levels at Three Virginia Libraries

Topics		Levels in Percents			Brief-Test	Self-Rated	Match
	1	*2*	*3*	*4*	*Level*	*Level*	
Art and Architecture							
Architectural History (ART111)							
Jefferson-Madison Regional Library	0	10	0	0	1a	2a/1b	Lower
Piedmont Virginia Community College	0	0	0	0	0	1a/0	Same
University of Virginia	90	90	100	70	4	3c/4	Same
History							
American History:							
Colonial Times to the Present							
(HIS394, HIS397, HIS403,							
HIS404, HIS407, HIS411)							
Jefferson-Madison Regional Library	80	50	10	0	3a	2a	Higher
Piedmont Virginia Community College	70	20	20	0	2a	2b,1b/2a,1a	Same
University of Virginia	90	90	90	20	3c	4,5/4,5	Lower
Russian / Soviet History (HIS124)							
Jefferson-Madison Regional Library	70	0	0	0	1b	1b	Same
Piedmont Virginia Community College	80	20	0	0	2a	1b	Higher
University of Virginia	100	100	70	60	4	4	Same
20th Century British History (HIS046)							
Jefferson-Madison Regional Library	30	0	0	0	1a	2a/1b	Lower
Piedmont Virginia Community College	40	0	0	0	1a	2b/2a	Lower
University of Virginia	100	100	92	92	4	4	Same
Literature							
Postmodern American Novel							
(LLL244, LLL250, LLL468)							
Jefferson-Madison Regional Library	70	10	0	0	2a	1b/1a	Higher
Piedmont Virginia Community College	20	20	0	0	1a	2a	Lower
University of Virginia	100	100	80	80	4	4	Same
18th Century British Fiction (LLL230)							
Jefferson-Madison Regional Library	10	0	0	0	1a	2a/1a	Same
Piedmont Virginia Community College	30	20	0	0	1a	2a/0	Lower
University of Virginia	100	100	100	100	4	4	Same
German Literature: Late 18th Century -							
Early 19th Century (LLL198)							
Jefferson-Madison Regional Library	40	10	0	0	1a	0/0	Higher
Piedmont Virginia Community College	40	10	0	0	1a	1a	Same
University of Virginia	90	100	80	80	4	4	Same
Philosophy							
Philosophy 1 (PHD001)							
Jefferson-Madison Regional Library	20	10	10	0	1a	1a	Same
University of Virginia	100	100	70	70	4	3c	Higher
Medical Ethics (MED092)							
Jefferson-Madison Regional Library	10	10	0	0	1a	1a	Same
University of Virginia	90	40	30	30	2a	2	Same
Social Sciences							
Criminology (SOC022)							
Jefferson-Madison Regional Library	10	0	0	0	1a	2a	Lower
Piedmont Virginia Community College	0	0	10	10	1a	1b/1a	Same
University of Virginia	100	100	50	40	3c	3b/4	Same
Cultural Anthropology 1 (ANT000)							
Jefferson-Madison Regional Library	20	10	0	0	1a	1a/1b	Same
Piedmont Virginia Community College	10	40	0	0	1a	1a	Same
University of Virginia	100	100	60	70	4	4	Same
Developmental Psychology (PSY019.5)							
Jefferson-Madison Regional Library	10	10	0	0	1a	1b/1a	Same
Piedmont Virginia Community College	40	20	10	0	1a	2b/1b	Lower
University of Virginia	90	100	80	60	4	4	Same
Economics 1 (BUD090)							
Jefferson-Madison Regional Library	30	10	0	0	1a	1b/2a	Lower
University of Virginia	100	100	100	70	4	3c/4	Same
Library and Information Science (LIS000)							
Jefferson-Madison Regional Library	30	20	0	0	1a	1a	Same
University of Virginia	70	70	80	10	3c	3c	Same

TABLE 5.5 *(continued)*

Topics		Levels in Percents			Brief-Test Level	Self-Rated Level	Match
	1	*2*	*3*	*4*			
Science							
Math / Physics (PHY078)							
Jefferson-Madison Regional Library	40	10	0	0	1a	1a/0	Same
Piedmont Virginia Community College	40	20	0	0	1a	1b	Lower
University of Virginia	100	100	90	80	4	4	Same
Genetics 1 (BID061)							
Jefferson-Madison Regional Library	10	0	0	0	1a	1a	Same
University of Virginia	100	90	100	70	4	4	Same

Moreover, even when a test is used to verify a single line, the subject match between line and test may be only approximate; for instance, SOC022 is broader than the criminology test, and PSY019.5 is broader than the developmental psychology test.

The agreement between test results and self-ratings on the WLN scale is summarized in Figures 5.2 and 5.3. In both, the columns correspond to brief-test results. In the upper figure, the rows correspond to claimed collection levels (CL); in the lower, to current acquisition commitments (AC). The cells hold counts of joint outcomes on the two scales. Exact matches are counted in the darkly shaded diagonal cells; matches off by only half a level are in those lightly shaded.

Good Congruence

The following points may be made in asserting good congruence between tests and ratings over the 43 trials.

Virtually all outcomes in both tables show disagreements of no more than one level between self-rating and test result. The great majority either wholly agree or diverge by no more than half a level; for example, a 2b is claimed, and the test result is 2a. In Figure 5.2, 79 percent of all outcomes lie within the shaded cells, and 44 percent are exact matches. Agreement in Figure 5.3 is even better: 86 percent of the outcomes are within the shaded cells, and 56 percent are exact matches. There are no cases in which a library claims a collection at Level 1 or 2 that the brief test puts at Level 4. The reverse is true also.

Brief-test levels are thus highly correlated with self-rated levels, whether the latter are for existing collection strength or current acquisition commitment. These data all derive from ordinal scales, for which Spearman's rho is a standard measure of correlation. The rho for Figure 5.2 is 0.81. For Figure 5.3, it is 0.82. Both correlations are statistically significant at $p < .001$, making it highly unlikely that the degree of association observed between brief-test levels and self-rated levels was produced by chance. Rather, test scores are systematically co-varying with librarians' judgments on their collections.

The tests discriminate sharply between the research collections of the University of Virginia and the nonresearch collections of the other two institutions. The

FIGURE 5.2

Claimed Collection Level by Brief-Test Level

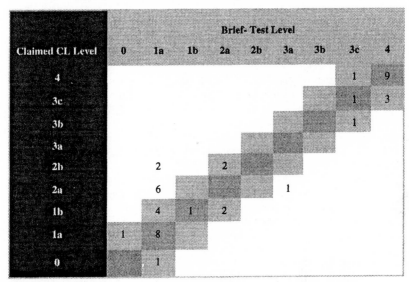

Claimed CL Level	0	1a	1b	2a	2b	3a	3b	3c	4
4								1	9
3c								1	3
3b								1	
3a									
2b		2			2				
2a		6			1				
1b		4	1	2					
1a	1	8							
0		1							

FIGURE 5.3

Claimed Acquisition Commitment Level by Brief-Test Level

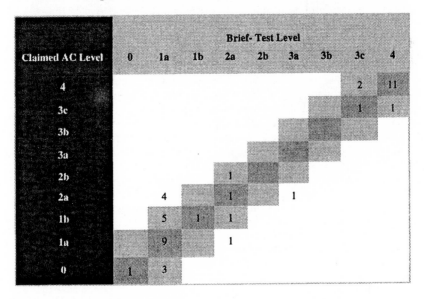

Claimed AC Level	0	1a	1b	2a	2b	3a	3b	3c	4
4								2	11
3c								1	1
3b									
3a									
2b				1					
2a		4		1		1			
1b		5	1	1					
1a		9		1					
0	1	3							

university's self-ratings and its test scores are always at the high end of the WLN scale; its outcomes occupy the upper right cells of the figures exclusively. In contrast, the self-ratings and the test scores of the other two libraries are never at the high end of the WLN scale; their outcomes occupy the lower left cells of the figures exclusively. Almost no claims of Level 3a or 3b collections, such as would support undergraduate programs, were up for verification in these trials, and the test results clearly show the absence of midrange collections. Outcomes in the two figures tend to be high or low, with a gap in between.

Brief tests agree remarkably well with ratings at the University of Virginia. Again and again, either they confirm the levels its librarians claim, or they point toward plausible reconsiderations. For example, the university's collection in American history, while strong (3c on the test), is probably not as strong as librarians thought when they gave it a 4 or even a 5. American history, with its enormous literature, is a difficult area in which to claim comprehensiveness, and the brief test is simply reminding us of this fact.

There is rather more disagreement between brief-test results and self-ratings at the two smaller libraries than at the university. The commonest brief-test reading for their collections is 1a (Minimal Level, Uneven Coverage), which is often somewhat lower than their claims. There are, however, some considerations to be noted. The collections they were rating for existing strength are all fairly small, according to their own title counts. Although the WLN quantitative guidelines hold that anything less than 2,500 titles is no more than a 1b collection, Jefferson-Madison and Piedmont assigned Levels 1a through 2b to collections that averaged about 256 titles each and that comprised about 900 titles at most.

One can argue that it is the WLN guidelines that err rather than the libraries, by being simply too high for many literatures. But even on their own terms, the libraries were somewhat inconsistent in assigning levels to different-sized collections. For instance, Jefferson-Madison assigned a 2a to its 186 titles in British history but a 1b to its 198 titles in general North American history. Piedmont assigned a 1b to its 900-item collection in social pathology (which includes criminology), but a 2b to its 556-item collection in colonial American history. It seems highly unlikely that these discrepancies are deliberate, reflecting proportions of literatures of different size. If not, convergence in verification trials is bound to be affected by inconsistent judgments.

Essentially, brief tests are indicating that many of the collections at Jefferson-Madison and Piedmont are both small and unevenly developed. Note that the University of Virginia had no trouble passing exactly the same tests at Levels 1a through 2b and on through higher levels. This implies the presence of larger and more evenly developed collections in Charlottesville that can be used as standards for comparison. The message for Jefferson-Madison and Piedmont is that some of their ratings of existing collection strength may be too high—for example, in architectural history, twentieth-century British history, and eighteenth-century British fiction. On the other hand, a fair number of their ratings agree with the tests, and some are actually lower than what the tests reveal; for example, the test in German literature shows that this subject is not out of scope for Jefferson-Madison, as its librarians apparently thought.

Finally, for the smaller collections, a few disagreements may be attributed more to the brief-test scoring mechanism than to real differences. One needs to examine the data and make a judgment; having results from more than one institution helps. The test scores yielding a 3a for American history at Jefferson-Madison are the weakest possible, and the 2a claimed by the library seems a more sensible judgment. Likewise, that library's claim of 1b/1a in the postmodern American novel should probably be favored over the test's weak 2a. In developmental psychology both Jefferson-Madison and Piedmont score 1a by test, but the latter's collection is obviously somewhat better, tending toward 1b at least, if not the 2b claimed.

Details aside, the tests produced informative results under fairly rigorous real-world conditions. The effort involved two sets of collaborators wholly unknown to each other. The coordinator of the Virginia assessment heard about brief tests by chance. After requesting a batch of them from me, she used her own judgment in fitting them to existing subject collections. The persons who created the tests did not know that their products would later be used in Virginia libraries, nor did they have specific Conspectus lines or the WLN scale in mind as they worked. The persons who administered the tests in Charlottesville had no prior acquaintance with the methodology and no connection with the test makers or with me; over the course of the assessment I simply received their results by mail while they remained anonymous. Their tallies and my scoring of them are here opened to public view. Under such conditions, the showing of the methodology reflects the fundamental soundness of the idea of power-testing collections. Improvements are possible, no doubt, but the idea has held up through trials in which most of the participants were indifferent to its success and merely following directions.

NOTES

1. This is another contingency of how and where brief tests were developed. For several reasons it was impractical to ask selectors, in diverse locales, to base their tests on the hard-copy or electronic Conspectus. Not being an RLG member, Drexel could not provide easy access to it. The rare hard-copy version, best for browsing, must be tracked down in staff offices in large research libraries. The online version requires training and an RLIN account to use. Thus, in order to make an already complex task as easy as possible, selectors were allowed to use their own judgment as to appropriate titles, whether or not these lay within the boundaries of Conspectus lines.

2. Ratings at Penn and Temple were transcribed from Conspectus-based collection policy manuals consulted on-site. A few Penn ratings show a third level, for *desired* collection intensity. Language codes, such as "F" or "E," also appear, but brief tests do not address these.

3. The "preferred" method of Table 5.3 had not been devised when the Charlottesville libraries used the tests and so does not figure in their reporting. It was devised in preparing this book, for consideration by future users of the WLN scale.

CHAPTER 6

Gains in Strength through a Consortium

INTRODUCTION

Intuition tells us that three college library collections should be better than one. Not only are more copies of the same works available, but each library adds uniquely held works to the general pool. Substantiating intuition, however, brief tests provide concrete data on how a joint collection improves on separate collections in areas corresponding to disciplines or broad subjects.

The Bryn Mawr, Haverford, and Swarthmore college libraries in the Philadelphia suburbs have made their collections jointly accessible in the Tri-College Consortium since 1991. One of the major effects of Tripod, their online union catalog, is to present their separate collections as a unified whole. This chapter, which originated as part of a larger study of the effects of automation in the Tri-College Consortium, shows the gains in collection strength brought about by unification.

Brief tests were used to assign the libraries separately and jointly a score for existing collection strength in a subject area. In each case it was possible to compare the joint B-H-S score with the separate scores (B, H, and S) to determine relative improvements in collection strength. There was often a clear benefit for at least one of the three libraries involved, in that, by participating in the Tri-College Consortium, it gained access to a higher-level collection than it would have been able to provide alone. The combined collections of the three colleges at this writing amount to almost 1.4 million titles, which means that the Consortium can play in the same league as members of the Association of Research Libraries.

METHODOLOGY

The seven subject areas to be tested were chosen by a committee of Tri-College librarians in 1989. By informal agreement, the American history test was to be augmented with one on American studies, construed to mean cultural, intellectual, and social history in contrast to political and military history. So eight tests were created during 1988–1992, all of which appear in Appendix A:

Humanities	*Social Sciences*	*Natural Sciences*
American history	Cultural anthropology	Genetics
American studies	Policy studies	Mathematics
Classical music		
French literature		

While Bryn Mawr, Haverford, and Swarthmore librarians had not actually assigned level-codes to their subject collections in these areas, it was known that no area was out of scope. Neither, however, was any collected exhaustively at Level 5. It was thus an open question as to what level, from 1 to 4, had been attained.

For this study, "longer" brief tests were created by combining the input of more than one selector per subject area. Selectors included librarians or academics whose subject expertise could be presumed. Several came from librarians or information specialists while they were enrolled as graduate students in the College of Information Science and Technology at Drexel University. Other selectors were from Temple and Penn in Philadelphia, and, more distantly, the University of Florida, Princeton, Harvard, and the University of California at Berkeley. I contributed tests in American studies and in French literature after selectors in those areas proved hard to find.

In most subject areas, two 40-title tests were combined into 80-title tests before being divided into quartiles, and so percentages are based on 20 items per level rather than 10. Some of these instruments were tried in settings other than the Tri-College Consortium and have already been introduced in an earlier chapter: genetics 1 and 2, mathematics and physics/math, and cultural anthropology 1. Other instruments are new: cultural anthropology 2 and both halves of the tests in classical music, French literature, and policy studies. The classical music test includes both books and musical scores. Policy studies are represented with a mixture of political science titles and analyses of specific undertakings in the public sector.

For American history, a broad and diverse field, three 40-title tests were combined to yield 120 titles, or 30 per level. These included the tests covering the 1760–1860 and 1861–1865 periods already seen in Chapter 4, plus one not seen there that runs "from colonial times to the present." American studies were addressed with a standard 40-item instrument.

The 120-item test in American history nicely demonstrates the qualitative effect of ordering titles by their OCLC counts. While the inner two levels, 2 Basic and 3 Instructional, are not clearly distinguishable, the outer levels, 1 Minimal and 4 Research, have very different characters. As I wrote earlier, the Level 1 titles are typically "always in print" and "found in chain bookstores"; the Level 4 titles are "advanced, localized, foreign, academic, obscure, or simply old." This effect parallels one frequently observed when human subjects are asked to rank a long list of items according to some principle: it is relatively easy to distinguish the top from the bottom items, but those in between are harder to order, and the rankings seem more arbitrary even to the subjects.

The test in French literature has 80 titles, but half of them were obtained in a somewhat unusual fashion. They are my own judgment sample from Jeffry Larson's thousand-item checklist for the RLG verification study briefly described in Chapters 1 and 2. I attempted to capture its substance and relative emphases and also to pick 40 titles with a variety of counts to reflect the four levels. To these were added 40 further choices of mine that are not on Larson's list.

The 80-item test in French literature reappears in the next chapter, which examines the performance of the brief-test methodology when it takes a small subset of titles from a large checklist and uses them in its distinctive way. (Can the much shorter test produce better results than the checklist?)

The design of Larson's list is complex, as will be seen. Most of his titles, in addition to being in French, are highly scholarly and specialized (cf. remarks by Benaud and Bordeianu, 1992). Yale University, his employer, had only 62 percent of them. Overall, they make the French literature test quite demanding as tests go.

The eight test instruments named here were used across the three individual college collections and again across the joint consortium collection for a total of 32 evaluations. Titles were searched on Tripod, and holdings were recorded as of mid-July 1992. Occasional anomalies appeared in using Tripod—for example, an item not found in a title search might be found under author—and items not found initially were rechecked. In some cases any edition of a monographic work was deemed acceptable; in other cases, a particular edition had to be owned to be credited. Numerous serial titles appear in the tests; for these, a library had to have a current subscription to receive credit.

RESULTS

In all tests, the Tri-College Consortium achieves at least a Level 2 Basic collection. Table 6.1 reveals the outcome of pooling the collections.

It will be recalled that, by hypothesis, library collections grow cumulatively:

TABLE 6.1

Collection Levels Achieved by Tri-College Consortium

Basic	Instructional	Research
French literature	American history	American studies
Policy studies	Cultural anthropology	Classical music
	Mathematics	Genetics

TABLE 6.2

Detailed Scores across Levels for Colleges Singly and Jointly

Percentages per Level

	1	2	3	4	Level Attained
American History (30 titles per level)					
Bryn Mawr	97	53	53	30	3
Haverford	83	57	40	30	2
Swarthmore	83	67	60	23	3
B-H-S Combined	**97**	**77**	**70**	**43**	**3**
American Studies (10 titles per level)					
Bryn Mawr	80	70	70	50	4
Haverford	90	60	60	60	4
Swarthmore	70	100	50	40	3
B-H-S Combined	**100**	**100**	**80**	**80**	**4**
Classical Music (20 titles per level)					
Bryn Mawr	85	80	55	35	3
Haverford	80	85	50	35	3
Swarthmore	90	90	85	60	4
B-H-S Combined	**100**	**100**	**95**	**80**	**4**
Cultural Anthropology (20 titles per level)					
Bryn Mawr	100	100	50	30	3
Haverford	70	65	25	15	2
Swarthmore	95	95	75	30	3
B-H-S Combined	**100**	**100**	**85**	**30**	**3**
French Literature (20 titles per level)					
Bryn Mawr	50	35	35	25	1
Haverford	60	40	10	5	1
Swarthmore	90	50	10	5	2
B-H-S Combined	**100**	**75**	**40**	**25**	**2**
Genetics (20 titles per level)					
Bryn Mawr	95	55	40	25	2
Haverford	100	70	55	55	4
Swarthmore	95	65	40	25	2
B-H-S Combined	**100**	**95**	**75**	**65**	**4**
Mathematics (20 titles per level)					
Bryn Mawr	75	45	40	20	1
Haverford	65	60	35	20	2
Swarthmore	95	85	55	35	3
B-H-S Combined	**100**	**95**	**75**	**45**	**3**
Public Policy (20 titles per level)					
Bryn Mawr	70	40	20	0	1
Haverford	65	25	20	0	1
Swarthmore	80	45	20	15	1
B-H-S Combined	**100**	**80**	**40**	**15**	**2**

ability to claim a given level rests on ability to claim all lower levels. The hypothesis predicts, for example, that if a library has sufficient titles to support advanced research, it will also have at least as many titles to support instructional and basic reference activities. In all 32 trials, this cumulative pattern was evident at Bryn Mawr, Haverford, and Swarthmore.

The full data appear in Table 6.2, which has the percentaged scores for the three colleges singly and jointly. The base of all percentages within a subject area—the number of titles per level—is given after the subject area's name. In American history, for example, Bryn Mawr had 97 percent (or 29) of the 30 titles representing a Level 1 collection. It had 53 percent (or 16) of the 30 titles at Level 2. All percentages for individual colleges are read similarly, though the numeric base per level varies by subject. For example, there were only 10 titles per level in American studies, and Bryn Mawr had 80 percent or eight of those at Level 1. The highest level attained in each trial is presented at right. (As usual, a library must hold at least 50 percent of titles at a given level in order to claim it.) The boldfaced percentages for the joint collection (B-H-S Combined) reflect the fact that at least one of the colleges has a particular title.

There is a general result to be observed across subjects in Table 6.2. At any given level, the consortium's collection is necessarily as good as that of its best member. But it is very often better than that, because of the pooling effect. For example, all three colleges are below the 50 percent threshold at Level 2 in public policy. But by pooling, the consortium reaches 80 percent—enough to claim the level handily.

It should also be said that the consortium might have done even better had it not been for the stringency of two of the tests. I have already noted that the items drawn from the Larson checklist make the French literature test hard. If the test is confined to my own 40 choices, rather than being increased to 80 with the Larson items, the joint B-H-S collection scores at Level 3 instead of Level 2. (Larson, needless to say, is not responsible for this outcome.)

The 80-item test in policy studies is also difficult. Again, the reason is that, unintentionally on the selector's part, one of the 40-item tests in it has an abundance of titles held by relatively few libraries. Based on follow-up trials with 40-item instruments of their own devising, two of my students have independently reported Level 3s in policy studies for the joint B-H-S collection. Although in this chapter I have let stand the outcomes presented to the consortium in a technical report (White, 1992a), it nonetheless seems likely that, for practical purposes, the consortium collections can support undergraduate instruction in French literature and in policy studies. If they are Level 2 Basic, it is a rich Basic. Probably a WLN-style rating of 3a would not be amiss.

In Table 6.2 the collection level achieved by each college individually may be contrasted with that achieved by the consortium. Table 6.3 summarizes the evidence that the individual collections at Bryn Mawr, Haverford, and Swarthmore were frequently weaker in the eight subject areas than the consortium's combined collection. In 14 (or 58 percent) of the 24 tests of individual collections, a college gained at least one level by participating in the consortium.

The column totals show the gains by magnitude. In 11 tests a college went

TABLE 6.3

Number and Magnitude of Gains per College

	Up One Level	Up Two Levels	*Totals*
Bryn Mawr	3	2	5
Haverford	6	0	6
Swarthmore	2	1	3
Totals	11	3	14

up one level; in three tests, up two levels. According to the row totals, Bryn Mawr and Haverford benefitted the most from the new alliance: Haverford gained six times and Bryn Mawr, five, to Swarthmore's three. Of course, these are gross measures, and the pattern is complex; every possible pair of collections has to be examined to see which (if either) contributes more.

TEST DIFFICULTY DISPLAYED

It is possible to convey how difficult the various tests are, using the device shown earlier for two hypothetical instruments in Figure 3.1. The key point there was to show the holdings-count ranges associated with each level of two or more tests so that comparisons could be made. Recall that, in any test, the titles for Levels 2 Basic, 3 Instructional, and 4 Research make up three-fourths of the total instrument. If this three-fourths draws largely on titles from the low, difficult end of the holdings-count scale, then libraries are going to have more trouble attaining them: relatively many titles with low holdings counts mean harder tests. As a graphic equivalent, when the holdings-count ranges of harder tests are plotted against the scale of possible counts, their higher levels look compressed compared to those for easier tests.

This effect is quite visible in Figure 6.1, which renders the higher levels of the tests used in this chapter in various shadings, while leaving the lowest level white. It is the shaded levels, not the white, that are the focus here. (The width of the Level 1 portion of the bars is determined by the holdings count of the most widely-held item, such as Darwin's *Origin of Species* in the genetics test; it should not be taken as particularly significant in this context.) The holdings-count scale runs along the bottom of Figure 6.1 as a standard. The tests with the two most highly compressed upper levels are French literature and policy studies.

As I shall explain in the final chapter, counts for the Research, Instructional,

FIGURE 6.1

Actual Tests with Different Ranges of Difficulty

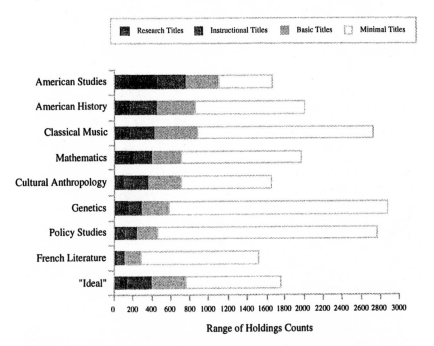

Range of Holdings Counts

and Basic levels in any brief test should ideally be distributed over a range of counts from 1 to around 750. The tests in American history, classical music, cultural anthropology, and mathematics in Figure 6.1 approximate the ideal.

In contrast, the titles at these three levels in policy studies have counts with a ceiling of only 465, and the titles at the same levels in French literature have counts with a ceiling of only 285, making the latter difficult indeed. At the other extreme, the comparable titles in my test in American studies have counts with a ceiling of 950, making it seem very easy by comparison. However, none of this was known when the tests were created. In the future, test makers will be able to draw on greater knowledge about the holdings-count scale as an absolute standard if they wish. See Chapter 8.

A GRAPHIC CODA

The many numbers of Table 6.2 are translated into line graphs in Figures 6.2 through 6.9. Those who are not interested in the Tri-College results per se may nevertheless find in these figures a useful model for presenting their own test data, since they are readily explained to most audiences and more palatable than tables of numbers.

On the horizontal axes are the four collection levels. The vertical axes allow the percentage of test items held at each level to be marked. When the marks are connected across the four levels, patterns become easy to detect. Almost always the profile descends rightward, indicating the falloff in holdings as titles become more specialized. The 50 percent threshold is shown by an arrow-headed line. Points on or above this threshold indicate levels that are claimable; point below it, levels that are not.

Superior collections show up clearly. In two subject areas, one college conspicuously helps the other two attain Research level. These are Swarthmore in classical music and Haverford in genetics. In mathematics, Swarthmore helps the other two attain Instructional level. Further details will be left to the captions.

This style of analysis is readily transferable to other settings. C. Suzanne Cole used it as a Drexel student in 1994 to compare holdings on social theory at Bowdoin, Bates, and Colby, a consortium of colleges in Maine. Her brief test was conducted via the Internet. Her results in Figure 6.10 show clearly how the joint collection, unlike individual ones, attains Research level.

FIGURE 6.2

American History

% of Titles Held

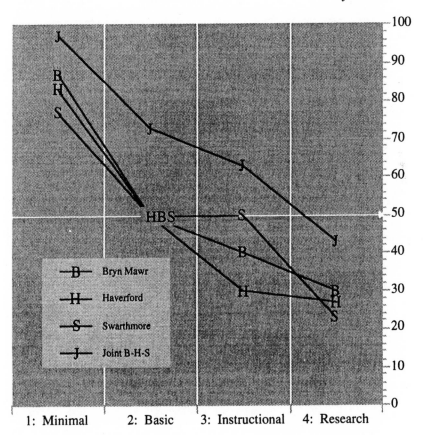

The colleges have similar collection strengths in American history, as shown by the closeness of their profiles. The superior joint collection results from the unique titles each brings to the consortium, an effect that appears throughout these figures.

FIGURE 6.3

American Studies

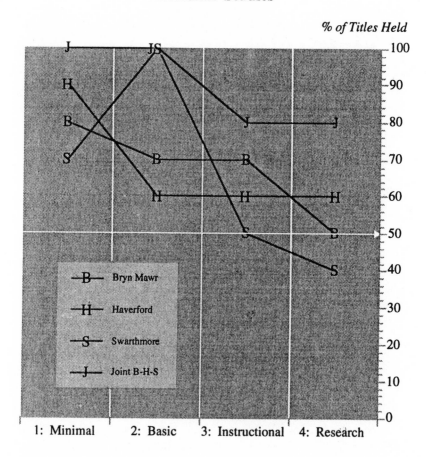

% of Titles Held

All the colleges did well in American studies. Swarthmore's pattern (rising from Level 1 to 2 before falling again) is atypical, the only one of its kind in the 32 tests of this study. The fact that the scoring profiles are mostly above the 50 percent cutoff indicates that this is a relatively easy test for these libraries. Profiles that plunge steeply below the cutoff in other figures indicate tests that were relatively difficult.

FIGURE 6.4

Classical Music

% of Titles Held

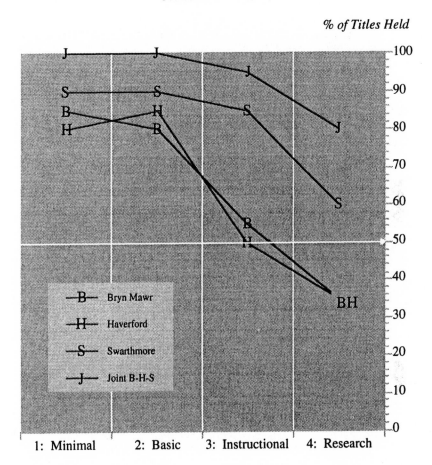

Bryn Mawr and Haverford have very similar profiles here. The enhancement brought about by Swarthmore is evident.

FIGURE 6.5

Cultural Anthropology

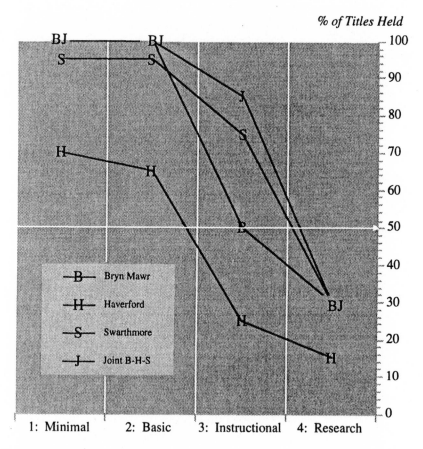

% of Titles Held

1: Minimal   2: Basic   3: Instructional   4: Research

Bryn Mawr and Swarthmore contribute to a Level 3 collection in an area in which Haverford is not as strong.

FIGURE 6.6

French Literature

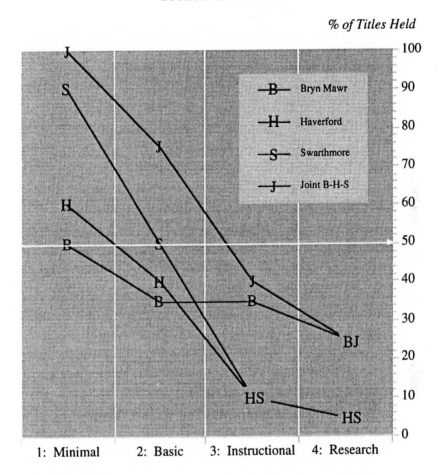

% of Titles Held

1: Minimal   2: Basic   3: Instructional   4: Research

Bryn Mawr has an odd pattern here—less developed than the other two colleges on Levels 1 and 2, more developed on 3 and 4, but still marginal. This is one type of the "long, thin collection" mentioned earlier in the book.

FIGURE 6.7

Genetics

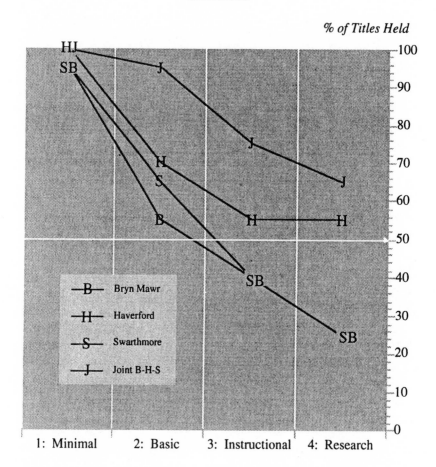

Haverford strengthens the genetics collection as the upper levels, bringing it to Research strength.

FIGURE 6.8

Mathematics

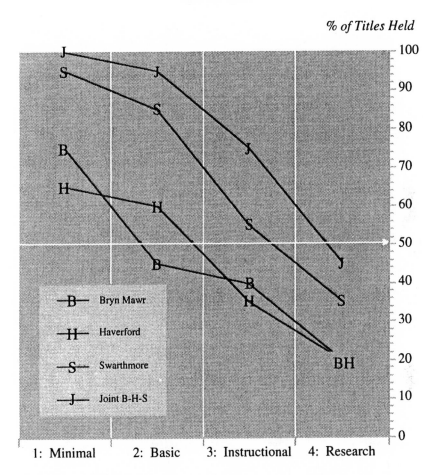

Swarthmore is clearly the dominant collection in mathematics, but note that the joint collection is even better than Swarthmore's because of the contributions of the other two schools.

FIGURE 6.9

Policy Studies

% of Titles Held

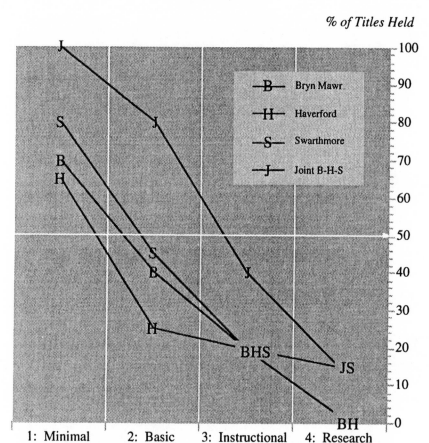

Singly, no college has even a Level 2 collection, but jointly they do, owing to relatively little overlap of holdings. All are only 20 percent at Level 3, and Bryn Mawr and Haverford actually show no holdings at Level 4 (the only time in the study this happens), perhaps because the large literature in policy studies is very diffuse.

FIGURE 6.10

Social Theory

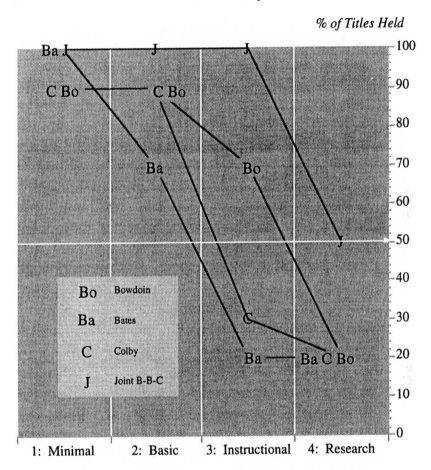

% of Titles Held

The joint collection of these three colleges just makes Level 4—a clear example of the benefit of pooling, since none of the libraries is even close to having a Level 4 collection in social theory on its own. Bowdoin's collection is Level 3, and those of Bates and Colby are Level 2.

CHAPTER 7

The French Literature Test

INTRODUCTION

In 1983 the Research Libraries Group conducted a thousand-item study to verify levels claimed by 20 members, plus the Library of Congress, in French literature. In 1992–1993 I constructed an 80-item brief test on the same topic and administered it in the same libraries. This chapter compares the results. As usual, the methodology is on trial, not the libraries.

The test in French literature was introduced in the last chapter, as part of the Tri-College assessment, and may be examined in Appendix A. Recall that it consists of 40 titles taken from the checklist created for the 1983 study by Jeffry Larson, a humanities bibliographer at Yale, and 40 other titles I chose ad libitum.

Larson's 1983 checklist measures coverage while leaving level undetermined. In contrast, the brief test yields readings on levels and so is a true verification instrument. Unlike the checklist, however, it is not tied to the subdivisions (mainly chronological) of French literature in the Conspectus. It addresses the field in general and thus cannot verify subdivision levels set by RLG libraries; for example, one cannot use it to verify claims about holdings in Old French only or nineteenth-century literature only, because it contains too few items per category. But extension to those (and all other) lines is straightforward: one simply needs new tests that are category-specific.

Although the larger-scale checklist study (Larson, 1984) was undertaken with considerable care, it should not be regarded as giving "true" or "definitive" results that the brief test simply tries to duplicate with less effort. It represents one methodology for evaluating collections, and the brief test represents another. The important question is how well the two converge on some kind of truth about collection levels. This chapter shows that they converge pretty well and that the results of the brief test are at least as useful as those of the 1983 checklist study. Obviously, the brief test's greater feasibility then becomes an important consideration.

THE 1983 VERIFICATION STUDY

The 1983 study, while big, is highly idiosyncratic. As one becomes immersed in its details, it is easy to forget that it excludes works by or about most of the leading French authors, such as Villon, Rabelais, Montaigne, Molière, Voltaire, Balzac, Hugo, Flaubert, Baudelaire, Proust, Sartre, and Camus, not to mention others. Its general design is somewhat similar to that of Allan and Jakubs's earlier RLG verification study for English literature (described in Gwinn and Mosher, 1983). In both studies, the designers believed they could not properly represent their vast domains even with a thousand titles each, and so they drew samples from subliteratures—Allan and Jakubs, judgment samples; Larson, random samples (cf. Coleman, 1992). Larson drew works by or about 10 authors, who were chosen in pairs to represent centuries and then genres judged typical of those centuries. He also drew works representing Old French and francophone linguistics. The sampling frame in each case was the best available monographic bibliography, updated as necessary by selections from the annual listings of the Modern Language Association. (There is no equivalent to the *New Cambridge Bibliography of English Literature* to serve as a sampling frame for French belles-lettres as a whole.)

Table 7.1, adapted from Larson,[1] maps the samples to Conspectus categories in linguistics, languages, and literatures (LLL). Presumably, the entire thousand items address the "general literature" category, LLL 79.

TABLE 7.1

The RLG French Literature Sample

Conspectus Categories	Literary Type	Subliteratures
LLL 76 French language		Phonology
LLL 79 French literature		
LLL 80 Old French	*chantefable*	Aucassin et Nicolette
LLL 81 16th century	*poetry*	Joachim Du Bellay and Clément Marot
LLL 82 17th century	*drama*	Jean Racine and Jean (de) Mairet
LLL 83 18th century	*polymathy*	Denis Diderot and Bernard de Fontenelle
LLL 84 19th century	*novel*	Jules Verne and Emile Zola
LLL 85 20th century	*criticism*	Jacques Derrida and Jacques Riviére

The thousand references are further divided into 566 titles that appeared in serials and 434 that appeared as monographs. This is roughly a 55 percent to 45 percent split, but the proportions of serials vs. monographs vary considerably across the 12 subliteratures.

BACKGROUND OF THE TEST

My initial idea was to create a brief test with 80 to 100 items drawn solely from Larson's checklist and preserving roughly his proportions of the subliteratures. The intent was to see whether such a test could outperform the thousand-item study, in the sense of being more informative and more efficient, in trials at some or all of the RLG libraries named in Larson (1984). Work toward that end went forward, and a version of that test exists. However, when the Tri-College project required an evaluation of the French literature collections at Bryn Mawr, Haverford, and Swarthmore, I changed the brief test markedly for two reasons.

First, many of Larson's titles turned out to have low OCLC counts. If retained, they would have made the test too rarefied for liberal arts colleges with strong undergraduate teaching functions. Second, even with these titles eliminated, there were still too few Minimal- or Basic-type items suitable for American college settings, such as English-language translations or studies of French classics. Related to this was my sense that a somewhat wider range of authors needed to be represented, even if by a single work, than what Larson had allowed. The compromise I reached was to retain three or four titles from each of his authors (or subliteratures) in Table 7.1 and then to raise the total to 80 by adding 40 titles that seemed complementary. My usual procedure was to think of authors and then to find works by or about them in the OCLC database.

Ironically, a fair number of my choices also turned out to have low OCLC counts, so that even the revised version of the French literature test is difficult, as the last chapter noted. It could, of course, be made easier by including more English translations and more text-blind choices of classics (e.g., any edition of *Tartuffe* in French). But that tendency could quickly go wrong as well, to the point of slighting everything in a literature that literary people care about. Moreover, given the notorious monolingualism of Americans, it is surely the case that *any* foreign-language literature is going to produce relatively difficult tests for U.S. libraries.

Balancing Items

What is wanted is some sense of balance between easy and hard items. The revised brief test exhibited balance in trials at Bryn Mawr, Haverford, and Swarthmore in the sense that, while it revealed their strengths, it did not put them *too high:* had it shown them with Level 4 collections, it would have failed to differentiate them from libraries whose French literature holdings are known to be vastly greater. (If the test places, say, Haverford and the Library of Congress on the same level, then for knowledgeable observers, comparisons become meaningless.) On this ground, I decided to use the test from the Tri-College evaluation on the research libraries participating in Larson's study. No less difficult a test seems appropriate for some of the most distinguished libraries in the country.

The issue of comparability is another matter. Table 7.2 provides data from Larson on percentages of sample items that are assigned to the eight Conspectus categories and the corresponding percentages from the brief test. With only 80 items apportioned over eight categories, the brief test is, of course, not a representative sample of the literatures involved (nor is it supposed to yield an inference of coverage). The comparison with Larson's sample is merely a convenient way of showing its composition.

In most categories, test and sample are quite similar. One pronounced difference is the test's relatively greater emphasis on the twentieth century. (The nine-

TABLE 7.2

The RLG Sample and the Brief Test in French Literature Compared

Conspectus Categories	% of Sample	% of Brief Test
LLL 76 French language	8.3%	5.0%
LLL 79 French literature		5.0%
LLL 80 Old French	4.2%	6.0%
LLL 81 16th century	12.5%	12.5%
LLL 82 17th century	16.7%	14.0%
LLL 83 18th century	18.8%	14.0%
LLL 84 19th century	27.0%	16.0%
LLL 85 20th century	12.5%	27.5%
	100.0%	100.0%
	N = 1,000	N = 80

teenth century has the largest share of titles in Larson's sample not because of its presumed greater importance but simply because of the combined magnitude of the Zola and Verne bibliographies, which he used as sampling frames, relative to the others.) The emphasis on twentieth-century literature in the brief test reflects my own, initially unconscious bias toward more recent authors and literary movements (which, however, I think many users of academic libraries will share). A few of my titles (Dupee's *Great French Short Novels*, Turnell's *The Novel in France*, and the serials *Yale French Studies* and *Lire*) could not be assigned to any single century; therefore they were assigned to the category LLL79, French literature in general.

A major difference not apparent in the table is that only 21 percent of the test titles are volumes or runs of serials, as opposed to 55 percent of those on the checklist. Moreover, many of Larson's titles are not assignable to French linguistic and literary studies per se, but are merely, in rare instances, supportive of them—for example, the *New Yorker* and the *Magazine of Fantasy and Science Fiction*. Thus, the checklist favors collections with deep multidisciplinary serial holdings. In contrast, the brief test focuses mostly on monographs and serials obviously relevant to French literature; it took over only a few "extradisciplinary" serial titles from Larson. One should be aware of this dissimilarity between measuring instruments when outcomes are compared.[2]

Catalogs on the Internet

The years between the RLG study and the brief test saw the emergence of many of the nation's research library catalogs in electronic form on the Internet. This remarkable development meant that, in December 1992, I could duplicate the work of a platoon of 1983 data gatherers simply by sitting at a microcomputer in my office. Every one of the 21 libraries participating in the original study had made an online public-access catalog (OPAC) available by then, and I was able to check holdings at all 21, throwing in, for good measure, a test of holdings at Harvard, which withdrew from the RLG in 1978. Harvard's French literature collection was introduced to see whether the test would confirm its putative status as Level 4.

On the whole, OPACs are extremely useful for testing holdings, although some are more congenial than others in design. They vary also in whether they include older materials, which are plentiful in this test. For those that do, one may conclude (subject to correction) that if an older title cannot be found, it is not held. Each item not initially found was searched on the OPAC in more than one way; for example, if title failed, a search by author or editor or series was undertaken. Thus, initial misses may have been turned into hits. Moreover, at 11 of the libraries[3] I supplemented the OPAC searches with lookups in antecedent card or book catalogs. In Harvard's case I used the online catalog of older Widener materials.

These searches took place in late 1992 and early 1993 and invariably improved the libraries' holdings scores. For the remaining libraries,[4] which I could not visit personally, I sent a letter in summer 1993 asking local collection development librarians to check for materials that I had not already found in their OPACs. In all cases they responded with the additional titles held. Thus, the following results should be reasonably fair to all participants.

In my own searches I may sometimes have failed to find titles that a more knowledgeable local librarian could turn up. Nevertheless, the scores seem accurate enough for my purpose, which is to indicate the promise of the methodology for future work. In this regard, I ask readers to focus on the overall outcomes and not to become bogged down in the rightness or wrongness of particular data points. (The risk one runs in administering brief tests as an outsider is that they

FIGURE 7.1

French Literature Test Results for 22 Libraries

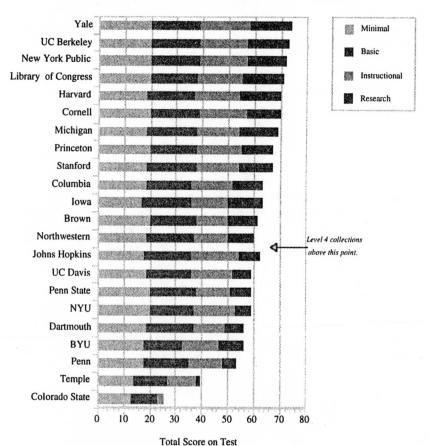

Total Score on Test

are fully replicable by peevish insiders.) As in previous chapters, the point is not to definitively rank the libraries involved but to show that some such ranking is both attainable and meaningful. If one person can do what is shown, then on-site library committees should be able to avoid whatever errors I have made and bring brief-test results to a fine accuracy.

RESULTS

Figure 7.1 is meant to convey a broad impression of the numerical details to follow. Against an 80-item scale, it presents the libraries' scores at each of the four levels as a stacked bar graph. Note how the stacked bars capture the notion of cumulativeness from Chapter 4. Again the data show strength built on strength: whatever level of collection the libraries attain, they have solid underpinnings on all lower levels. The library with a rare *Oeuvres complètes* of Racine is not going to lack an English translation of *Madame Bovary.*

The main question to be answered from any such evaluation is which libraries truly excel and which do not. The ordering of libraries high to low reflects their total scores on the test. No institution held all 80 titles; for example, Yale at top had 74; Colorado State at bottom had 25. As usual, however, the main criterion is not total score but performance on each of the four levels. To claim a level, 50 percent or more of its items must be held. These are all big libraries, and almost all of them can claim at least a Level 3 on the French literature test. What really distinguishes them is how well they do on the items representing Level 4.

On this most difficult of levels, only 13 of the 22 have scores of 50 percent or higher. The libraries above the arrow in Figure 7.1—those from Northwestern on up—held at least 50 percent of the items at all four levels, and so, according to the test, have Research-level collections in French literature. Harvard, the nonparticipant in the original study that was used as a check case, is among those attaining Level 4, as expected. The libraries below the arrow held less than 50 percent of the items at Level 4, and are all Instructional level, except Colorado State, which held less than 50 percent at Level 3 and is Basic level.[5]

Johns Hopkins presents a slight anomaly, in that it actually held more of the titles on the test overall than Northwestern or Brown immediately above it. However, it had only 40 percent of the Level 4 titles, and thus its collection scores as only a Level 3. Interestingly, that is precisely the level its librarians claimed when they estimated the collection subjectively for the Conspectus, as will be seen later.

Higher Performers

The superior performance of libraries attaining Level 4 is clearer if we divide them from the remainder and show the median percentage scores for each group separately as in Figure 7.2. The higher group outperforms the lower at all levels,

FIGURE 7.2

**Median Percentages of French Literature Holdings for
Two Groups of Libraries across RLG Scale**

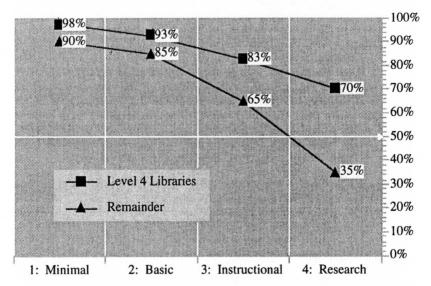

but, because of the increasing rarefication of test titles, the gap between their scores is greatest at Level 4, where the higher group is 20 points above the 50 percent threshold, and the lower group is 15 points below it. The ability to discriminate between Level 4 and lower-level collections is a major goal of the RLG verification studies, and here we see the brief test discriminating nicely.

Table 7.3 has the actual percentages of individual libraries across the four levels and the levels attained and claimed. A glance at the percentages across levels shows the power-test aspect operating very strongly (perhaps as a result of having 80 rather than 40 items on the test). As the levels rise in difficulty from 1 to 4, all percentage scores either fall or stay the same (i.e., are monotonically decreasing), with only one minor exception in the case of Iowa—another corroboration of theory.

Agreement in Levels

The libraries are ranked in Table 7.3 by level attained. In 18 of the 22 cases, including that of Johns Hopkins, the level attained and the level claimed agree. The finding that brief tests confirm librarians' estimates in 82 percent of the cases strongly encourages further experimentation with these tests as verification tools.

TABLE 7.3

Percentage Scores and Levels Claimed and Attained in the French Literature Test

Library	Minimal	Basic	Instructional	Research	Attained	Claimed
Yale	100%	95%	95%	80%	4	4
UC Berkeley	100%	95%	90%	80%	4	4
New York Public	100%	95%	90%	75%	4	4
Library of Congress	100%	90%	85%	80%	4	4
Harvard	95%	90%	85%	80%	4	4
Cornell	100%	95%	90%	65%	4	4
Michigan	95%	95%	80%	75%	4	4
Stanford	95%	95%	80%	65%	4	4
Princeton	100%	90%	85%	60%	4	4
Columbia	95%	85%	80%	55%	4	4
Iowa	85%	95%	70%	65%	4	4
Brown	100%	90%	60%	55%	4	4
Northwestern	95%	90%	65%	50%	4	4
Johns Hopkins	90%	90%	90%	40%	3	3
UC Davis	95%	85%	80%	35%	3	4
NYU	100%	85%	80%	30%	3	3
Penn State	100%	90%	65%	40%	3	4
Dartmouth	95%	90%	50%	35%	3	3
BYU	90%	75%	70%	45%	3	3
Penn	90%	85%	65%	25%	3	4
Temple	70%	65%	55%	5%	3	3
Colorado State	65%	50%	10%	0%	2	3

The four cases of disagreement are UC Davis, Penn State, Penn, and Colorado State, all of which claimed one level higher than they attained on the brief test. The message to librarians in these cases would be to reconsider their ratings in light of the data from other comparable libraries.

We should also note, however, that, if scored in the more liberal fashion devised for the WLN scale in Chapter 5, UC Davis, Penn State, and Penn would actually be Level 3c (or "4 minus") and Colorado State would be Level 3a (or "3 minus"). On this reading, the brief-test results come even closer to the original claims, although still not fully agreeing with them.

The fact that some libraries failed to attain Level 4 should not be taken to mean that they are deficient in supporting research in French literature on their campuses. A client-centered measure might uncover such deficiencies, but collection-centered brief tests do not. While the collection-building prowess they tap is not insignificant (scholarly eminence may rest on it), it is less important than a commitment to forestalling student and faculty complaints. The absence of those would be a better indicator of library success than high scores on brief tests.

1983 AND 1993 FINDINGS COMPARED

For librarians with collections involved, the main concern in an evaluation like this is the credibility of results for their own libraries. Their main question is

TABLE 7.4

Total Counts and Rankings in 1983 Verification Study and 1993 Brief Test in French Literature

Library	Count 1993	Count 1983	Rank 1993	Rank 1983
Yale	74	616	1	3
UC Berkeley	73	619	2	2
New York Public	72	597	3	5
Library of Congress	71	620	4	1
Cornell	70	549	5	7
Michigan	69	523	6	8
Princeton	67	603	8	4
Stanford	67	479	8	10
Columbia	63	555	10	6
Iowa	63	502	10	9
Johns Hopkins	62	416	11	13
Brown	61	400	12	14
Northwestern	60	457	13	12
UC Davis	59	365	15	16
NYU	59	338	15	18
Penn State	59	307	15	20
Dartmouth	56	374	18	15
BYU	56	308	18	19
Penn	53	476	19	11
Temple	39	346	20	17
Colorado State	25	163	21	21
Harvard	70	NA		

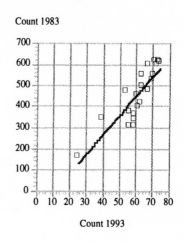

Count 1983 / Count 1993

likely to be: do the results square with my preconceptions? While that question cannot be answered here, one can at least point out that the brief-test results from 1992 are remarkably congruent with Larson's findings on number of titles held in 1983. Table 7.4 presents the counts and the resulting rankings.

Minor shifts in rank within the top 10 and bottom 11 libraries in the two studies should not be taken too seriously, since the brief-test rankings are often based on differences of a single title. The key finding is that, in number of titles held, none of the libraries in Larson's top 10 leave the top 10 of the brief test. The same is, of course, true for the bottom 11 in both studies. The library with the largest single shift in ranking is Penn, which drops from 11th place in Larson to 19th place here.

The 1983 counts, reflecting titles held out of 1,000, were used to rank-order the libraries in Table 2.1, whereas in Table 7.4 counts from the brief test are used. The two orderings are by no means identical, but the Pearson r correlation figure for the counts is 0.84. The accompanying scatterplot of counts from the two studies shows the strong linear relationship. If ranks are used instead of counts, the Spearman rho correlation is 0.88. Thus, the brief test provides, as a by-product, much the same information as the checklist study, while better addressing the matter of level attained.

The Long and Short of It

The brief test is less than one-twelfth the size of the checklist. It may therefore be useful to state once more why the two studies converge as well as they do. To reiterate, it is not claimed here that an 80-item random sample performs as well as a 1,000-item random sample in estimating the true percentage of a literature covered. However, that kind of estimation is not the intent of brief tests. It is not even clear that it was the intent of Larson's study. That is, while Larson's checklist was apparently intended to yield estimates of coverage, it is not a random sample from the whole of French literature. Given its distinctive design, it seems, indeed, almost more like a *test*—an extremely long test that accomplishes its aim of differentiating libraries by brute force, piling on items until the true nature of their collections is revealed.

The brief test accomplishes the same aim by grading items as to difficulty: it is structured so as to be maximally informative for the effort involved. It yields results similar to those of the checklist because relatively few items, identified by their OCLC holdings counts as Instructional- or Research-level, can tell the same tale as hundreds of such items on the checklist. The latter simply repeat the tale over and over again.

Of many possible analogies, we may take one from women's figure skating. To learn how good a skater is, one could observe her performance on the ice over many hours of practice, or one could ask her to skate a short program in which figures known to be difficult are compulsory. Presumably, the two test modes would yield similar results, but the reader will know which was chosen for the Winter Olympics.

Someone might argue that the brief test yields results similar to those of the checklist because 40 of its items are actually *from* the checklist. However, that opens the intriguing possibility that, had those items been structured as a brief test to begin with, we could have gained much the same information with 40 titles as we gained with 1,000, which is probably not something the persons who did the checking in 1983 want to contemplate.

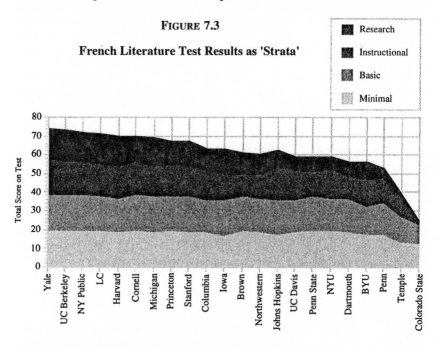

FIGURE 7.3

French Literature Test Results as 'Strata'

Research

Instructional

Basic

Minimal

A METAPHOR FOR COLLECTIONS

Figure 7.3 re-presents the information in Figure 7.1 in such a way as to suggest a new metaphor: that of collections as strata or "layers of books." We must, of course, bear in mind that Figure 7.3 depicts scores on an 80-item test and not measures made on 22 French literature collections in their entirety. Nevertheless, it raises an interesting question: if the results of the brief test look like this, would not measures made on entire subject collections yield a similar picture?

The 22 libraries in Figure 7.3 are ordered by their total scores on the French literature test, Yale at left being highest. Two major impressions derive from the gra￢h as it stands. The first, oft noted here, is the cumulativeness of collections. It is simply a fact that collections are built from the bottom up—Colorado State in this regard is no different from Yale—and that each higher level rests on holdings, not absence of holdings, beneath it.

The second impression is the pattern of decline in holdings: it is from the top down. That is, over these 22 libraries, holdings at the Research level are the first to fall away and fall away most steeply; those at Instructional level are next, and so on. While the actual shapes in Figure 7.3 derive solely from the 22 libraries that were tested, and the drop at right would change with the substitution of stronger collections than Temple's and Colorado State's, the principle of *decline from the top down* would very likely not. Suppose we were able to include in Figure 7.3 the many American libraries with French literature holdings, preserving the present ordering by total score on the brief test. Presumably, we would see a very gradual decline across all the levels, with Research-level titles disappearing first, then Instructional, then Basic, and finally Minimal, like a coastal plain sloping into the sea.

That, essentially, is what I believe we would also observe if we had a graph showing not brief-test scores, but data on total collections drawn from subject literatures. If subject literatures are defined by Conspectus lines, it is still an open question as to how one would define the RLG levels within them so as to produce a graph like that of Figure 7.3, at least for limited sets of libraries. Whether one simply divided the literature into quartiles or used some other definitional mechanism, what one would probably see in the graph is a pattern of stratification that tapers very gradually downward, from collections approaching comprehensive coverage to those for which the subject is very nearly out of scope. Libraries holding Research-level collections would be least numerous, and collections at each lower level would be progressively more numerous.

The shading of Figure 7.3 makes the Research-level holdings look like topsoil and the Minimal-level holdings look like bedrock. That is not a bad metaphor to consider. For example, library "topsoil" is fragile (erodible?) in the sense that it contains works with relatively few copies, distributed over the scarce Research-level collections. Library "bedrock" is much less fragile, in that it comprises works with relatively many copies, distributed over the numerous collections with Minimal-level holdings. However, Figure 7.3 somewhat belies the true nature of these relationships by running together as continuous "strata" collections that are, in geographic fact, widely dispersed. A truer rendering might show subject collections as scattered elevations of various heights over the surface of the United States, or some part of it. Such mapping is, of course, feasible on personal computers even now, but it has not yet been much used by the library community in depicting collections of subject literatures.

NOTES

1. I also had the benefit of RLG's own tables for the French literature verification study, copies of which were kindly supplied me by RLG's statistician, Jim Coleman. These contain data for the Library of Congress not reported by Larson. I have included LC in my tables.

2. Chapter 2 mentioned the problem of deciding whether a checklist should comprise works clearly belonging to a subject or merely somehow connected to it. The latter group is much larger and is tapped when a checklist is drawn from scholars'

footnotes and bibliographies rather than from a literature consistently identified as to subject (e.g., by an LC class range). Thus, the *Magazine of Fantasy and Science Fiction* appears in Larson's checklist not because it ordinarily has anything to do with French literature but because it published something on Jules Verne as a science fictionist. In bibliometric terms, Larson's sampling technique is picking up items from the tail, rather than the core, of a Bradford distribution.

There is no doubt that scholars need materials from fields outside their own to conduct their research (cf. Metz, 1983); and studies of library abilities to supply such materials have appeared in the collection evaluation literature at least since Coale (1965). (Coale drew citations from monographs or articles in Latin American history, and then determined whether Chicago's Newberry Library could have provided the titles cited, regardless of subject matter.) Nevertheless, there is a real question as to whether checklists containing titles from a variety of fields are appropriate for Conspectus verification studies. I would argue that they are not—that verification checklists ought to contain only titles clearly belonging to a subject, because what is being verified is the rating given to a subject collection as defined by Conspectus lines. That means that, in the future, titles for the checklists ought not to be drawn from scholars' footnotes or from the tails of Bradford distributions. Instead, they ought to be drawn from the Conspectus lines they are intended to verify, as I suggested in Chapter 5. Studies such as Coale's remain valuable, but not for verification.

3. Penn, Temple, Princeton, Columbia, New York University, New York Public Library, Yale, UC Berkeley, UC Davis, Stanford, Johns Hopkins, and the Library of Congress.

4. Michigan, Penn State, Brown, Dartmouth, Iowa, Cornell, Northwestern, Brigham Young, and Colorado State. The assistance of responding librarians at these institutions is gratefully acknowledged.

5. Incidentally, the total counts from this brief test fit well with the "quartile" scheme, discussed in Chapter 2, for converting total checklist scores into levels on the RLG scale. That scheme, arguably the best in Figure 2.4, equates Level 4 collections with checklist scores of at least 76 percent. The Level 4 libraries here hold between 75 and 92.5 percent of the 80 titles on the brief test. In the "quintile" and "Gwinn-Mosher" schemes, also shown in Figure 2.4, those scores would make some libraries Level 4 and others Level 5.

PART THREE

The OCLC Database and Holdings Counts

CHAPTER 8

Creating New Tests

INTRODUCTION

With the information in the past chapters, new selectors should readily be able to create tests like those in Appendix A. To go beyond this stage, however, one needs greater control over the difficulty of titles as test items. Difficulty is set by the number of OCLC libraries holding them; easy items are held by many libraries; hard items, by few. But counts of holding libraries must also be mapped onto the four-point version of the RLG scale. How best to do it? The answer lies in knowing more about the OCLC database from which the counts are obtained. Here we will break some new ground; the aspects of OCLC to be discussed seem not to have been taken up in print before.

In typical brief tests thus far, 40 items have simply been ranked by their counts, cut into 10s, and mechanically assigned to Levels 1 through 4. This procedure has worked surprisingly well during the early trials of the methodology. Nevertheless, it produces serious problems of calibration—the "rubber yardstick problem" noted in Chapter 3. For example, on one selector's list, a title held by 600 libraries might be assigned to Level 4; on another's, to Level 3; on yet another's, to Level 2, simply because of its position relative to mechanically derived cutpoints on those different lists.

We need a way of mapping counts to the four-point scale that is absolute rather than relative. With it, a test maker could equate Levels 1 through 4 with fixed ranges of counts in the OCLC database, rather than with ranges that vary from test to test. The advantages are considerable. First, one could accept only titles whose counts match desired levels of difficulty, rather than passively accepting, as now, whatever outcomes occur. Second, the levels would have a consistent interpretation in test-retest situations. Third, it would be possible, once the OCLC counts of books and serials have stabilized, to assign them to RLG levels automatically and thus to have succinct summaries of their reception by libraries. I mentioned the possibility, for instance, of calling the *Statistical Abstract of the*

United States a "quintessential Minimal-level work" on the basis of the many libraries that hold it. Other works could similarly be assigned by their counts to the Basic, Instructional, or Research levels.

But how many libraries must hold a title to place it at a certain level? In the present collection of brief tests, the counts of holding libraries run from 1 to approximately 3,000. (Figures above 3,000 may result from summing the counts for multiple editions of a work.) The following OCLC count scale conveys this range, marked off in hundreds. The problem is to divide it into four subranges defining the "width" of the levels on the RLG scale, which is also shown. (The latter runs backward here, of course, because of its inverse relationship with the scale of holdings counts.) More specifically, the problem is to set cutpoints on the OCLC count scale so that we have approximately equal numbers of titles at each of the four RLG levels, just as we have when we divide any selector's list into four groups of 10 or 20. The subranges encompassing these equal groups define the "width" of each RLG level.

0 1 2 3 4 5 6 7 8 9 10 11 12 13 14 15 16 17 18 19 20 21 22 23 24 25 26 27 28 29 30

Hardest   4   3   2   1   *Easiest*

Persons who have worked with computerized statistical packages such as SPSS or SAS will recognize the problem as deciding how to recode (or "collapse") one scale into another. We have ratio-level values of 1 to 3,000 on the holdings-count scale, and we want to recode them into the much cruder ordinal-level values of 4 to 1 on the RLG scale. But what nonoverlapping blocks of numbers on the first scale should we tell the computer to assign to each of the four levels of the second?

A HYPOTHETICAL DISTRIBUTION OF COUNTS

Holdings counts have their own frequency distribution, which we want to divide into four parts with equal numbers of titles in each. The question thus becomes: what is the distribution of the counts? If we plotted it on the line above, would it be approximately normal? Roughly rectangular?

The counts reflect the number of times titles have been chosen by librarians. It is well known in library and information science (L&IS) that frequency distributions of counts involving human choices (books borrowed, authors cited, and so on) are neither normal nor rectangular. They are highly skewed rightward, reflecting the uneven distribution of preferences. Items chosen seldom are numerous; items chosen frequently are few. In the present case, one would expect titles not widely held to be numerous, titles increasingly widely held to decline in frequency, and titles acquired by librarians everywhere—"superworks" like the *Statistical Abstract of the United States*—to be relatively few.

On the basis of L&IS theory, I made the diagram in Figure 8.1 before there were any data. The shaded triangle renders the prediction of the last paragraph: a decrease in the number of titles as the number of holding libraries increases. (The

FIGURE 8.1

Hypothetical Frequency Distribution of Titles Held by Various Numbers of Libraries

Frequency of Titles

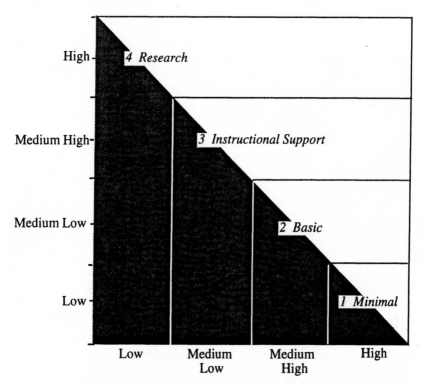

Number of Libraries Holding a Title

linear decrease in the figure was a crude approximation, not a prediction of the exact shape of the curve.) Although this is another inverse relationship (the first was between the holdings-count scale and the RLG scale), the two halves of Figure 8.1 are easy to interpret. Think of the shaded triangle as a four-level "mountain" that is less and less easy to climb the higher one goes, corresponding to the increasing difficulty of test items. Note that in ascending its levels from 1 to 4, one moves backward over the holdings-count scale, from the high end to the low, which reflects one of the inverse relationships. Next, think of the unshaded triangle as four different-sized "pools" from which titles may be drawn. There are many titles to choose from at the Research level but progressively fewer as one moves down to the Minimal-level pool at lower right. It is in the latter, of course, that one finds titles that are standard, indispensable, or classic; and its smallness suggests their relative scarcity. This trade-off between "mountain" and "pools" is the other inverse relationship.

AN EMPIRICAL DISTRIBUTION OF COUNTS

As brief tests by students and others accumulated, the holdings counts from them were put into machine-readable form. Eventually, the sample comprised 2,145 counts from 53 tests. (Because a few tests have "irregular" numbers of titles, such as 44, the sample size is not an exact multiple of 40.) This sample is, of course, based on convenience rather than on known probability of selection. Hence, its estimates of parameters in the population of holdings counts may err to an unknown degree. It must nevertheless do until we have something more representative. It does include the titles spontaneously chosen by more than 50 persons, and the titles represent a wide range of subject literatures from the sciences, social sciences, and humanities.

As the sample increased, various analyses were run on independent subsets, so as to compare results. The last comparison involved two subsets of more than a thousand titles each. Results were highly similar. For brevity's sake, therefore, only the figures from the full sample are presented here.

Titles (editions of works) are the unit of analysis, and the variable of interest is how many OCLC-member libraries hold them. The frequency distribution of the latter is given in Figure 8.2. The horizontal scale has counts grouped in intervals of hundreds, from 1 to 25 and beyond. The vertical scale shows how frequently various counts in the intervals occurred. The distribution is not approximately normal (like that of Table 1.2) nor roughly rectangular (like that of Table 1.5). It is one with high positive skew, resembling many others in library and information science (Pratt, 1975).

The hypothetical inverse relationship between the count scale and the frequency scale is confirmed: titles decrease in frequency as the number of libraries holding them increases. The curve of decrease is hyperbolic or "reverse-J" rather than linear, which accords well with L&IS theory. In plain words, the sample shows OCLC to have relatively many titles with low holdings counts and relatively few with high holdings counts. More qualitatively, there are huge numbers of works that are too specialized to be widely held by libraries (such as Gene H. Allrecht's *Craniofacial Morphology of the Sulawesi Macaques*), but far fewer "superworks" that turn up everywhere (such as Jane von Lawick-Goodall's *Chimpanzees of the Gombe*).

CONTROLLING DIFFICULTY

The goal is to gain more control over the difficulty of titles as test items. In practice this means no longer assigning items to levels on the basis of where they

FIGURE 8.2

Empirical Frequency Distribution of Titles Held by Various Numbers of Libraries

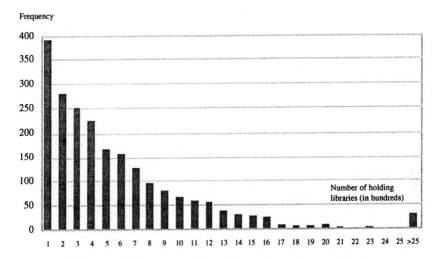

happen to be ranked in one's own test. Rather, one will seek at least 10 titles that fit within each of four predetermined ranges on the holdings-count scale.

It is a simple matter to divide the distribution in Figure 8.2 into quartiles with approximately equal numbers of titles in each. When that is done, the "raw" cutpoints are as in the first row of Table 8.1.

TABLE 8.1

Levels of RLG Scale Mapped to Ranges on Holdings-Count Scale

Cutpoints	Level			
	4 Research	3 Instructional	2 Basic	1 Minimal
Raw	to 146	to 363	to 710	over 710
Adjusted	to 157	to 393	to 751	over 751
"Mnemonic"	to 150	to 400	to 750	over 750

If one were making up a brief test and wanted to know how difficult particular titles would be as test items, one would err little in using the "raw" cutpoints of Table 8.1 as predetermined ranges. The second, "adjusted" row raises the cutpoints a bit, on the basis of a discriminant analysis to be explained below. The third, "mnemonic" row rounds the adjusted cutpoints to the nearest 50 to make them easy to remember.[1]

Recast as directions for makers of brief tests, Table 8.1 can be read as follows:

• To represent Level 1 Minimal, choose titles with counts of 751 or higher.
• To represent Level 2 Basic, choose titles with counts of 401 to 750.
• To represent Level 3 Instructional, choose titles with counts of 151 to 400.
• To represent Level 4 Research, choose titles with counts of 1 to 150.

Thus, if a search on OCLC reveals that only 124 libraries hold a title, it would go into the block of relatively difficult Research-level items. In contrast, a title held by 826 libraries would be a fairly easy item, suitable for a Minimal-level block.

Many titles can be assigned by their counts directly. However, when there is more than one OCLC record of one edition of a work, their counts need to be combined if complete accuracy is desired. Counts also need to be combined when a *work* is the selector's choice and the work exists in multiple editions, or when a test maker wants to create test-items with counts higher than some desired number, such as 750. Admittedly, this leaves much to discretion, but that cannot be helped. The bibliographic universe of OCLC is simply more complicated than many people realize.

In most cases it is unnecessary to combine the counts for *all* editions of established classics. If a work already has a count of something like 1,500, further additions to the count become superfluous: they produce no change in its level (Minimal) and little or no change in its rank within that level.

The test maker must decide when to stop adding counts. For example, one of my students picked as an item "any English translation of *Beowulf.*" In summing the actual counts for editions, she arrived at a total of *9,572,* which amounts to finding that this item is so easy as to be "off the chart"—and then finding it over and over again. She wrote me: "After being pigheaded about *Beowulf,* I decided to only [add counts for] the other minimal level books up to 1,000. The ranking in Level 1, therefore, may not reflect the actual holdings frequency."[2]

With the endpoints of the ranges set, another important consideration is the distribution of items *within* levels. Test makers might want to spread counts over the ranges as artfully as possible so as to avoid "bunching"—in other words, to choose titles with markedly different positions on the scale, so that test items would genuinely vary in difficulty. Thus, if two titles both turned out to have counts of 500, discarding one would permit another with a nonredundant count to be chosen.

Given a fixed scale, truly conscientious test makers may want to return to making tests in the way originally envisioned—by choosing titles that are appropriate to a level not only in their counts but also in their perceived content. The counts, in other words, would no longer be permitted to override one's judgment as to the correct level for a title. Rather, one would seek titles whose positions by virtue of their counts agreed with one's own notions of correct placement, and one would continue to do this until one had at least 10 titles at each level. One would need to know something of a literature, of course, so as to be fluent in proposing replacements for discarded titles.

ADVANTAGES OF CONTROL

Let me state what this new formulation gains us. Back in Chapter 2, I discussed some ways of converting percentages of coverage of a literature, as opposed to ranges of counts, into RLG levels. Of all the schemes presented in Table 2.4, I favored the one that simply equated Levels 1 through 4 with percentage *quartiles,* since it had the greatest number of desirable properties. But even it was blind to the qualitative differences of the RLG levels, in that percentages are fulfilled by abstract quanta of titles, rather than by particular sets of titles with particular characteristics. For example, two libraries might both have 20 percent of a literature and so qualify under the quartile scheme as having Level 1 or Minimal collections yet possess almost no works in common: one library could have mostly foundational titles, and the other, a mishmash of titles scattered over all the levels. It is true that, as coverage of a literature increases, there is less and less difference between a scale based on it and a scale based on holdings counts (none whatever when coverage stands at 100 percent). But for the vast majority of collections, any scale based solely on coverage would throw information away. We do not know *what* is covered in terms of the RLG levels. In any case, it would not be a constant set of titles from library to library.

Tying the RLG scale to holdings counts, on the other hand, increases information. Titles are assigned to particular levels by their counts, and whatever they have in common when they are ranked by those counts becomes observable. The scale thus highlights qualitative differences in titles that are appropriate to levels, while retaining all the advantages of the quartile scheme mentioned in Chapter 2: absolute rather than relative values, mutually exclusive divisions, a true zero point for registering Level 0 (Out of scope), and a puzzle-free interpretation of the Level 5 collection as one that achieves comprehensiveness (about 100 percent) by filling in gaps in Levels 1 through 4.

On this last point, recall the possibility, discussed in Chapter 2, of identifying the Comprehensive level with coverage of the last 15 percent or 20 percent of a literature. The counterproposal here is that the Comprehensive level be identified with gap-filling over Levels 1 through 4, *as defined for all libraries by the holdings-count scale,* rather than as a separate level in its own right. Thus, I have not defined a range of Level 5 titles. For libraries already at Level 4 and seeking comprehensiveness, "Level 5 titles" are simply any remaining desiderata. This eliminates the need to describe a "Comprehensive-type" item substantively, as we might, say, a "Basic-type" or a "Research-type" item. Indeed, given the annotations in Table 1.1, it is not unreasonable to ask whether the titles placed in Levels

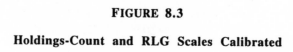

FIGURE 8.3

Holdings-Count and RLG Scales Calibrated

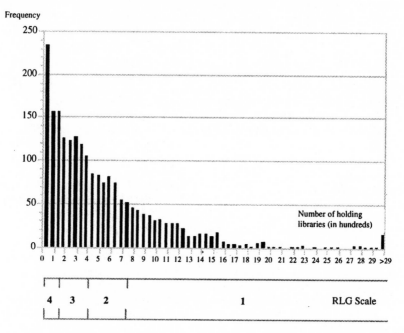

1 through 4 by their holdings counts are appropriately placed there, but such a question makes little sense for Level 5. What would make a title "Comprehensive-type"?

Sensitivity to qualitative differences in RLG levels cannot be dismissed as unimportant. As broad characterizations of the types of inquiry a library supports—see Table 1.1—these differences are central to RLG-style collection evaluation. They will be further discussed in later sections.

CALIBRATION

The new "mnemonic" cutpoints are used to calibrate the holdings-count scale and the RLG scale in Figure 8.3, which cumulates the previous figures in this chapter. To match the cutpoints, the horizontal scale is here incremented in fifties rather than Figure 8.2's hundreds. (It is still labeled in hundreds.) The associated histogram suggests the titles available for sampling at the various RLG levels. Figure 8.3 also conveys literally the inverse relationships between scales that were earlier presented fancifully as "mountain and pools." Values on both the RLG and the frequency scales are high when values on the holdings-count scale are low, and vice versa. Note the difference between mechanical division of a literature into quartiles or quintiles (as in Table 2.4) and Figure 8.3's division by cutpoints established from holdings counts. The former produces equal scale-ranges between cutpoints and equal numbers of titles within categories. The latter produces unequal scale-ranges between cutpoints and variable numbers of titles within categories. But the latter also imply important qualitative distinctions in titles at the RLG levels, something that mere percentage cutpoints cannot do.

Some may see the RLG levels thus defined as a linear version of a logarithmic scale. Indeed, when the raw holdings counts along the base of Figure 8.3 are converted into their logarithmic equivalents,[3] the frequency distribution of the 2,145 titles much more closely approximates a normal distribution. (As Pratt, 1975, observes, log-normal distributions are common in L&IS.) With this particular sample of 2,145, a somewhat better normalization is obtained by replacing each count with its own square root. (Log-normalization produces a marked negative skew, overcorrecting the positive skew.)

Figure 8.3 is, of course, a try-on, open to revision as better data become available. It should perhaps be recomputed for every subject literature—a possibility as OCLC or some other organization increases its power to summarize very large matrices. Meanwhile, however, the calibrated RLG scale permits the making of brief tests with standardized levels of difficulty. In effect, the library is given a sample of n questions (usually 10 or 20) from each of the four levels and then assigned a grade based on the highest level passed.

As previous chapters have shown, the brief-test methodology works tolerably well without these efforts at greater control. It seems only prudent, however, to learn what we can about matters affecting test difficulty. Figure 8.3 is helpful in this respect. It implies, for example, that a test consisting mostly of titles with counts over 400 would be unduly easy, while a test consisting mostly of titles with counts under 400 would be unduly hard.

Tests of both types are not mere possibilities; they exist in fact. Whether their creators would want them so is another question; at the time they were made, the information now being presented was not available. The situation is complex: certain literatures, such as that of intellectual property law, may simply not produce the range of counts seen in Figure 8.3, in that even their best-selling titles are held by only a few hundred libraries. Much, obviously, needs to be learned. Nonetheless, Figure 8.3 provides an initial pattern by which to judge empirical data as they come in.

The cutpoints on the holdings-count scale are arbitrary in that they do not obviously coincide with breaks in the qualitative nature of titles (at least not yet; see the later discussion). But while arbitrary to a degree, they are not capricious. Rather, they resemble the judgmental cutpoints that teachers use to translate students' test scores into the cruder categories of letter grades. With experience, teachers learn how to set cutpoints for different levels of students' performance. The same claim is made here for library collection testing. The calibration of the holdings-count and collection-level scales is already informed by a fair amount of empirical data and is capable of being corrected with more. The reader who believes that teachers can grade students fairly (borderline cases notwithstanding) should be able to accept a similar procedure when it is applied to collection evaluation.

ORIGIN OF THE CALIBRATED RLG SCALE

As noted, the process of assigning items to levels simply by cutting 40-item tests into 10s produces less than optimal results, in that titles with identical counts may be assigned to different levels in different tests. The calibrated RLG scale derives from an analysis that addressed this problem. The goal was to translate the four groups corresponding to RLG levels into mutually exclusive ranges on the holdings-count scale.

The input data were the counts for the 2,145 titles and the four groups, representing the RLG levels, to which they had been assigned by the "mechanical 10s" method. While these a priori groups are themselves mutually exclusive, the ranges of counts associated with them are not, as the "before" panel in Figure 8.4 shows. The four groups are rendered there with boxplots.[4] The undesirable overlap in distributions is clearly visible: different boxplots occupy the same parts of the holdings-count scale. Although by no means indistinguishable—note, for example, the nonalignment of their medians—they are not cleanly separate either. Ideally, they should be adjacent but separate on the scale.

To see how well each title's a priori membership in one of the four groups could be predicted on the basis of its count alone, a discriminant analysis was performed. This computerized classification procedure predicts which of the four groups a title belongs to on the basis of probabilities arising from the distribution of the counts over 2,145 titles. Given a count for a particular title and the overall distribution of counts, it computes the title's probability of membership in each of the four groups and then assigns the title to the group in which its probability of membership is highest.[5]

This way of assigning titles to levels uses more information than the a priori method of mechanical 10s. The predicted assignments can then be compared with the actual, a priori assignments in what is called a "confusion matrix." Such matrices show where the assignments produced by the two methods agree and disagree.

I take as correctly classified those titles on which the discriminant function and the mechanical 10s method *agree*. That is, agreement is held to indicate that a title has been placed in the "right" range of the holdings-count scale; disagreement, that the mechanical 10s method has placed a title too high or too low.

The Confusion Matrix

Table 8.2 gives the confusion matrix for the discriminant analysis. Percentages in the cells have been computed to the base of 2,145, the total number of titles (and not to column or row bases). Boldfaced down the main diagonal

are the percentages of cases in which the discriminant function's prediction agreed
with assignment by mechanical 10s over the four levels. Had agreement been perfect, each boldfaced figure would have been 25 percent (or close to it). As it is, the
agreements produce the largest percentages in any given column—i.e., 17.7, 13.2,

FIGURE 8.4

**Ranges of Holdings Counts Assigned to RLG Levels before and
after Discriminant Analysis of Titles**

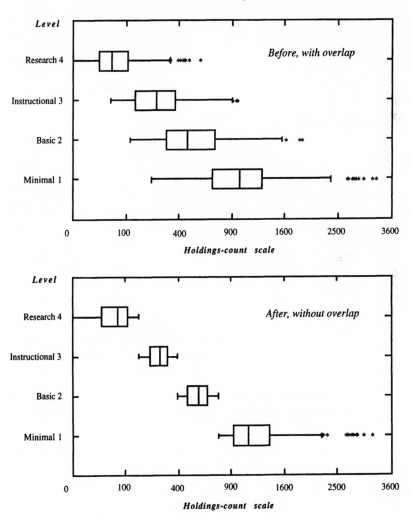

TABLE 8.2

Joint Prediction of Levels by Mechanical 10s Method and by Discriminant Function

Mechanical 10s Prediction	Discriminant Function's Prediction				
	1 Minimal	2 Basic	3 Instructional	4 Research	TOTAL
1 Minimal	17.7%	6.2%	1.0%	0.0%	24.9%
2 Basic	4.4%	13.2%	7.1%	0.4%	25.1%
3 Instructional	1.0%	3.9%	14.3%	5.9%	25.1%
4 Research	0.0%	0.5%	4.1%	20.3%	24.9%
TOTAL	23.1%	23.8%	26.5%	26.5%	100.0%

14.3, and 20.3 respectively. Jointly, these modal values add up to 65.5 percent; overall, about two in three titles are classified correctly. (The percentage correctly classified was even better in earlier versions of the Table, before I put in almost all of the tests I then had, including some odd ones.) The probability of obtaining such results by chance alone is less than one in a thousand by chi-square test. Fortunately for brief tests, even the mechanical 10s method performs fairly well.

Nevertheless, it is far from perfect. Disagreements or "confusions" of classification are found in the off-diagonal cells. The first row, for example, shows that, of the titles called Minimal by the mechanical 10s method, the discriminant function put 6.2 percent at Basic and 1 percent at Instructional. Row by row, these disagreements or confusions can be taken as another version of the undesirable overlap shown in the "before" panel of Figure 8.4.[6]

The overlap problem can be solved by rejecting the classification procedure along the rows—that of mechanical 10s—in favor of the classification procedure down the columns—that of the discriminant function. Both will be briefly described in turn.

The a priori mechanical 10s classification produces four unique groups of titles. The row marginals in Table 8.2 show each to be about 25 percent of the sample, which simply reflects the fact that mechanical 10s cuts each brief test into quartiles. (The small deviations from 25 percent arise from tests with nonstandard numbers of items.) If one then asks the computer to display the ranges of counts associated with each of these groups, one gets the following:

Research	*Instructional*	*Basic*	*Minimal*
0 to 601	49 to 1313	116 to 2286	218 to highest

In other words, if one regards the classification of title by the mechanical 10s method as correct, these four overlapping ranges are the result.

In contrast, one can regard the algorithmic classification of cases by the discriminant function as correct in all cases. This function predicts that each title most probably belongs, by virtue of the number of libraries that hold it, to one of the four input categories. The computer retains the predicted categories as a new variable, separate from the actual categories assigned by mechanical 10s. If one then asks for a display of the ranges of counts associated with this new variable, one gets the following:

Research	*Instructional*	*Basic*	*Minimal*
1 to 157	158 to 393	394 to 751	752 to highest

The predicted categories are thus four mutually exclusive ranges of the holdings-count scale. While the column marginals reflecting the number of titles in each predicted category are not quite equal (23 percent Minimal, 24 percent Basic, 26.5 percent Instructional, and 26.5 percent Research), they seem close enough for the present purpose of suggesting cutpoints. (If test makers hew to the proposed cutpoints in the future, the column marginals will presumably be an even 25 percent per level.)

After such a step, the ranges for the four levels appear as plotted in the "after" panel of Figure 8.4. The overlaps of the "before" version have disappeared. This method lets the discriminant function set the width of the four levels and yields the adjusted cutpoints of Table 8.1. The rounded version of the latter in the "mnemonic" row of Table 8.1 conveys my journalistic preference for numbers that are easy to remember. While both revised and mnemonic figures turn out to be not greatly different from the "raw" cutpoints obtained by simply quartering the distribution, they provide a clearer sense of where the mechanical 10s method has gone wrong.

This use of discriminant analysis is unorthodox. Ordinarily, one regards the a priori classification of cases as being optimal or standard and then tries to find variables that algorithmically classify cases in like fashion, with as few disagreements as possible. Here, however, the classification of titles produced by the mechanical 10s method is not regarded as optimal, and the information in the counts is being used as the standard by which to correct it.[7]

All this is improvisatory rather than rigorous, but my sense is that it yields a reasonable definition of the RLG levels in terms of holdings counts. Titles with counts above 750 will be adequately easy as test items; titles with counts below 150 will be adequately hard; and titles with counts between 150 and 750 will be adequately middling.

The 400-Library Point

The midpoint for all counts, an interesting value, can be variously estimated. Simply halving the raw counts of the sample gives a median of 363, while the "adjusted" median set by the discriminant analysis is 393. I have used 400 as the "mnemonic" midpoint. (The mean lies somewhere near 400, depending on which technique one uses to eliminate the undue influence of the relatively few counts at the high end of the scale—above, say, 2,500.) *Some* point in this vicinity divides the distribution of titles in half. Its significance, regardless of the exact count associated with it, is that it can be used to operationalize what is perhaps the haziest concept in the present RLG scale—the break between the Minimal and Basic levels on the one hand, and the Instructional and Research levels on the other. Very likely there are important qualitative differences to be found in the broad groups of titles on either side of this median. Discovering what they are will advance our capabilities for collection assessment.

Marshall (1994, p. 17), a short piece on why academic books are no longer edited to make them readable, independently mentions 400 libraries as a cutpoint for judging the appeal of titles.

Says Liz Maguire, senior editor at Oxford University Press: "Most editors think, 'Well, if this is an academic monograph for this author's peers and about 400 research libraries, is it really going to benefit from my editing?'" Maguire and her peers agree that only the few works that seem likely to sell between 3,000 and 10,000 copies get serious attention from senior editors.

In other words, Maguire, who should know, intuitively equates a market of 400 or fewer libraries with highly specialized books. Academic titles that sell 3,000 to 10,000 copies throughout the world would be well on the other side of the spcialization divide. Their sales to American libraries alone would probably make them Minimal-level titles.

A cutpoint of 400 libraries is also intuitively used by the director of the Penn State Press. Regarding titles that sell almost exclusively to the library market, Thatcher (1995, p. B2) writes, "American university presses might buy some time if they were willing to follow the example of European publishers and raise book prices to cover the full cost of small print runs—to, say, $150 for a 250-page book with a print run of 400 copies." Other figures in his article are roughly consistent with the cutpoints in Table 8.1 and the general description of OCLC holdings counts presented in this chapter. Of 150 books of literary criticism published by his press since 1985, he writes (p. B1), "65 per cent have sold fewer than 500 copies and 91 per cent have sold fewer than 800. Only 3 per cent (generally those dealing with American literature or gender issues) have sold more than 1,000 copies." Again, these would mostly be sales to libraries rather than to individual scholars.

QUALITATIVE DIFFERENCES IN LEVELS

The original RLG scale, or something like it, is clearly valuable for grading collections. The definitions of levels in Table 1.1 are nevertheless open to improvement now that we can divide titles into large, discrete groups by their holdings counts and learn their characteristics. Since the definitions of RLG levels apply to whole subject collections, we should indeed seek the characteristics of groups of titles, not individual titles, to improve the definitions.

Suppose a Conspectus-defined subject literature (or a large random sample of titles) has been divided into non-overlapping groups with cutpoints along the lines of those in Table 8.1. What further can be discovered? Presumably that certain characteristics will vary in frequency across the levels, and that such variation exhibits definite patterns. One would certainly expect interpretable variation at the two extremes: the Research-level group, with counts under 150, will have characteristics that recommend them only to specialists (such as having a foreign imprint), and the Minimal-level group, with counts over 750, will have characteristics that recommend them to wide readerships (such as being in English). But the differing characteristics of the two inner groups, Basic and Instructional, are less easy to predict and are likely to emerge only through computerized analysis of OCLC records.

The large-scale empirical analysis needed to characterize groups of titles has not yet been done. It would involve whole literatures and represents a potential further stage in brief-tests research. Here I can only point out how the methodology reflects our intuitions about what the different levels should contain. But I shall also suggest measurable differences to look for in the future—differences that, if found, would more firmly distinguish the levels than the present definitions of Table 1.1.

GLOSSING THE LEVELS

Librarians know how to interpret those definitions without taking everything at face value. For example, the statement that a Basic-level collection "is not sufficiently intensive to support any courses or independent study" should probably be discounted. Many teachers would be delighted to have their students read a few items from holdings of the most Minimal-level sort. Imagine a literature collection consisting of a single volume, the plays of Shakespeare; or an Islamic studies collection consisting solely of the Koran; does anyone doubt that a course could be given or independent study conducted with those alone? Vladimir Nabokov gave a famous course at Cornell in which the students simply read novels like *Bleak House* and *Madame Bovary* to his counterpoint from the lectern; surely such titles would be found in even Minimal-level fiction collections. And how many people have learned nonparametric statistics or experimental design by independent study of a single textbook, such as Sidney Siegel's or B. J. Winer's, that belongs to the Minimal-level canon of a field? Similarly dubious is the statement that "major periodicals" in a subject appear only at Basic level and not lower down, at Minimal level. For a small library, subscriptions to such periodicals—e.g., *Library Journal* for librarianship, *National Geographic* for geography, *Scientific American* for the natural sciences—may be almost the only things that stand between having *something* on a subject and declaring it out of scope.

The real point here is to accept the RLG scale (in some version) without necessarily accepting the present definitions of the levels. Sympathy with their intent should not deter us from giving them greater empirical content. As a preliminary, let me state what I, and I think many librarians, would infer about items appropriate to the levels (cf. Atkinson, 1986; Henige, 1987; Coffey, 1992).

Minimal: the works one should have if anything at all is held on a subject; the kind of foundational titles that appear in the *Reader's Adviser.* Famous works and classics, both old and new. The most popular serials.

Basic Information: Minimal items, plus standard bibliographic and factual reference books on the subject; key serials; major monographs—i.e., works of established reputation. Core collection items, as in *Books for College Libraries.*

Instructional Support: Minimal and Basic items, plus enough depth in monographs, serials, and reference works that one can usually supply, without special ordering, the items that teachers put on reading lists, including newer works not yet established and hence not on core collection lists.

Research: Items from the three lower levels, plus all the rest of the universe of publications and quasi-publications that typically interest only students in advanced degree programs and postdoctoral specialists. Items that are collected in case they are needed, but that may be used infrequently or never. (In academic libraries, they are usually in the stacks rather than on reserve.)

AMBIGUITIES OF REFERENCE

There are ambiguities in what these RLG scale labels refer to. In the main, they are supposed to designate librarians' intentions as to levels of inquiry their collections will support. But it is next to impossible to keep them from also implying types of materials suitable for the different levels of inquiry. Indeed, brief tests instantiate them with individual works, mechanically characterized as "minimal," "basic," "instructional," or "research" in nature. Unfortunately, it is then hard not to conflate these labels further with our common notion of levels of difficulty of a subject, such as "elementary," "basic," "intermediate," and "advanced." (Or perhaps "high school," "lower-division college," "upper-division college," and "postgraduate.")

I have already said that selectors often seem to have such a scale in mind when they assign titles to levels before OCLC searching. It cannot be stressed enough that levels as defined by OCLC holdings-counts may not square with ordinary notions of levels of difficulty of subject matter. Many academic subjects are difficult for most people even in their rudiments. Thus, if the subject is recent French literary theory, the Minimal-level counts will lead not to something like *My First Book of Deconstruction* but directly to writings by Derrida, Barthes, Kristeva, and so on, which few would call easy. Or, as we shall see in Table 8.3, *Science* and *Nature* are both Minimal-level journals for contemporary genetics by their counts, yet both are far from being "minimal" in the demands they place on readers. (Even popularizations like the Time-Life *Genetics,* which some would consider truly minimal in difficulty, would be considered by others forbiddingly highbrow.) Conversely, other collectible literatures (e.g., American cookbooks, children's picture books, Victorian erotica) would be easy enough to fathom even at Research level. Thus, any identification of librarians' intended levels solely with levels of difficulty of content cannot be sustained. However, the broader identification—of librarians' intended levels with types of materials suitable to those levels— seems to me inevitable, as long as it is understood that suitability will be decided on grounds not limited to difficulty of content.

EXPECTED DEMAND

While these grounds are multidimensional, it is appropriate to set them against a unifying concept: expected demand. In collection development, librarians bring publications to more or less permanent clienteles, whose interests will determine the subject matters and form classes collected. These clienteles represent demand, both past and future. Librarians' images of local people's wants, both changing and unchanging, are probably the most important determinant of what they buy. That is why many collection developers automatically buy items published by certain presses or reviewed in certain periodicals; they know that their clienteles monitor these sources and that demand is shaped accordingly. An image of demand can be sharply individual—of, say, a particular bespectacled Colley Cibber expert; or it can be general and relatively faceless—for example, "the materials engineering department" or "term-paper writers." But it is always there when something is purchased or subscribed to (or even foregone because of cost). When it is absent—that is, when publications simply evoke a blank in terms of likely users—then chances are they will not be acquired. Librarians differ, by clienteles, as to which titles within literatures bring on this negative state, and it is this variation, more than anything else, that the levels of the RLG scale will capture.

To some extent, expected demand for a work correlates with its fame: people tend to ask for what is already well known. Fame is, of course, various: it could be local, as when a textbook is a perennial in a professor's classes; sudden, as when something is mentioned on television; fleeting, in the case of many best-selling titles; permanent, in the case of classics. But culturally literate librarians will recognize most works within these categories, including established monographs and long-running serials. These are the kinds of works likely to be assigned to Minimal or Basic level when holdings counts are ranked. Selections whose counts put them on the Instructional or Research levels will probably be less well known, unless they happen to be particular editions of a famous work that are not necessarily famous in themselves.

POLAR OPPOSITES

In Appendix A the titles in the subjects of the Tri-College study are ranked by their holdings counts. In Table 8.3 the three highest Minimal titles in all subjects are set against the three lowest Research titles, which is the greatest possible contrast for these data. It does not fail to bring out sharp qualitative differences.

The highest-ranked titles include classics (Flaubert, Darwin, Celine), American best-sellers (Wills, Freeman, Naisbitt), established introductory texts (Commager, Howard, Turnell), standard encyclopedias and handbooks, and several very well-known serials. The British journal *Nature,* for example, published the paper

TABLE 8.3

Titles Ranked Highest and Lowest in Eight Brief Tests

Three Highest-Ranked	*Three Lowest-Ranked*

American History

American heritage magazine	Danielson. Lincoln's attitude toward Prohibition
American historical review	Lemonnier. Histoire du Far-West: les Mormons
Boatner. Civil War dictionary	Luraghi. Storia della guerra civile americana

American Studies

Inge, ed. Handbook of American popular culture	Campbell. Establishing Zion: the Mormon church ...1847–1869
Wills. Inventing America	Maledicta, the international journal of verbal aggression
Commager. The American mind	Dictionary catalog, Schomburg collection of Negro literature and history

Classical Music

Musical Americana	Ragtime: World's favorite music and songs (Scott Joplin scores)
International cyclopedia of music and musicians	Paleographie Musicale
Howard. Our American music	Repertoire international des sources musicales

Cultural Anthropology

Less & Vogt, eds. Reader in comparative religion	Reche. Rasse und Heimat der Indogermanen
Johanson & Edey. Lucy: The beginnings of humankind	Professional papers of Franz Boas (microfilm)
Freeman. Margaret Mead in Samoa	Balandier. L'anthropologie appliquée aux problemes des pays sous-developpé

French Literature

Flaubert. Madame Bovary (Steegmuller translation)	de Vigny. Servitude et grandeur militaires (1835 ed.)
Celine. Death on the installment plan (English eds.)	Racine. Oeuvres complètes (1825 ed.)
Turnell. The novel in France	Marivaux. Une comédie inconnue de Marivaux: La provinciale (1922 ed.)

Genetics

Darwin. On the origin of species (any ed.)	Advanced bacterial genetics: A manual of genetic engineering
Nature	Molecular cloning: A laboratory manual
Science	Genetic recombination: Thinking about it in phage and fungi

Mathematics

Handbook of mathematical functions..	Faith. Algebra (2 vols.)
McGraw-Hill encyclopedia of science and technology	Flhugge. Handbuch der Physik/Encyclopedia of physics
CRC handbook of chemistry and physics	American Mathematical Society translations

Policy Studies

Naisbitt. Megatrends	ABC News transcripts (microform)
Statistical abstract of the United States	Public policy and labour markets in the Ecowa
Barone et al. Almanac of American politics	El Salvador: The making of a U.S. policy, 1977–1984 (microform)

in which James Watson and Francis Crick announced the double-helical structure of DNA. The monographs among them were multiply reviewed; the classics have spawned book-length studies in their own right. All of them are in English, and all except *Nature* come from American publishers. All are currently in print in hard copy (as opposed to microform), and none would be particularly difficult to buy. All are intended for broad (if well-educated) readerships, and most of the non-fictional items seem broad-gauged in their subject matter. It is easy to imagine uses for them.

In contrast, the lowest-ranked titles are much more specialized and limited in their appeal. (Compare the comprehensive *American Heritage Magazine* with *Maledicta*, a journal devoted to analyses of insult humor; or *Musical America* with the *Repertoire International des Sources Musicales*, a journal published in Germany and containing scores from the period before 1700.) The highest-ranked items in Table 8.3 presumably include a good many that the reader recognizes, whereas the lowest-ranked set may include none, and it would be hard or impossible to find reviews. More than one title in the latter is "archival" in nature, and three actually appear in microform. Quite a few are in foreign languages, or come from foreign publishers, or both. Few trade publishers are represented. The three French literary titles are confined to editions long out of print. There is a collection of piano scores (Scott Joplin's), and two laboratory manuals. Generally, it seems fair to conclude that this set of titles would pose far more problems to acquire than the highest-ranked set.

These observations indicate some of the characteristics by which "types of materials suitable for the four levels" might be judged. They are all binary characteristics hypothetically associated with the four levels. Table 8.4 gives a fuller array, and states the hypotheses they suggest. These hypotheses are as yet untested, and the list is neither complete nor closed to revision.

Some of these variables could be immediately operationalized; others need further definition. Nevertheless, we can see more clearly now why *expected demand* is relevant to a consideration of the levels. Expected demand varies inversely with specialization, and the variables in Table 8.4 are crude indicators of specialization, low to high. At the high end they single out works that require unusual training to know, unusual bibliographic competence to find, unusual language skills to read, and so on. As increasing specialization filters out progressively more people, the publics for comparably specialized materials decrease correspondingly. (This is reminiscent of the saying that every mathematical equation in a piece of writing cuts the readership by half.) Thus, in any given place there are many persons who will sometimes need a general encyclopedia or dictionary, but relatively few who will need a Russian-language bibliography on futurism or a national science policy study from Canada. In an entire nation there might be only one person who knows enough about Colley Cibber to require certain eighteenth-century playbills, but thousands of persons who need a particular atlas. As a professional task, librarians judge the size of groups to which particular titles will appeal. (They could, of course, put the likely demand at zero.) The claim of brief-test theory is that, once stabilized, OCLC holdings counts summarize estimates of demand quite nicely.

TABLE 8.4

Hypotheses on Variation in Characteristics of Titles at RLG Levels 1 through 4

The lower the level, the greater the proportion of	*The higher the level, the greater the proportion of*
Titles from trade presses	Titles from academic presses Titles from association and small presses Titles from U.S. governments (federal, state, local) Titles from international organizations
Titles in hard copy	Titles in microform
Titles with U.S. publishers Tiles in English (or English translations)	Titles with foreign publishers Titles in foreign languages
Titles in print five years after first edition Serials still published	Titles out of print five years after first edition Serials no longer published
Titles with more than one edition Titles in "best" or "core" lists Titles judged widely known Titles judged useful to many persons Titles receiving one or more reviews Serials with high impact factors	Titles with one edition Titles not in "best" or "core" lists Titles judged little known Titles judged useful to relatively few persons Titles receiving no review Serials with low impact factors
Titles without mathematical or statistical content Titles without notation requiring training to read	Titles with mathematical or statistical content Titles with notation requiring training to read

POTENTIAL MEASURES

Table 8.4 sets forth *titles* as units of analysis and assumes that measures would be made on them within a given literature as defined by a Conspectus line. Assuming they are assigned to levels by a scheme like that in Figure 8.3, one would expect systematic variation by level in the frequencies with which a particular characteristic is present or absent. To take one idealized example, one would expect a decrease in the in-print status of titles over the four levels, as illustrated in Table 8.5. As holdings counts fall, in-print status—another measure of popularity among libraries—falls as well. The table is contrived to show majorities of titles in print at Minimal and Basic levels, and minorities in print at Instructional and Research levels. While this particular effect may be absent in real data, at least some of the variables in Table 8.4 should perform as hypothesized.

At present, however, it is not clear that any variable will define the levels or their cutpoints less arbitrarily than was done in Figure 8.3. It is easy to establish qualitative differences among titles at polar ends of the holdings-count scale, as in Table 8.3. It is harder to distinguish among titles within *neighboring levels*—Minimal and Basic, Basic and Instructional, and Instructional and Research—on the basis of some feature or set of features that is present in one set and absent in the other. Indeed, it may not always be possible. (Stielow and Tibbo (1989) note "particular confusion" between Levels 1 and 2 for their informants; Coffey (1992) says that Level 3 "is the most difficult to understand.") Works whose counts put them on the boundaries of the levels focus the problem acutely: does any observable difference in their characteristics mark the transition from one level to the next? Where really, for example, does Basic level end and Instructional level begin?

Here we confront a difficulty now widely recognized by writers on categorization: lack of strict criteria for determining categorical membership. In the present case, there may be no criterial features, other than holdings counts, that will serve to assign works uniquely to one of the RLG levels. (Certainly the definitions in Table 1.1 are not adequate in this regard.) At best one would expect bundles of features that, to some degree, co-occur within the levels, but that are inconstant from work to work. Thus, category members exhibit Wittgenstein's "family resemblances" rather than strictly equivalent features, and even across the levels there are simply diminishing resemblances rather than sharp breaks. Those exhibiting most of the features within a category would be taken as prototypical. For example, words I used earlier to describe my notion of prototypical materials at Level 1 included "popular, standard, indispensable, classic," and at Level 4, "advanced, localized, foreign, academic, obscure, old." But such features, assuming they are somehow measurable, would occur in varying combinations within levels, rather than in all-or-none fashion, and would be attenuated across levels, rather than disappearing completely.

It is less easy to characterize prototypical works at Levels 2 and 3, or even to distinguish the criterial features of the two inner levels. One notion worth exploring is that, for any given subject literature, there may be different "in-print status zones," defined by the publication dates of titles and whether they remain available from their publishers. Titles at least, say, five years old but still in print might also have holdings counts that put them at the Basic or Minimal level. They would have had time to gain reputations sufficient to keep them in print, and their

Table 8.5

Hypothetical Distribution of In-print Status by RLG Level

Status	RLG Level			
	Minimal	Basic	Instructional	Research
In print	80%	60%	40%	20%
Out of print	20%	40%	60%	80%
	100%	100%	100%	100%

counts would have had time to grow accordingly. In contrast, titles still in print but less than five years old should occur largely in the Instructional or Research levels. They have not yet reached maturity, so to speak, or perhaps they are simply not destined for widespread acceptance. Finally, titles out of print and not being reprinted should, by this logic, occur most heavily at Research level. It would be interesting if some such "zonal analysis" reinforced the cutpoints I have set between levels. In particular, it might help differentiate the inner two, which are less well defined with regard to each other than the outer two. (If this notion is viable, the proper age at which to check "in-print status" needs to be found empirically; it may not be five years.)

Types of Libraries

An analysis of types of libraries holding titles is another possible differentiator of levels in many literatures. Once the three-letter holders' codes attached to OCLC bibliographic records are translated, the types of libraries they designate can be determined. For the vast majority of monographs and serials placed by low holdings counts in Research level, the predominant holders should be *academic* libraries serving *universities* (or other research-oriented institutions). For titles on the Instructional, Basic, and Minimal levels, the proportion of *nonresearch* libraries in the overall mix of holders should systematically increase. The difference between Research and Instructional levels, for example, could be the latter's greater share of titles held by libraries at *teaching* institutions, such as liberal arts colleges and community colleges. A distinguishing feature of the Basic and Minimal levels, relative to those on the other side of the median, might be increasing shares of *public* libraries. At the Minimal level, a complement of smaller *public* and *school* libraries should appear, provided they report holdings to OCLC.

Such a scheme would account for the increase in number of holding libraries

TABLE 8.6

Hypothetical Mixes of Libraries Contributing to Holdings Counts at Different Levels

Level	Types of Libraries
Research 4	Research libraries
Instructional 3	Research libraries; college and special libraries
Basic 2	Research libraries; college and special libraries; larger public libraries
Minimal 1	Research libraries; college and special libraries; larger public libraries; smaller public libraries; school libraries

across the four RLG levels. That is, what drives up the counts are acquisitions by increasingly various types of libraries—different library markets—with the result that each level has a different mix of holders, as in Table 8.6. Titles such as Strunk and White's *The Elements of Style* have counts over 750 because they appeal to the widest range of library types, while titles such as *Who's Who in Finnish Librarianship* have counts under 150 because they appeal to the narrowest.

The very shape of the entries in Table 8.6 recalls the "mountain" shape presented earlier in Figure 8.1. That is because, as displayed, it captures the notion of cumulative collections seen in the data of past chapters. Research libraries hold titles on all four levels, college and some special libraries on three, larger public libraries on two, and school and smaller public libraries on one. Essentially, the world of titles with counts above the median is identified with public and school librarianship. That world, *plus* the world of titles with counts below the median, is identified with academic and special librarianship.

The ultimate intent here is to define the RLG levels not solely by the intuitions of a committee, as they are now, but with the help of hard data on the organizational affiliations of thousands of collection developers. The view in Table 8.6 is, of course, overschematized, but its goodness of fit is open to empirical test. "Instructional-level" collections, for example, have been somewhat difficult for developers to define. As noted earlier, it seems plausible that titles with counts in the second quartile (here, from 151 to 400) will be held not only by big research libraries, but also by numerous academic libraries that support undergraduate teaching rather than graduate and postgraduate research; and that these two kinds of academic libraries will predominate among holders. Should this turn out to be the case, it would imply that titles in this range of counts are indeed Instructional in nature (teaching goes on even at research universities), and thus we could operationalize the concept of Instructional-level collections.

Exactly how to score holders as to type and how to get computers to generate the results need not concern us here. The main thing is that there may be regularities in the different mixes of holding libraries over the different levels. If so, these regularities could afford another check on the levels as set with holdings counts. More grandly, they could be used to relate levels of literatures to the standard types of librarianship.

QUALITATIVE DIFFERENCES IN TITLES

It remains to be added that, once the levels are set with holdings counts, we can use them to classify individual works, as mentioned above. This needs a bit of explaining.

Clearly the RLG scale of Table 1.1 is not intended to describe individual works; it is intended to describe collections. To architects of the Conspectus, the idea that one might speak of a Research-level monograph or a Minimal-level serial represents a confusion. However, there is no denying that individual works have holdings counts, that these can be used to fix them on a holdings-count scale, that that scale can be mapped onto the RLG levels, and that the names of the levels thus become applicable to individual works. Therefore it appears we *can* speak of such things as Minimal-level monographs or serials, and the belief that the RLG scale describes only collections becomes too simple. It is still true that its main use is to describe collections, but we can also use it now to characterize specific works as well.

The trouble is that the names of the RLG levels, which were created to describe collection developers' intentions, may not accord well with the nature of specific works to which they are applied. Earlier I noted that most observers cannot help equating the levels with a scale of difficulty of content. Thus, they are dismayed when a Research-level item (by its count) turns out to be an ABC book, or when a Minimal-level item (by its count) turns out to be over most readers' heads. Other ironies are readily imaginable, such as a textbook titled *Advanced Physics* put at Basic, or a pornographic novel called Instructional. The inescapable conclusion is that the existing names of the RLG levels will sometimes—by no means always—seem distorted or counterintuitive or simply wrong if we take them as literal descriptions of the content of individual works.

Since the levels will probably not be renamed in the foreseeable future, the only remedy is to make such statements as, "This is an *x*-type work" mean primarily, "This work is suitable for *x*-level collections." That is, the labels pertain first to the level of inquiry the work supports, and only provisionally to the work itself. By this logic, a phrase like "a Research serial" is just a short way of saying "a serial suitable only for Research-level collections" or "a serial needed to support only the most specialized level of interest." It will not necessarily imply anything about what the serial contains. A magazine about pop music stars for Japanese teenage girls would be a Research serial in the American context. Of course, if such labels agree with our intuitive notions of content—as they often should—so much the better.

An interesting prospect for this type of labeling lies in identification of Minimal- and Basic-level works on the basis of high holdings counts. The reason is that it would allow us to obtain titles for core collection lists algorithmically. At present we do not know the most-held titles within subject classes in American libraries. We can make educated guesses, but with OCLC's present online technology we cannot ask for a ranking of titles in a subject. If we could, the top-ranked titles—library best-sellers—would constitute a de facto core collection based on the judgments of many librarians.

It is likely that Minimal- and Basic-level titles in a given literature would heavily overlap those appearing now in collection-development tools such as *The Reader's Adviser* and *Books for College Libraries*. If so, lists from OCLC might in time replace these printed tools by serving the same purpose with quicker updates and input from far more people. From a slightly different standpoint, it also is likely that Minimal- and Basic-level titles include many standard reference works, such as encyclopedias, dictionaries, directories, and atlases. Thus OCLC-generated lists would probably do at least as well as present-day textbooks in specifying the titles that reference librarians most need to know—the "repertoire," as discussed in White (1992b), that should be inside their heads.

The *OCLC Newsletter* now annually lists in rank order the titles most widely cataloged in a given period by member libraries. As a printed feature, however, this information is simply perishable journalism. What is important is the capability to generate those lists, particularly if anyone could generate them anywhere, any time, for any subject. Such a capability could have numerous uses if it were part of generally available software.[8]

AUTOMATIC GRADING OF COLLECTIONS

Speaking of advances in software, it is possible that the entire business of assigning collections to levels on the RLG scale or the WLN scale could be automated. Then librarians whose collections are computer-analyzable would no longer have to worry about setting or verifying Conspectus levels themselves; software would do it for them. The need for brief tests would consequently disappear. (They might still play a role in less computerized libraries.)

Among the measures to be automated, two stand out. It is inherently desirable for collection developers to know what percentage of titles in a subject literature the library has covered. The first evaluative task, therefore, is to establish *coverage*, both as a summary of collection strength and as an indicator of local effort toward a goal. Next, one wants finer-grained summaries of holdings—the percentages of titles held at each of the RLG levels over many subject literatures—and a conversion algorithm so that *level* might be claimed. The data on both coverage and levels should be directly comparable among libraries, so that relative standing can be determined.

Toward these ends, one of the most useful—and perhaps underappreciated—innovations of the Conspectus movement has been the creation of the Conspectus lines, which group titles as subject literatures by using ranges of the Library of Congress (or Dewey) classification scheme. Conspectus lines operationalize the notion "subject literature" as it applies to monographs and serials. Unadapted, the hierarchical categories of the LC scheme are often too narrow or too broad to frame subject literatures well. The Conspectus lines bring out their major themes as grouping devices, while retaining them as building blocks, thereby avoiding the problems of an entirely new classification scheme.[9]

Moreover, when Conspectus lines define membership, each title can belong to only one subject literature, and the literatures that result are mutually exclusive. (The literatures defined by LC subject headings or by citation linkages are not, which complicates practical analysis.) Admittedly, these mutually exclusive literatures are the creation of nonspecialists, who classify works on the basis of superficial examination rather than reading, and they may differ greatly from literatures nominally on the same subject but defined by citation linkages of specialists in the field. But the commonsensical literatures defined by the Conspectus lines are formed long before citation-based literatures exist, and there is no reason to think the lines will be bettered or supplanted by some new system.

Having good definitions of subject literatures permits unambiguous measurement of their sizes and rates of growth (in number of titles), two parameters with obvious consequences for libraries. Having good definitions *in common* insures that measures specific to libraries, such as coverage, will be comparable, again with obvious consequences for collection development. Note, for example, that the full set of titles associated with a Conspectus line becomes the "ideal" or "target" set against which any library's coverage can be measured. The set so defined is clear, permanent, and consistent across libraries.

The same set is also a total population of writings rather than a sample. As such, it could replace published bibliographies—or samples drawn, perhaps idiosyncratically, from them—as the standard for comparison. In other words, there would no longer be a need to simulate literatures with titles drawn from an arbitrary mix of bibliographies, such as are appended to the *WLN Collection Assessment Manual*. As I argued in the previous chapter, such a move would produce fairer assessments of coverage than those that include in the "ideal" set any writing somehow connected to a literature rather than just those clearly constituting it.

Algorithmic Reports

If a Conspectus line, then, is used to define a subject literature, the holdings of various libraries can be defined as subsets of this literature, ranging from the null set (Out of scope) to the complete set (Comprehensive). Expressed as a percentage, the fraction of the literature held by a library is that library's coverage of the literature. However, as previously explained, a simple coverage figure is insensitive to the qualitative differences in RLG or WLN levels and so is not optimal for conversion to a rating. On the other hand, titles ranked by their holdings counts do reflect those differences, and this chapter has shown how titles so ranked can be mapped onto the levels of the RLG scale. Once that ranking and mapping is done—by computer, of course—it should be a simple enough task to ask the computer for percentages of holdings within the levels and for an algorithmic conversion of percentages into ratings or "grades" for subject collections, along the lines seen in this book.

Librarians would soon learn to read a report resembling those we have seen with brief tests:

Level	*1*	*2*	*3*	*4*
% Held	52%	16%	0%	0%

and to distinguish that Level 1 collection from, say, a "long, thin" collection:

Level	*1*	*2*	*3*	*4*
% Held	37%	21%	27%	3%

or from very strong holdings capable of supporting doctoral and postdoctoral research:

Level	*1*	*2*	*3*	*4*
% Held	98%	94%	81%	73%

What makes this reporting system plausible is that all the data for it are already present in machine-readable form in OCLC. Indeed, the ability to create *coverage* figures for Conspectus lines is already possible through OCLC/ AMIGOS Tape Analysis, and the ability to assign *levels* to collections might develop simply as an extension of existing software, as a by-product of reports to OCLC. The vital next step is a program that ranks the titles within a Conspectus line by their OCLC holdings counts, giving every title in the line an ordered place. The ordered titles could then be partitioned into RLG (or WLN) levels by formulae like—though not necessarily the same as—those seen in this book. The titles held by individual libraries would be computer-matched against the titles defining particular levels, so that percentages of titles held per level could be computed, as above. Finally, another algorithm would convert those percentages into a rating, such as "4" or "2b," that could be claimed for the subject collection.[10]

In working with literatures rather than 40- or 80-item brief tests, an important unsettled question is the percentage of items that must be held in order to claim a level. Just as the "general" cutpoints for holdings-count distributions shown in Table 8.1 may need to be recomputed for each subject literature, so may the thresholds for claiming levels. Here let me simply assume that the 50 percent threshold can be used and leave the matter in soft focus. To hold a minimum of 50 percent of the titles at each of the four levels—enough to claim them—a research library would need to have only an appropriately distributed 50 percent of titles overall, as shown by the black segments:

This does not seem to me excessively demanding, despite my colleague's remark, quoted in an earlier chapter, that requiring such coverage at Level 4 may be "too severe." Nevertheless, we are indeed now talking about coverage of parts of a whole literature, and not merely "getting five out of 10" on a brief test. As of yet, the sizes and holdings-count distributions of most literatures are obscure, so it is too early to determine the most suitable scoring procedures.

The key to such advances in software is to learn more about OCLC holdings counts, especially about their patterns of growth and stabilization. I have largely bracketed the fact that the counts change over time, since it apparently has not impeded work with brief tests so far. However, it seems likely that, for purposes such as core collection lists, the dynamism of the counts needs to be controlled. New titles work their way up the ranks constantly, and one might want to list only titles that were, say, three or more years old in order to give their counts a chance to stabilize. But three years is the merest guess; we do not presently know much about the diffusion of titles over libraries as a historical process. What are the factors that determine the way the counts change? Are any simply artifacts of the OCLC reporting system? Are they the same for all subjects? Do they result in more or less the same distribution for each subject literature, or do literatures differ markedly in this regard? Do some counts change quickly and others slowly? When do they stop changing? These are the sorts of questions that need to be pursued if the holdings counts, a resource with considerable informational potential for librarians, are to be properly exploited.

A SUMMARY

Presumably the counts would best be exploited in computerized collection management systems offered worldwide by bibliographic utilities such as OCLC, RLG, or WLN. This book contributes some new lore to that possibility. In particular, it indicates that power-tests of library holdings, through checklists scaled to reflect the difficulty of items, are an idea worth developing further.

Brief tests, the sole examples of power-testing to date, have been shown to be an economical alternative to more labor-intensive methods of collection evaluation. To make them, a subject expert names 40 or so titles according to directions, and a PRISM searcher obtains OCLC holdings counts for the titles so that they can be rank-ordered. Someone then checks the ranked titles in a library's catalog, calculates percentages, and translates the percentages into readings on level. That is all. Yet even when the tests are constructed without the refinements proposed in this chapter, they almost always yield results that librarians can use. The scores are informative in assessing collections of any size, in any subject, in any type of library. They measure collection developers' aptitudes quickly and unobtrusively. They can be obtained in one library, as a check on private judgments, or across libraries, for purposes of public comparison.

In Chapter 4 we saw that these scores generally made sense in light of the different kinds of libraries being tested (which is one check on validity). We also saw that when independent tests with similar subject matters were administered to the same collections, the results tended to converge (another check on validity).

Moreover, aggregated results strongly confirm the hypothesis that the nation's library collections are *cumulative* over the levels of the RLG scale: they are built from Minimal level up. The counterhypothesis—that "higher-level" libraries ignore "lower-level" collecting—is false. While the devisers of the RLG and WLN scales assumed that collection development is cumulative, no previous research has produced evidence that this is indeed the case.

The verification trials in Chapter 5 took place in libraries both small and large. Regardless of collection size, we saw that brief-test readings quite often confirmed the RLG or WLN levels set earlier by librarians. When tests and librarians disagreed, the different estimates tended to be no more than one level apart, strengthening the conjecture that tests and librarians are "measuring the same thing" (a third check on validity). The outcome is all the more encouraging in that the tests of Chapter 5 were only roughly matched with the subject collections whose ratings were being verified. Librarians and tests might agree even more often if the test for a given subject comprised only titles from its Conspectus line rather than anything supplied by a selector.

We saw in Chapter 6 that brief tests are useful in demonstrating the effect of combining library collections in a consortium. Chapter 7 showed that an 80-item brief test in French literature produced results that compared favorably in informativeness with those of an earlier 1,000-item checklist study when administered to many of the nation's leading libraries.

This final chapter has set forth a scheme to give test makers greater control over the difficulty of brief tests, along with some not-too-utopian ideas for future research and development. Not least among the latter is the idea of defining a subject literature as the titles in a Conspectus line that are several years old, ranking those titles by their now-stabilized OCLC holdings counts, partitioning the titles into RLG or WLN levels calibrated to the holdings-count scale, and exploring qualitative differences in titles at the different levels. My surmise is that titles with large differences in holdings counts will often have marked differences on other indicators in their bibliographic records as well, and that computer-generated reports on these differences will considerably enrich librarians' knowledge of collections, making relationships explicit that are now only dimly sensed. The chief interest of brief tests in the long run may be that they led to the discovery of holdings-count scales, whose useful properties this book only begins to record.

NOTES

1. In order to have approximately equal numbers of titles in each interval in a highly skewed distribution, the intervals must progressively widen, and that is what we observe in Table 8.1. In the "Mnemonic" row, for example, the Research interval has a range of about 150; the Instructional, a range of about 250 (from 151 to 400); the Basic, a range of about 350 (from 401 to 750); and the Minimal is open-endedly large, to include titles whose library sales can run from 751 into the thousands. If, instead, the intervals are kept fixed in width, the number of titles in them progressively declines, as Figures 8.1 and 8.2 imply.

2. As a practical note, trial cutpoints of 150, 400, and 750 (or 200, 400, and 800) were presented in offerings of my course during 1994, and all enrollees used them easily enough in making their tests. Rather than laboriously compiling counts above the 750 mark, one student simply approximated them with figures like "over 1,500" and "over 2,200." Officially I encourage stricter standards, but as long as the figures can be rank-ordered, there seems no great harm in this; his test worked despite the inexactness.

3. With base-10 logarithms, a count of 10 would convert to 1, a count of 100 to 2, a count of 1,000 to 3, and so on.

4. Boxplots convey the midpoint and spread of distributions on a scale. The median is the vertical line within a box. The width of the box shows the spread of the inner 50 percent of cases around the median. The spread of all remaining cases that are not outliers is shown by the "whiskers" attached to the box. Outliers are shown by asterisks. The less symmetrical the overall boxplot, the more skewed the distribution.

5. Discriminant analysis assumes that predictor variables are normally distributed, which is not the case with the counts. For this study, the skewed distribution of Figure 8.1 was normalized by taking the square root of each original value. Results were returned to the original values by squaring, as the distinctive holdings-count scales in Figure 8.4 imply. (While no standard transformation fully normalizes these data, the square-root conversion comes closest. It is a milder transformation than log-normalization, which, as noted, overcorrects.)

6. Disagreements or confusions occur in all the cells of the two inner categories, Basic and Instructional, but there are no cases in the two outer categories, Minimal and Research, in which one classification method puts a title at Level 1 and the other puts it as far away as Level 4. This implies that a title with a count from somewhere in the middle of the holdings-count scale—say, 500—can end up at any of the four levels by

the mechanical 10s method; but a title with a count toward the end of the holdings-count scale is not going to end up at the other end of the RLG scale, even by the relatively sloppy method of mechanical 10s. As categories grow more distant from each other, overlaps between them become less probable.

7. Typically one would compute a discriminant function using half of one's cases, and then test it on the other half to see how well its predictions matched the a priori classification. Here, I have used all the cases to compute the discriminant function rather than randomly splitting the sample into halves. In some trials, however, the sample was in fact randomly split and the discriminant function from the first half used to classify cases in the second. The results were quite stable: for the second half as well as the first, about 65 percent of cases overall were classified correctly. This accords with the results for both halves combined.

8. If OCLC had an online "sort" command like that of some other vendors, a searcher could form the set of all documents in a subject literature (defined by LC class, for example) and then rank-order them by counts in the field for number of holding libraries. The OCLC/AMIGOS Collection Analysis CD provides a foretaste of this capability through its "Holdings Distribution" feature. The counts seen there reflect the LC-classed acquisitions of more than 900 academic libraries over a recent 10-year period, which is a relatively small subset of the data in the full OCLC online union catalog.

9. Cf. Coleman (1992). Whether Dewey or LC is the base, use of Conspectus lines to define subject literatures is not without difficulties. For notes on those, which my account glosses over, see Underwood (1992).

10. Though unrelated to the present scheme, the work of Nisonger (1985) and Sanders et al. (1988) sets precedents for using information from both OCLC and RLG in collection evaluation.

Eight Specimen Brief Tests

Here are listed the titles and counts of the tests used in Chapters 6 and 7. They are typical working documents of the brief-test project of the early 1990s. None follows the guidelines for test construction seen in Chapter 8. Persons wishing to try them might update or revise the counts to their own satisfaction through recourse to OCLC's PRISM system.

Selectors of titles have been credited. This does not necessarily imply their endorsement of the brief-test methodology in general or the particular uses to which their selections have been put. Selections are here merged in unified tests.

Slight variations in selectors' bibliographic styles have been left unchanged.

American History

Selectors: *Early American History, 1760–1860*

John M. Powell, Reference Librarian
Wolfgram Memorial Library
Widener University
Chester, PA

American Civil War, 1861–1865

Sidney G. Dreese, Interlibrary Loan Clerk
Hagerty Library
Drexel University
Philadelphia, PA

American History from Colonial Times to the Present

Janet Panzer, Librarian
Roslyn Branch, Abington Public Library
Abington, PA

Minimal Level

2012	American Heritage: The Magazine of History (Serial).
1926	American Historical Review (Serial).
1490	Mark Mayo Boatner. Civil War dictionary. McKay: 1959 or any later edition.
1441	Bruce Catton. Centennial history of the Civil War. 3 vols. Doubleday: 1961–1965 or any later ed.
1425	Dumas Malone. Jefferson and his time. 6 vols. Little, Brown: 1981.
1411	Catherine Drinker Bowen. John Adams and the American Revolution. Little, Brown: 1950.
1396	Bruce Catton. A stillness at Appomatox. Doubleday: 1953.
1314	Frank Freidel, ed. Harvard guide to American history. Harvard University Press: 1974.
1304	Journal of American History (Serial).
1298	The West Point atlas of the Civil War. Praeger: 1962.
1272	Page Smith. John Adams. Doubleday: 1962.
1259	Allan Nevins. The ordeal of the Union. 2 vols. Scribner's: 1947 or any later ed.
1195	Henry Commager. The blue and the gray: The story of the Civil War as told by participants. 2 vols. Bobbs-Merrill: 1951 or any later ed.
1195	Walter Lord. The good years: From 1900 to the first world war. Harper: 1960.
1193	William Manchester. The glory and the dream: A narrative history of America, 1932–1972. Little, Brown: 1974.
1178	Richard Beringer. Why the South lost the Civil War. University of Georgia Press: 1986 or any later ed.
1159	Douglas Southall Freeman. Lee's lieutenants: A study in command. 3 vols. Scribner's: 1942–1944.
1140	Chadwick Hansen. Witchcraft at Salem. Braziller: 1969.
1139	Roger Butterfield. The American past: A history of the United States from Concord to Hiroshima, 1775–1945. Simon and Schuster: 1947 or any later ed.
1107	Mortimer J. Adler and Charles Van Doren, eds. The annals of America. 23 vols. Encyclopedia Britannica: 1976.
1070	Harry L. Coles. The War of 1812. University of Chicago Press: 1965.
1061	James G. Randall and David Donald. The Civil War and Reconstruction. Heath: 1937 or any later ed.
1050	Carl Bridenbough. Vexed and troubled Englishmen, 1590–1642. Oxford University Press: 1968.
1013	Perry Miller. The life of the mind in America, from the Revolution to the Civil War. Harcourt, Brace and World: 1965.
1000	Frank Burt Freidel. The splendid little war. Little, Brown: 1958.
983	Angie Debo. A history of the Indians in the United States. University of Oklahoma Press: 1970.
967	Richard Morris, ed. Encyclopedia of American history. Harper and Row: 1982.
961	Carl Van Doren. Benjamin Franklin. Garden City Publications: 1941.
961	Clement Eaton. History of the southern Confederacy. Macmillan: 1954.
898	Gordon Carruth et al. The encyclopedia of American facts and dates. 7th ed. Crowell: 1979.

Basic Level

857   William and Mary Quarterly: A Magazine of Early American History and Culture. (Serial).
824   James I. Robertson, Allan Nevins and Bell I. Wiley. Civil War books: A critical bibliography. 2 vols. Louisiana State University Press: 1967–1969.
814   E.B. Long. Civil War day by day. National Historical Society: 1985 or any later ed.
798   James Thomas Flexner. Washington, the indispensable man. Little, Brown: 1974.
770   Stewart Sifakis. Who was who in the Civil War. 2 vols. Facts on File: 1988.
759   Lester J. Cappon, ed. The Adams-Jefferson Letters: The complete correspondence between Thomas Jefferson and Abigail and John Adams. University of North Carolina Press: 1959.
741   Stephen G. Kurtz. The presidency of John Adams: The collapse of Federalism, 1795–1800. University of Pennsylvania Press: 1957.
739   Ned Bradford. Battles and leaders of the Civil War. New American Library: 1956 or any later ed.
730   The Adams papers (Adams family collection). Massachusetts Historical Society: 1954.
714   Early American Life (Serial).
697   Richard Beale Davis. Intellectual life in Jefferson's Virginia, 1790–1830. University of North Carolina Press: 1964.
677   John R. Howe. The changing political thought of John Adams. Princeton University Press: 1966.
677   Alice Tyler. Freedom's ferment: Phases of American social history to 1860. University of Minnesota Press: 1944
656   Dictionary of American biography. 17 vols. Scribner: 1988.
651   Bruce Cumings. The origins of the Korean war: Liberation and the emergence of separate regimes, 1945–47. Princeton University Press: 1981.
647   Mary Massey. Bonnet brigades. Knopf: 1966.
643   Jack Greene. The quest for power: The lower houses of the assembly in the southern royal colonies, 1689–1776. University of North Carolina Press: 1963.
630   Francis Paul Prucha. The sword of the republic: The United States army on the frontier, 1783–1846. Macmillan: 1969.
619   Journal of American Studies (Serial).
592   Civil War History (Serial).
592   James Randall. Civil war and reconstruction. Heath: 1969.
587   Linda K. Kerber. Federalists in dissent: Imagery and ideology in Jeffersonian America. Cornell University Press: 1970.
585   Durand Echeverria. Mirage in the west: A history of the French image of American society to 1815. Octagon Books: 1966.
571   Stuart Gerry Brown, ed. Autobiography of James Monroe, 1758–1831. Syracuse University Press: 1959.
560   Domingo Sarmiento. Travels in the United States in 1847. Princeton University Press: 1970.
P555   George Smith. Life in the North during the Civil War: A source history. University of New Mexico Press: 1966.

498   Thomas Jefferson. Notes on the state of Virginia. University of North
        Carolina Press: 1955.
493   Thomas Thayer. War without fronts: The American experience in Vietnam.
        Westview Press: 1985.
489   Charles Austin Beard. The rise of American civilization. Macmillan: 1933.
471   Philip Van Doren Stern. When the guns roared: World aspects of the
        American Civil War. Doubleday: 1965.

Instructional Level

467   Peter Thomas. British politics and the Stamp Act crisis: The first phase of
        the American Revolution, 1763–1767. Clarendon Press: 1975.
455   Charles Maurice Wiltse. The Jeffersonian tradition in American democracy.
        Hill and Wang: 1950.
453   John Bach McMaster. A history of the people of the United States. 8 vols.
        Appleton: 1913.
44C   George Washington. The diaries of George Washington, 1748–1799.
        Houghton Mifflin: 1925.
436   Robert E. Spiller. The American literary revolution, 1783–1837. New York
        University Press: 1967.
418   The war of the rebellion: A compilation of the official records of the Union
        and Confederate armies. 70 vols. GPO: 1880–1901.
395   Fairfax D. Downey. Indian wars of the U.S. Army, 1776–1865. Doubleday:
        1963.
389   Frederick M. Binder. The color problem in early national America as viewed
        by John Adams, Jefferson, and Jackson. Mouton: 1969.
381   Edward Stackpole. They met at Gettysburg. Eagle Books: 1956 or any later
        ed.
354   David T. Gilchrist and W. David Lewis, eds. Economic change in the Civil
        War: Proceedings. Eleutherian Mills–Hagley Foundation: 1965.
335   Thomas Adams. American independence, the growth of an idea: A biblio-
        graphical study of the American political pamphlets printed between Great
        Britain and her colonies. Brown University Press: 1965.
318   Frank Moore, ed. The rebellion record: A diary of American events. 11
        vols. Putnam: 1861–1868 or any later ed.
306   Civil War Times Illustrated (Serial).
305   Frank Welcher. The Union army, 1861–1865: Organizations and opera-
        tions. Indiana University Press: 1989.
292   Garold L. Cole. Civil War eyewitnesses: An annotated bibliography of
        books and articles, 1955–1986. University of South Carolina Press: 1988.
290   Wesley Frank Craven. The colonies in transition, 1660–1713. Harper and
        Row: 1967.
287   Louise Arnold. The era of the Civil War, 1820–1876. U.S. Army Military
        History Institute/GPO: 1982.
278   James Ford Rhodes. History of the Civil War, 1861–1865. Macmillan:
        1917.
276   John Raimo. A guide to manuscripts relating to America in Great Britain and
        Ireland. Meckler Books: 1979.
267   Edmund C. Burnett. Letters of members of the continental congress. Smith
        Publications: 1963.

260   James McPherson. Battle chronicles of the Civil War. 6 vols. Macmillan: 1989.

260   Carl Russell Fish. The American Civil War: An interpretation. Longmans, Green: 1937.

236   R. Ernest Dupuy. The compact history of the United States army. Haw-thorn Books: 1973.

232   Henry Steele Commager. The defeat of the Confederacy: A documentary survey. Van Nostrand: 1964.

231   Henry Adams. History of the United States during the administrations of Jefferson and Madison. A. and C. Boni: 1930.

230   Dudley Taylor Cornish. The sable arm: Black troops in the Union army. University Press of Kansas: 1987.

205   Gilman M. Ostrander. The rights of man in America. University of Missouri Press: 1969.

198   William Leonard Langer and Sarrell Gleason. Undeclared war, 1940–41. Published for the Council on Foreign Relations by Harper: 1953.

185   Henry Eugene Simmons. The concise encyclopedia of the Civil War. Bonanza Books: 1965 or any later ed.

Research Level

180   John Cushing. A bibliography of laws and resolves of the Massachusetts Bay, 1642–1780. Massachusetts Historical Society: 1984.

179   James Madison. Notes of debates in the federal convention of 1787. Ohio University Press: 1984.

168   John Quincy Adams. The life of John Adams. Lippincott: 1871.

134   Shelby Foote. The Civil War: a narrative. 3 vols. Vintage Books: 1958–1963 or any later ed.

123   Stanley C. Johnson. A history of emigration from the United Kingdom to North America, 1763–1912. G. Routledge and Sons: 1913.

119   Harper's pictorial history of the Civil War. 2 vols. Harper: 1866-1868 or later ed.

118   James T. Flexner. George Washington: the forge of experience, 1732–1775. Little, Brown: 1965.

110   Durand, of Dauphiné. A Huguenot exile in Virginia; or voyages of a Frenchman exiled for his religion, with a description of Virginia and Maryland (from the Hague edition of 1687). Press of the Pioneers: 1934.

107   Horace Greely. The American conflict: A history of the Great Rebellion in the United States of America, 1860–'65; its causes, incidents, and results; intended to exhibit especially its moral and political phases, with the drift and progess of American opinion respecting human slavery from 1776 to the close of the war for the Union. 2 vols. O.D. Case: 1864–66.

101   Amerikastudien/American Studies (Serial).

91   Campaigns of the Civil War. Scribner: 1881–1883.

88   Henry Adams. Albert Gallatin. Lippincott: 1879.

79   J. T. Headly. The great rebellion: a history of the Civil War in the United States. 2 vols. Hurlbut, Williams/E. B. and R. C. Treat: 1863–1866.

61   Alberto Maria Carreno. La diplomacia extraordinaria entre Mexico y Estados Unidos, 1789–1947. Editorial Jus: 1961.

51   Albert Sheldon Pennoyer. Locomotives in our lives: Railroad experiences of

three brothers for more than sixty years, 1890–1951. Hastings House: 1954.

49 Nikolai N. Bolkhovitinov. Stanovlenie Russko-Amerikanskikh Otnoshenii, 1775–1815 (The beginnings of the Russian-American relations, 1775–1815). Nauka: 1966.

49 Orra Eugene Monette. First settlers of ye plantations of Piscataway and Woodbridge, olde east New Jersey, 1664–1714, a period of fifty years. Part 6. Leroy Carman Press: 1934.

44 Ozora S. Davis. John Robinson, the pilgrim pastor. Pilgrim: 1903.

41 Ulane Bonnel. La France, les Etats-Unis et la guerre de course, 1797–1815. Nouvelles Editions latines: 1961.

35 Hubert Galle. La "Famine du coton" 1861–1865: Effets de la guerre de Secession sur l'industrie cotonniere gantoise. Institut de sociologie, Université libre de Bruxelles: 1967.

34 Deborah Norris Logan. Memoir of Dr. George Logan of Stenton by his widow. Historical Society of Pennsylvania: 1899.

32 Lombardo Agostino. Italia e Stati Uniti nell'eta del Risorgimento e della Guerra civile. La nuova Italia: 1969.

28 Erwin Holzle. Russland und Amerika: Aufbruch und Begegnung zweier Weltmachte. R. Oldenbourg: 1953.

23 Bob Bjoring. Explorers' and travellers' journals documenting early contacts with native Americans in the Pacific northwest, 1741–1900. University of Washington Libraries: 1982.

12 Sam Alewitz. Sanitation and public health: Philadelphia, 1870-1900. Case Western Reserve University: 1981 (Dissertation).

9 Luke Gridley. Luke Gridley's diary of 1757 while in service in the French and Indian war. Hartford Press: 1906. (Acorn Club Publication No. 10)

7 Hilarion Frias y Soto. Mexico y los Estados Unidos durante la intervencion francesca; rectificaciones historicas. Impr. del comercio de J. E. Barbero: 1901.

7 J. A. Danielson. Lincoln's attitude towards prohibition. Barnes Press: 1927.

7 Leon Lemonnier. Histoire du Far-West: Les Mormons. Gallimard: 1927.

3 Raimondo Luraghi. Storia della guerra civile americana. Rizzoli Editore: 1985.

American Studies

Selector: Dr. Howard D. White, Professor
College of Information Science and Technology
Drexel University
Philadelphia, PA

Minimal Level

1667 M. Thomas Inge, ed. Handbook of American popular culture. 3 vols. Greenwood Press: 1978 or later ed.

1530 Garry Wills. Inventing America: Jefferson's Declaration of Independence. Doubleday: 1978.

1497 Henry Steele Commager. The American mind: An interpretation of American thought and character since the 1880s. Yale University Press: 1950 or later ed.

1413 Richard Hofstadter. Anti-intellectualism in American life. Knopf: 1962 or later ed.

1350 Christopher Jencks, et al. Inequality: a reassessment of the effect of family and schooling in America. Basic Books: 1972.

1339 Andrew Hacker, ed. U/S: A statistical portrait of the American people. Penguin Books: 1983.

1262 Joel Garreau. The nine nations of North America. Houghton Mifflin: 1981.

1180 Morton White. Science and sentiment in America: Philosophical thought from Jonathan Edward to John Dewey. Oxford University Press: 1972 or later ed.

1168 Martin L. Gross. The psychological society: A critical analysis of psychiatry, psychotherapy, psychoanalysis and the psychological revolution. Simon and Schuster: 1978.

1135 Gay Talese. Thy neighbor's wife. Doubleday: 1980 or later ed.

Basic Level

1094 Perry Miller. Errand into the wilderness. Belknap Press of Harvard University Press: 1956 or later ed.

1058 Russell Lynes. The lively audience: A social history of the visual and performing arts in America, 1890–1950. Harper and Row: 1985.

1033 Nathan Glazer and Daniel P. Moynihan. Beyond the melting pot: The Negroes, Puerto Ricans, Jews, Italians, and Irish of New York City. M.I.T. Press: 1963.

1027 Bernard Rosenberg and David Manning White, eds. Mass culture: The popular arts in America. Free Press: 1957.

959 Albert Krichmar. The women's rights movement in the United States, 1848–1970: A bibliography and sourcebook. Scarecrow: 1972.

906 Thomas Jefferson Wertenbaker. The Puritan oligarchy: The founding of American civilization. Scribner: 1947 or later ed.

865 Kenneth C. Davis. Two-bit culture: The paperbacking of America. Houghton Mifflin: 1984.

841   America: History and Life (Serial).
768   Richard McLanathan. The American tradition in the arts. Harcourt, Brace and World: 1968 or later ed.
758   Louis Harris. Inside America. Vintage: 1987.

Instructional Level

756   Walter Dean Burnham. Critical elections and the mainsprings of American politics. Norton: 1970.
711   American Statistics Index (Serial).
703   National Journal (Serial).
701   Robert F. Spencer, Jesse D. Jennings, et al. The Native Americans: Ethnology and backgrounds of the North American Indians. 2d ed. Harper and Row: 1977.
639   The Pacific rivals: A Japanese view of Japanese-American relations, by the staff of the Asahi Shimbun. Weatherhill/Asahi: 1972.
615   William Filby, ed. Passenger and immigration lists index. [Not the bibliography with the same title] 3 vols. Gale: 1981.
568   Wilbur Zelinsky. The cultural geography of the United States. Prentice-Hall: 1973.
533   Bertram Gross, ed. Social intelligence for America's future: Explorations in societal problems. Allyn and Bacon: 1969.
524   Lawrence Ferlinghetti and Nancy J. Peters. Literary San Francisco: A pictorial history from its beginnings to the present day. City Lights Books and Harper and Row: 1980.
496   Richard A. Apostle, Charles Y. Glock, Thomas Piazza, Marijean Suelzle. The anatomy of racial attitudes. University of California Press: 1983.

Research Level

457   Robert H.Walker. American studies: Topics and sources. Greenwood Press: 1976.
453   Robin M. Williams, Jr. American society: A sociological interpretation. 3rd ed., revised and reset. Knopf: 1970.
433   Benjamin M. Compaine, ed. Who owns the media? Concentration of ownership in the mass communications industry. 2nd ed. Harmony Books/Knowledge Industry Publications: 1982.
347   Hispanic American Periodicals Index (Serial).
252   Patricia Nelson Limerick. Desert passages: Encounters with the American deserts. University of New Mexico Press: 1985.
215   H. Richard Niebuhr. The social sources of denominationalism. Holt: 1929 or later ed.
184   Godey's Lady's Book (...and Ladies' American Magazine, 1840–1858 and 1887–1892) (...and Magazine, 1859-1887) (Microform serial).
164   Eugene E. Campbell. Establishing Zion: The Mormon Church in the American West, 1847–1869. Signature Books: 1988.
139   Maledicta (Serial).
88   New York Public Library. Dictionary catalog of the Schomburg collection of Negro literature and history. NYPL: 1962.

Classical Music

Selectors: *Music 1*

Richard M. Duris, Music Librarian
Paley Library
Temple University
Philadelphia, PA

Music 2

Paula Morgan, Music Librarian
Firestone Library
Princeton University
Princeton, NJ

Minimal Level

2727 Musical America (Serial).
2093 Oscar Thompson, ed. International cyclopedia of music and musicians.. Dodd, Mead: 1952 or other ed.
1685 John Tasker Howard. Our American music: Three hundred years of it. Crowell: 1939 or other ed.
1575 Donald J. Grout. History of western music. Dent: 1980 or other ed.
1520 New Grove dictionary of music. Macmillan/Grove's Dictionaries of Music: 1968 or later ed.
1464 Theodore Baker. Baker's biographical dictionary of musicians. 7th ed. Schirmer/Collier Macmillan: 1984 or later ed.
1329 Aaron Copeland. What to listen for in music. McGraw-Hill: 1957 or later ed.
1272 Milton Cross. Complete stories of the great operas. Doubleday: 1952.
1200 Julius Mattfeld. Variety music calvacade, 1620–1950: A chronology of vocal and instrumental music popular in the United States. Prentice-Hall: 1952 or later ed.
1160 Paul Henry Lang. Music in western civilization. Dent: 1942 or later ed.
1154 Opera News (Serial).
1126 Musical Quarterly (Serial).
1110 Walter Piston. Harmony. Gollancz: 1949 or later ed.
1100 The new Grove dictionary of American music. Grove's Dictionaries of Music: 1986 or later ed.
1100 New Harvard dictionary of music. Belknap Press of Harvard University Press: 1986 or later ed.
1066 Sybil Marcuse. Musical instruments: A comprehensive dictionary. Doubleday: 1964 or later ed.
1010 Maynard Solomon. Beethoven. Schirmer Books: 1977.
910 Igor Stravinsky. Poetics of music in the form of six lessons. Random House: 1947 or other ed.
910 Alfred Einstein. Mozart, his character, his work. Oxford University Press: 1965 or other ed.

905   International who's who in music and musician's directory. Melrose Press:
        1975 or later ed.

Basic Level

873   Joseph Kerman. Opera as drama. Vintage Books: 1952 or other ed.
833   Desireé DeCharms. Songs in collections: An index. Information Service:
        1966 or other ed.
812   Gunther Schuller. The history of jazz. Oxford University Press: 1968 or
        later ed.
800   Arthur Loesser. Men, women, and pianos: A social history. Dover: 1954 or
        later ed.
766   David Ewen. Encyclopedia of opera. Hill and Wang: 1963 or other ed.
750   Wolfgang Schmeider. Thematisch-systematisches Verzeichnis der musikal-
        ischen Werke von Johann Sebastian Bach. Breitkopf and Hartel: 1990 or
        other ed.
722   Hector Berlioz. Evenings with the orchestra. (Jacques Barzun, trans.). Uni-
        versity of Chicago Press: 1973.
716   Notes (the Quarterly Journal of the Music Library Association) (Serial).
716   Archibald Davision. Historical anthology of music. 2 vols.
706   Alexander Wheelock Thayer. The life of Ludwig van Beethoven. The
        Beethoven Association: 1925 or later ed.
699   Donald Francis Tovey. Essays in musical analysis. 6 vols. Oxford
        University Press: 1935 or later ed.
690   Ludwig van Beethoven. Complete piano sonatas. Dover: 1975.
627   Music Index (Serial).
600   Journal of the American Musicological Society (Serial).
597   Heinrich Schenker. Free composition. Longman: 1979.
580   Anna Heyer. Historical sets, collected editions and monuments of music: A
        guide to their contents. American Library Association: 1938 or later ed.
570   Robert Donington. The interpretation of early music. Faber and Faber:
        1989 or other ed.
552   Sydney Charles. Handbook of music and music literature in sets and series.
        Free Press/Collier-Macmillan: 1973 or later ed.
540   Vincent H. Duckles. Music reference and research material: An annotated
        bibliography. Free Press of Glencoe: 1964 or other ed.
462   Wolfgang Amadeus Mozart. The marriage of Figaro. Vocal score, English
        and Italian. G. Schirmer: 1951.

Instructional Level

431   Albert Schweitzer. J. S. Bach. 2 vols. A. and C. Black: 1911 or later ed.
416   RILM abstracts of music literature (Serial).
411   Mary Vinquist. Performance practice: A bibliography. Norton: 1971 or
        later ed.
389   Walter Gerboth. An index to musical Festschriften and similar publications.
        Norton: 1969 or other ed.
388   Johann Sebastian Bach. The six Brandenburg concertos and the four
        orchestral suites. Dover: 1976.

383	Die Musik in Geschichte und Gegenwart. Barenreiter: 1949–86.
365	Johannes Brahms. Complete symphonies in full orchestral score. Dover: 1974.
341	Johann Sebastian Bach. Neue Ausgabe samtlicher Werke. Barenreiter: 1954– .
321	Donald Jay Grout. A short history of opera. 3rd ed. Columbia University Press: 1988.
303	Wolfgang Amadeus Mozart. Neue Ausgabe samtlicher Werke. Barenreiter: 1955- .
275	Janet Baker. Full circle: An autobiographical journal. Penguin: 1982 or other ed.
271	Alban Berg. Wozzeck. Universal: 1955 (Score).
262	Acta Musicologia (Serial).
254	Arnold Schonberg. Samtliche Werke. Schott: 1966– .
237	Ludwig Kochel. Chronologisch-thematisches Verzeichnis samtlicher Tonwerke Wolfgang Amade Mozarts. J.W. Edwards: 1947.
211	Ludwig van Beethoven. Werke herausgaben vom Beethoven-Archiv, Bonn. 1961- .
200	Ludwig van Beethoven. Autograph Miscellany from *circa* 1786 to 1799: British Museum Additional Manuscript 29801, ff. 39–162 (The "Kafka Sketchbook"). British Museum: 1970.
180	Franz Schubert. Neue Ausgabe samtlicher Werke. Barenreiter: 1964– .
176	Paul Hindemith. Ludus tonalis. Associated Music Publishers: 1943 or other ed. (Score).
176	Richard Wagner. Siegfried in full score. Dover: 1983.

Research Level

175	Peter Ilich Tchaikovsky. Fourth, fifth and sixth symphonies. Dover: 1979.
162	Claude Debussy. Three great orchestral works. Dover: 1983.
156	Sergei Prokofiev. Peter and the wolf. Kalmus: 1936 or other ed. (Score).
142	Carl Philipp Emanuel Bach. Six symphonies. Garland: 1982 (Score).
131	Guiseppe Verdi. The works of Guiseppe Verdi. 1983– .
121	Karl Orff. Der Mond. Schott: 1947 or any other ed. (Score).
116	Gustav Mahler. Samtliche Werke; kritische Gesamtausgabe. Universal Edition: 1900 or any later ed. (Score).
112	Leonard Bernstein. Fancy free. Schirmer: 1968 or other ed. (Score).
110	Joseph Haydn. Complete London symphonies. Dover: 1985.
108	Igor Stravinsky. Agon: ballet for twelve dancers. Boosey and Hawkes: 1957 or other ed. (Score).
85	Edward Elgar. Elgar complete edition. Novello: 1981.
73	Frederic Chopin. Complete preludes and etudes. Dover: 1980.
70	John Dowland. Ayres for four voices. Stainer and Bell: 1970 or other ed. (Score).
65	Bela Bartok. Bluebeard's castle. Boosey and Hawkes: 1952 or other ed. (Score).
29	George Crumb. A haunted landscape. Peters: 1984 or laterr ed. (Score).
17	Johann Sebastian Bach. Four-part chorales. Terry, Riemenschneider, or Mainous and Ottman eds. Oxford University Press: 1929 or later ed.
16	Recent researches in the music of the Baroque era (Serial).

10   Alexander Shealy, comp. Ragtime: World's favorite music and songs.
       Ashley Publications: 1973 (Score of Scott Joplin's music).
7   Paleographie Musicale (Serial).
4   Repertoire Internationales Sources Musicales (Serial).

Cultural Anthropology

Selectors: *Cultural Anthropology 1*

Dorothy Koenig, Head
Lowie Anthropology Library
University of California
Berkeley, CA

Cultural Anthropology 2

Dr. Fred J. Hay, Reference and Acquisitions Librarian
Tozzer Library
Harvard University
Cambridge, MA

Minimal Level

1647   William Armand Lessa and Evon Z. Vogt, eds. Reader in comparative religion: An anthropological approach. Row, Peterson: 1958 or later ed.
1620   Donald C. Johanson and Maitland A Edey. Lucy: The beginnings of humankind. Simon and Shuster: 1981.
1364   Freeman, Derek. Margaret Mead in Samoa: The making and unmaking of an anthropological myth. Harvard University Press: 1983 or later ed.
1265   Claude Levi-Straus. The savage mind. University of Chicago Press: 1962 or later ed.
1053   American Anthropologist (Serial).
1045   Sarel Eimerl and Irven DeVore et al. The primates. Time-Life Books/Life Nature Library: 1965.
1011   Columbia University contributions to anthropology. (Monographic series)
1003   Colin M. Turnbull. The forest people. Chatto and Windus: 1961 or later ed.
955   Marvin Harris. The rise of anthropological theory: A history of theories of culture. Columbia University Press: 1968.
923   John Pfeiffer. The emergence of man. Harper and Row: 1969.
916   David E. Hunter and Phillip Whitten, eds. Encyclopedia of anthropology. Harper and Row: 1976.
916   Jules Henry. Culture against man. Random House: 1963 or later ed.
912   E. Adamson Hoebel. The Cheyennes: Indians of the Great Plains. (Case studies in cultural anthropology) Holt: 1960.
875   James Deetz. Invitation to archaeology. Natural History Press: 1967.
853   Franz Boas. The mind of primitive man. Macmillan: 1911 or later ed.
838   Current Anthropology (Serial).
823   Black Elk speaks: Being the life story of a holy man of the Oglala Sioux, as told through John G. Neihardt. W. Morrow: 1932 or later ed.
817   Clifford Geertz. Interpretations of cultures: Selected essays. Basic Books: 1973 or later ed.
771   E. E. Evans-Pritchard. The Nuer: A description of the modes of livelihood and political institutions of a Nilotic people. Clarendon Press: 1940 or later ed.
769   Handbook of Middle American Indians (including supplements). University of Texas Press: 1981.

Basic Level

705   Charlotte Seymour-Smith. Dictionary of anthropology. G. K. Hall: 1986.
700   Ruth Benedict. Patterns of culture. Houghton Mifflin: 1934 or later ed.
695   James L. Gibbs, ed. Peoples of Africa. Holt, Rinehart, and Winston: 1965
        or later ed.
672   V. Gordon Childe. Man makes himself. New American Library: 1951 or later
        ed.
663   Lowell D. Holmes. Quest for the real Samoa: Assessing the Mead/Freeman
        controversy. Bergin and Garvey: 1987 or later ed.
646   Edward Sapir. Selected writings in language, culture and personality.
        University of California Press: 1949 or laer ed.
622   Charles Wagley. Welcome of tears: The Tapirape Indians of central Brazil.
        Oxford University Press: 1977 or later ed.
614   Robin Fox. Kinship and marriage: An anthropological perspective. Pen-
        guin: 1967 or later ed.
585   American Antiquity (Serial).
528   Man (Serial).
520   Edmund Ronald Leach. Political systems of highland Burma: A study of
        Kachin social structure. Harvard University Press: 1954 or later ed.
516   American Journal of Physical Anthropology (Serial).
505   Victor Turner. The forest of symbols: Aspects of Ndembu ritual. Cornell
        University Press: 1967 or later ed.
499   Julian Stewart. Theory of culture change: The methodology of multilinear
        evolution. University of Illinois Press: 1955 or later ed.
492   Margaret Mead. Coming of age in Samoa: A psychological study of prim-
        itive youth for western civilization. Morrow: 1928 or later ed.
488   David Bidney. Theoretical anthropology. Columbia University Press: 1953
        or later ed.
461   Alan Dundes. Every man his way: Readings in cultural anthropology.
        Prentice-Hall: 1968.
430   George Peter Murdock. Ethnographic bibliography of North America. 5
        vols. 4th ed. Human Relations Area Files Press: 1975 or later ed.
406   Elsie Clews Parsons. Mitla, town of souls and other Zapoteco-speaking
        pueblos of Oaxaca, Mexico. University of Chicago Press: 1900 or later ed.
375   Serial publications in anthropology. University of Chicago Press: 1973– .

Instructional Level

369   Charles Franz. The student anthropologist's handbook: A guide to research,
        training, and career. Schenkman: 1972 or later ed.
358   Edmund Ronald Leach. Social anthropology. Oxford University Press: 1982.
340   John Van Maanen. Tales of the field: On writing ethnography. University
        of Chicago Press: 1988.
325   Robert Wuthnow. Meaning and moral order: Explorations in cultural
        analysis. University of California Press: 1987 or later ed.
322   LARG (Library-Anthropology Research Group). Anthropological bibli-
        ographies: A selected guide. Redgrave: 1981.
315   Weston LaBarre. Muelos: A Stone-Age superstition about sexuality.
        Columbia University Press: 1984.

296	C. H. Fairbanks and J. T. Milanich. Florida archaeology. Academic Press: 1980.
269	Nelson H. H. Graburn. Readings in kinship and social structure. Harper and Row: 1971.
267	Walter Willard Taylor. A study of archaeology. American Anthropological Association: 1948.
219	Ino Rossi, ed. People in culture: A survey of cultural anthropology. Praeger: 1980.
219	Anthropological index of current periodicals in the Museum of Mankind Library, London (Serial).
199	A.L. Kroeber and Clyde Kluckhohn. Culture: A critical review of concepts and definitions. Random House: 1950 or later ed.
196	Anthropological Literature (Serial).
176	Elizabeth Benson, ed. Dumbarton Oaks conference on Chavin, October 26–27, 1968. Dumbarton Oaks Research Library and Collection, Trustees for Harvard University: 1971.
166	Fredrik Barth. Process and form in social life. Routledge and Kegan Paul: 1981.
166	International directory of anthropologists. 2 vols. 2nd ed. National Research Council: 1940.
160	Marvin Harris. Cultural anthropology. Harper and Row: 1983 or later ed.
153	Carol B. Stack. All our kin: Strategies for survival in a Black community. Harper and Row: 1974 or later ed.
138	Thomas L. Mann, general editor. Biographical directory of anthropologists born before 1920. Garland: 1988.
129	Author and title catalogs of the Tozzer Library. Cumulated microfiche edition, 1988. (Or its earlier hard-copy equivalent, Peabody catalog, 1963– and the serial *Anthropological Literature*.)

Research Level

104	Claude Levi-Strauss. Structures elementaires de la parenté. Presses universitaires de France: 1949 or later edition in French.
99	Ales Hrdlicka. Practical anthropometry. Wistar Institute of Anatomy and Biology: 1939 or later ed.
88	Mary Tew Douglas. Purity and danger: An analysis of concepts of pollution and taboo. Routledge and Kegan Paul: 1966.
81	Lewis Henry Morgan. Systems of consanguinity and affinity of the human family. Smithsonian Institution: 1870.
61	Zeitschrift für Morphologie und Anthropologie (Serial).
52	John Eric Thompson. Civilization of the Mayas. Field Museum of Natural History: 1927.
44	Author and subject catalogues of the Tozzer library.
43	Bibliographic guide to anthropology and archaeology. G.K. Hall: 1987– .
40	Keebet von Benda-Beckmann and A. K. J. M. Strijbosch, eds. Anthropology of law in the Netherlands: Essays on legal pluralism. Foris Publications: 1986.
39	Stanley Diamond, ed. Culture in history: Essays in honor of Paul Radin. Published for Brandeis University by Columbia Univesity Press: 1960.
32	Papers of John Peabody Harrington in the Smithsonian Institution.

24   Dan Sperber. Le savoir des anthropologues: Trois essais. Hermann: 1982.
20   Walter Dostal, ed. On social evolution: Contributions to anthropological concepts. Proceedings of the symposium on the occasion of the 50th anniversary of the Wiener Institut für Volkerkunde, December 12–16, 1979. F. Berger: 1984.
14   Herbert Baldus. Lendas dos Indios do Brasil: Selecionadas e comentadas. Editora Brasiliense: 1946.
11   Bernabe Cobo, 1582–1657. Historia del nuevo mundo. Rasco: 1890 or later edition in Spanish.
11   M. J. Hardman-de-Bautista, Juana Vasquez and Juan da Dios Yapita. Aymara: Compendio de estructura fonologica y gramatical. Gramma Impresion: 1988.
6   Otto Reche. Rasse und Heimat der Indogermanen. J. F. Lehmann: 1936.
4   Microfilm collection of the professional papers of Franz Boas.
2   Georges Balandier. L'anthropologie appliquée aux problemes des pays sous-developpés. Cours de droit: 1955.
2   Claartje Gieben and Jan Ijzermans, eds. Music and dance in Surinam: A comprehensive collection of source liteature extracted from over 4,000 publications. Inter Documentation Company: 1989 (Microform).

French Literature

Selectors: *French Literature 1*

Dr. Howard D. White, Professor
College of Information Science and Technology
Drexel University
Philadelphia, PA

French Literature 2
White's judgment sample from checklist by

Jeffry Larson, Humanities Bibliographer
Yale University Library
New Haven, CT

Minimal Level

1524   Gustave Flaubert. Madame Bovary (Francis Steegmuller, trans.) Random House: 1957 or any ed. of this translation.

1008   Louis-Ferdinand Céline. Death on the installment plan. Any ed. in English.

955   Martin Turnell. The novel in France. Vintage: 1958 or later ed.

932   Wallace Fowlie. Age of surrealism. Alan Swallow: 1950 or later ed.

847   French review, v. 31 (1957-1958). (Phonology)

736   Modern Language Review, v. 50 (April, 1955). (Mairet)

672   Yale French Studies (Serial).

605   F. W. Dupee, ed. Great French short novels. Dial Press: 1952.

588   Eighteenth Century Studies, 4 (1970-1971). (Diderot)

564   Richard Macksey and Eugenio Umberto Donato, eds. The languages of criticism and the sciences of man; the structuralist controversy. Johns Hopkins Press: 1970. (Derrida)

547   Simone de Beauvoire. Le deuxième sexe. Paris: Gallimard, 1949 or later ed. in French.

538   Glyph 2. Johns Hopkins Textual Studies: 1977. (Derrida)

516   Morris Bishop. Ronsard, prince of poets. Oxford University Press: 1940 or later ed.

515   Albert Camus. Les justes. Librarie Gallimard: 1950 or later ed. in French.

468   Will Durant and Ariel Durant. The story of civilization; part 9: The age of Voltaire... Simon and Schuster: 1965 etc. (Diderot and Fontenelle)

454   Denis Diderot. Rameau's nephew (Jacques Barzun, trans). Any ed. of this translation.

426   John Cruickshank, ed. French literature and its background (1): The sixteenth century. Oxford University Press: 1968. (Du Bellay)

392   Maurice Bardèche. Balzac, romancier. Plon: 1947.

365   Choderlos de Laclos. Oeuvres complètes (Maurice Allem, ed.). Gallimard: 1943. Bibliothéque de la Plèiade.

307   André Schwarz-Bart. Le dernier des justes. Editions du Seuil: 1959 or later ed. in French.

Basic Level

285   Joan M. Miller. French structuralism: A multidisciplinary bibliography. Garland Press: 1981.
283   European Studies Review, v. 6 (1976). (Diderot)
272   Martin Turnell. Jacques Riviére. Yale University Press: 1953.
254   Aucassin et Nicolette... (Mario Roques, ed.). 2d ed. Champion: 1935 etc.
248   Diderot Studies, v. 14 (1971).
247   Marcel Proust. Pastiches et mélanges. Gallimard: 1949.
242   Antonin Artaud. Le théâtre et son double. Any ed. in French.
207   Neophilologus. 1955. (Marot)
197   Hispano Americano (Mexico). 63, no. 1629 (23 July 1973). (Zola)
189   Beril Becker. Jules Verne. Putnam: 1966.
188   Jacques Derrida. De la grammatologie. Editions de Minuit: 1967.
186   Tel Quel. (Serial, 1960-1982).
167   Stanford French Review, v. 3 (1979). (Verne)
159   Comtesse de Marie Madeleine de la Vergne La Fayette. The princess of Clèves (Nancy Mitford, trans). Penguin Books: 1978. Any ed. of this trans.
156   John C. Lapp. Aspects of Racinian tragedy. University of Toronto Press: 1964.
152   François Villon. Œuvres: Edition critique. Paris: 1923.
135   L'Infini. (Serial).
130   Floyd Francis Gray. La poetique de Du Bellay. Nizet: 1978.
127   M. Jean Plattard. François Rabelais. Boivin: 1932 or any ed. in French.
116   Robert Griffin. Coronation of the poet; Joachim Du Bellay's debt to the Trivium. University of California Publications in Modern Philology, 69: 1969.

Instructional Level

110   Bernard Le Bovier de Fontenelle. Entretiens sur la pluralité des mondes... (Alexandre Calame, ed.). Didier: 1967.
104   Travaux de linguistique et de litterature. 14, i (1976). (Phonology)
103   Henry Harrisse. L'Abbé Prévost: Histoire de sa vie et de ses oeuvres. Paris: 1896 or any later ed.
103   Joachim Du Bellay. L'Olive. (E. Caldarini, ed.) Droz: 1974.
102   Australian Journal of French Studies., v. 5 (May-Aug. 1968). (Verne)
96   Dominique Boutet. La litterature française du Moyen Age. PUF: 1978. (Que sais-je 145).
95   Robert Desnos. Domaine public. Editions Gallimard: 1953.
88   Maurice Blanchot. Faux pas. Paris: 1943, etc. (Racine)
86   Arnaud Rykner. Théâtres du nouveau roman: Sarraute-Pinget-Duras. Corti: 1988.
85   Raymond Ricard, ed. Corpus Racinianum; recueil-inventaire des textes et documents du XVIIe siecle concernant J. Racine. Paris: 1956.
81   Charles Arnaud. Les theories dramatique au XVIIe siècle; étude sur la vie et les oeuvres de l'abbé d'Aubignac. A. Picard: 1888. (Mairet)
80   Julia Kristeva. Les samourais. Fayard: 1990.
73   Jean (de) Mairet. La Sophonisbe (Charles Dedeyan, ed). Droz: 1945, etc.
69   Jacques Riviere. Carnets 1914-1917. Fayard: 1974.

64   Clement Marot. Oeuvres poetiques. (Yves Giraud, ed.). Garnier-Flamarion: 1973.

64   Pierre Chappuis. Michel Leiris. Seghers: 1974.

60   Molière. Le misanthrope; comédie. Librarie Larousse. Nouveaux classiques Larousse. (This ed. only.)

51   Jean Paulhan. Le marquis de Sade et sa complice... Lilac: 1951.

50   Clement Marot. L'Enfer; les Coq-a-l'ane; les Elegies. Ed. C. A. Mayer. Champion: 1977.

49   Ecarts; quatre essais a propos de Jacques Derrida. Fayard: 1973.

Research Level

44   Jean Wahl. Petite histoire de l'existentialisme. Club Maintenant: 1947

43   Charles Marie René Leconte de Lisle. Choix poèmes de Leconte de Lisle. Larousse: 1969. Nouveaux classiques Larousse.

43   Jean Laforgue. Poésies complètes (M. G. Jean-Aubry, ed.). 2 vols. Editions de Cluny: 1943.

43   Denis Diderot. Oeuvres complètes; edition chronologique. (Roger Lewinter, ed.). 15 vols. Club français du livre: 1969-73.

38   Andre Martinet. La pronunciation du français contemporain... Paris: 1945. (Phonology)

31.   Lire; le magazine des livres (Serial).

27   Zeitschrift für celtische Philologie, v. 31 (1970). (Aucassin et Nicolette)

24   Stephen Ullmann. Précis de semantique française. 2nd ed. Berne: 1959. (Phonology)

24   Marquise de Marie de Rabutin Chantal Sévigné. Lettres de Madame de Sévigné avec les notes de tous les commentateurs. Firmin Didot: 1844. (This ed. only.)

24   Annarosa Poli. George Sand vue par les Italiens: Essai de bibliographie critique. Edizioni Sansoni Antiquario; M. Didier: 1965. (IIe Serie; collection d'études bibliographiques, n. 8.)

20   Leon Blum. Stendahl et le beylisme. Ollendorff: 1914.

19   Charles-Augustin Sainte-Beuve. Tableau de la poésie au seizième siècle. 1876.

19   Jean Baptiste Racine. Théâtre. (P. Melese, ed.) 5 v. Richelieu: 1951.

17   Francois Marie Coquoz. L'évolution religieuse de Jacques Riviere. Editions Universitaires: 1963.

14   Wolfgang Storost. Geschichte des altfranzosischen und altprovenzalischen Romanzenstrophe. Romanistiche Arbeiten, 16. Halle: 1930. (Aucassin et Nicolette)

13   Les Cahiers naturalistes 2, no. 6 (1956). (Zola)

10   Emile Zola. Les Oeuvres complètes (Maurice Le Blond, ed.). 50 vols. Bernouard: 1927-29.

9   Alfred de Vigny. Servitude et grandeur militaires (Félix Bonnaire, ed.). Publications de la Revue des Deux Mondes: 1835. Victor Magen libraire. (This ed. only.)

6   Jean Baptiste Racine. Oeuvres complètes. 7 vols. Lefevre: 1825. Collection des classiques françois. (This ed. only.)

6   Pierre Carlet de Chamblain de Marivaux. Une comédie inconnue de Marivaux: La Provinciale. Sonor: 1922.

Genetics

Selectors: *Genetics 1*

                Dr. Laurie Tompkins, Professor
                Department of Biology
                Temple University
                Philadelphia, PA

                Genetics 2

                Dr. Greg Guild, Professor
                Department of Biology
                University of Pennsylvania
                Philadelphia, PA

Minimal Level

2868	Charles Darwin. On the origin of the species. (Any ed.)
1511	Nature (Serial).
1200	Science (Serial).
1130	Eric H. Davidson. Gene activity in early development. Academic Press: 1968 or later ed.
990	Proceedings of the National Academy of Sciences of the United States of America. Physical sciences. Washington: NASUSA.
967	James D. Watson, John Tooze, David T. Kurtz. Recombinant DNA: A short course. Scientific American Books: 1983.
935	Annual Review of Genetics (Serial).
894	Robert C. King and William D. Stansfield. A dictionary of genetics. 3rd ed. Oxford: 1985 or later ed.
862	Genetics (Serial).
787	Developmental Biology (Serial).
778	William Hayes. Genetics of bacteria and their viruses: Studies in basic genetics and molecular biology. Blackwell: 1964 or later ed.
772	Francois Jacob. The statue within: An autobiography. Basic Books: 1988.
760	Journal of Molecular Biology (Serial).
709	Arthur Kornberg. For the love of enzymes: The odeyssy of a biochemist. Harvard: 1989.
692	Benjamin Lewin. Gene expression. 2 vols. Wiley: 1974.
686	Advances in Genetics (Serial).
629	James D. Watson et al. Molecular biology of the gene. 4th ed. Benjamin/ Cummings: 1987.
601	Advances in Human Genetics (Serial).
589	Cell (Serial).
579	J. R. S. Fincham et al. Fungal genetics. Blackwell: 1963 or later ed.

Basic Level

567	Progress in Nucleic Acid Research and Molecular Biology (Serial).

554 James F. Crow. Genetics notes: An introduction to genetics. 8th ed. Macmillan: 1983.

553 Karl Drlica. Understanding DNA and gene cloning: A guide for the curious. Wiley: 1984 or any later ed.

455 Jeffrey H. Miller. Experiments in molecular genetics. Cold Spring Harbor Laboratory: 1972.

442 Genetics: Readings from Scientific American. Freeman: 1981.

439 Bruce Alberts et al. Molecular biology of the cell. 2nd ed. Garland: 1989.

435 M. Ashburner and E. Novitski, eds. The genetics and biology of drosophila. Academic Press: 1976.

431 James A. Shapiro. Mobile genetic elements. Academic Press: 1983.

380 Morgan Harris. Cell culture and somatic variation. Holt, Rinehart and Winston: 1964.

361 William Stansfield. Schaum's outline of theory and problems of genetics. McGraw-Hill: 1969.

359 Molecular and Cellular Biology (Serial).

353 Nucleic Acids Research (Serial).

348 Biochemical Genetics (Serial).

346 Heredity (Serial).

344 Dan L. Lindsley and E. H. Grell. Genetic variations of drosophila melanogaster. Washington: 1968.

339 Genetic Engineering: Principles and Methods (Serial).

324 Chromosoma (Serial).

323 Mark Ptashne. A genetic switch: Gene control and phage (lambda). Blackwell Scientific: 1986.

321 Jeffrey C. Hall et al. Genetic neurobiology. MIT Press: 1982.

321 Ernst-Ludwig Winnacker. From genes to clones: Introduction to gene technology (Horst Ibelgaufts, trans.). VCH: 1987.

Instructional Level

302 Genetic variations of drosophila melanogaster (Catalog).

301 The EMBO Journal (Serial).

298 Molecular and General Genetics (Serial).

293 James D. Watson. The double helix: A personal account of the discovery of the structure of DNA (Gunther S. Stent, ed.). Norton: 1980. (This ed. only.)

292 Behavior Genetics (Serial).

289 Gene (Serial).

281 Raymond L. Rodriguez and Robert C. Tait. Recombinant DNA techniques: An introduction. Benjamin/Cummings: 1983.

274 Recombinant DNA Technical Bulletin (Serial).

247 Roger W. Hendrix, ed. Lambda II. Cold Spring Harbor Laboratory: 1983.

243 Louis Levine. Papers in genetics: A book of readings. C. V. Mosby: 1971.

229 Trends in Genetics (Serial).

223 Freddy B. Christiansen and Marcus W. Feldman. Population genetics. Blackwell Scientific: 1986.

214 Benjamin Lewin. Genes IV. Oxford: 1990.

206 Raymond L. Rodriguez and David T. Denhardt, eds. Vectors: A survey of molecular cloning vectors and their uses. Butterworths: 1988.

203 Human Genetics (Serial).

194   Genes and Development (Serial).
179   Daniel L. Hartl and Andrew G. Clark. Principles of population genetics. 2nd ed. Sinauer Assoc.: 1989.
175   Scott F. Gilbert. Developmental biology. 2nd ed. Sinauer Assoc.: 1988.
166   Alexander Alland, Jr. Evolution and human behavior: An introduction to Darwinian anthropology. 2nd ed. Doubleday-Anchor: 1973.
165   Monroe W. Strickberger. Genetics. 3rd ed. Macmillan: 1985.

Research Level

160   Developmental Genetics (Serial).
158   James Darnell, Harvey Lodish, and David Baltimore. Molecular cell biology. Scientific American Books: 1990.
151   Drosophila Information Service (Serial).
150   David T. Suzuki et al. An introduction to genetic analysis. 4th ed. Freeman: 1989.
141   Journal of Molecular and Applied Genetics (Serial).
126   Japanese journal of genetics (Serial).
112   Elof Axel Carlson. Human genetics. Heath: 1984.
105   Stephen J. O'Brien, ed. Genetic maps. (Imprint varies; must have latest ed.)
102   Edward H. Simon and Joseph Grossfield. The challenge of genetics. Addison-Wesley: 1971.
90   Daniel L. Hartl, David Freifelder, and Leon A. Snyder. Basic genetics. Jones and Bartlett: 1988.
89   Soviet Genetics (Serial).
87   Veikko Sorsa. Chromosome maps of drosophila. CRC Press: 1988.
79   Genomics (Serial).
73   D. B. Roberts. Drosophila: A practical approach. IRL Press: 1986.
60   Journal of Neurogenetics (Serial).
51   Peter J. Russell. Genetics. 2nd ed. Scott-Foresman: 1990.
49   Ronald W. Davis, David Botstein, and John R. Roth. Advanced bacterial genetics: A manual of genetic engineering. Cold Spring Harbor Laboratory: 1980.
46   Neil A. Campbell. Biology. 2nd ed. Benjamin/Cummings: 1990.
29   Joseph Sambrook, E. F. Fritsch, and T. Maniatis. Molecular cloning: A laboratory manual. 2nd ed. Cold Spring Harbor Laboratory: 1989.
15   Franklin W. Stahl. Genetic recombination: Thinking about it in phage and fungi. Freeman: 1979.

Mathematics

Selectors: *Mathematics*

Agus Permadi, Librarian
Center for Scientific Documentation and Information
Jakarta, Indonesia

Mathematics/Physics

Rhea Mihalisin, Senior Literature Resources Assoicate
Literature Resources Center
Merck and Company Laboratories
Blue Bell, PA

Minimal Level

1963 M. Abramowitz and I. A. Stegun, eds. Handbook of mathematical functions with formulas, graphs, and mathematical tables. GPO: 1964 or later ed.
1426 McGraw encyclopedia of science and technology: An international reference work in twenty volumes including an index.   7th ed. McGraw-Hill: 1992.
1277 CRC handbook of chemistry and physics. CRC Press: 1977– .
1169 Carl B. Boyer. A history of mathematics. Wiley: 1968 or later ed.
1115 Glenn James and Robert C. James, eds. Mathematics dictionary. Digest Press: 1942 or later ed.
1100 Scientific American (Serial).
1100 Stephen W. Hawking. A brief history of time: From the big bang to black holes. Bantam: 1988.
1063 James S. Trefil. From atoms to quarks: An introduction to the strange world of particle physics. Scribner: 1980.
1010 Kiyosi Ito, ed. Encyclopedic dictionary of mathematics by the Mathematical Society of Japan. MIT Press: 1987.
1007 The American Mathematical Monthly (Serial).
937 American Journal of Physics (Serial).
915 Gary Zukav. The dancing Wu Li masters: An overview of the new physics. Morrow: 1979 or later ed.
914 General science index (Serial).
850 E. T. Bell. The development of mathematics. McGraw-Hill: 1940 or later ed.
835 Kosaku Yosida. Functional analysis. Springer-Verlag: 1965.
790 Charles Kittel. Introduction to solid state physics. Wiley: 1953 or later ed.
767 E.V. Condon and Hugh Odishaw, eds. Handbook of physics. McGraw-Hill: 1967.
757 P. G. Francis. Mathematics for chemists. Chapham and Hall: 1984.
729 Herbert John Ryser. Combinatorial mathematics. Wiley: 1963.

Basic Level

714 Physics Teacher (Serial).

699   Walter Rudin. Real and complex analysis. McGraw-Hill: 1966 or later ed.
685   Michael Riordan. Hunting of the quark: A true story of modern physics. Simon and Shuster: 1987.
603   William F. Lucas, ed. Modules in applied mathematics. Springer-Verlag: 1983.
602   Bernard R. Gelbaum and James G. March. Mathematics for the social and behavioral sciences: Probability, calculus, and statistics. Saunders: 1969.
601   Nathan Grier Parke. Guide to the literature of mathematics and physics including related works on engineering science. McGraw-Hill: 1947 or later ed.
594   Reviews of Modern Physics (Serial).
585   Physical Review Letters (Serial).
583   Jonathan L. Mayo. Superconductivity: The threshold of a new technology. Tab Books: 1988.
559   Elie M..Dick. Current information sources in mathematics: An annotated guide to books and periodicals (1960-1972). Libraries Unlimited: 1973.
549   The College Mathematics Journal (Serial).
528   Taro Yamane. Mathematics for economists: An elementary survey. Prentice-Hall: 1962.
522   D. T. Whiteside, ed. The mathematical papers of Isaac Newton. 6 vols. Cambridge University Press: 1967-1981.
522   J. Thewlis et al., eds. Encyclopaedic dictionary of physics. Pergamon: 1961-64.
508   Physics Abstracts (Serial).
503   Randy Simon and Andrew Smith. Superconductors: Conquering technology's new frontier. Plenum Press: 1988.
491   George Gamow. Thirty years that shook physics: The story of quantum theory. Doubleday: 1966.
487   M. Richardson. Fundamentals of mathematics. Macmillan: 1941 or any later ed.
464   Ronald S. Calinger, ed. Classics of mathematics. Moore: 1980.
456   A. R. Dorling, ed. Use of mathematical literature. Butterworths: 1977.
433   Edgardo Browne. Table of radioactive isotopes. Wiley: 1986.

Instructional Level

406   Mehdi Behzad and Gary Chartrand. Introduction to the theory of graphs. Allyn and Bacon: 1971.
398   James W. Armstrong. Elements of mathematics. Macmillan: 1970 or later ed.
391   Mary L. Boas. Mathematical methods in the physical sciences. Wiley: 1983.
381   K. Kuratowski. Topology (translation of French text). Academic Press: 1966-68.
376   Barbara Kirsch Schaefer. Using the mathematical literature: A practical guide. Dekker: 1979.
361   Joseph R. Shoenfield. Mathematical logic. Addison-Wesley: 1967.
324   Advances in Mathematics (Serial).
310   Joseph W. Dauben. The history of mathematics from antiquity to the present: A selected bibliography. Garland: 1985.
306   Journal of Fluid Mechanics (Serial).

300	L. Kuipers and R. Timman, eds. Handbook of mathematics. Pergamon Press: 1969.
298	P. Dembowski. Finite geometries. Springer-Verlag: 1968.
295	C. I. Palmer and S. F. Bibb. Practical mathematics: Being the essentials of arithmetic, geometry, algebra and trigonometry. Parts I-IV. McGraw-Hill: 1912 or later ed.
295	Encyclopaedia of mathematics: An updated and annotated translation of the Soviet "Mathematical encyclopaedia." 10 vols. and index. Kluwer Academic Publications.: 1988-1994.
293	Granino A. Korn and Theresa M. Korn. Manual of mathematics. McGraw-Hill: 1967.
289	G. W. C. Kaye, et al., compilers. Tables of physical and chemical constants and some mathematical functions. Longman: 1986 or later ed.
278	Max Born and Emil Wolf. Principles of optics: Electromagnetic theory of propagation, interference and diffraction of light. 6th ed. Pergamon: 1980.
270	Francis W. Sears. Thermodynamics, kinetic theory, and statistical thermodynamics. 3rd ed. Addison-Wesley: 1975.
260	George B. Arfken. Mathematical methods for physicists. 3rd ed. Academic Press: 1985.
217	R.D. Parks, ed. Superconductivity. M. Dekker: 1969.
210	Witold Nowacki. Thermoelasticity (translation of Polish text). Pergamon: 1962 or later ed.

Research Level

208	Transactions of the Moscow Mathematical Society (Serial).
195	Georg von Freiherr Vega. Seven place logarithmic tables of numbers and trigonometrical functions. Westermann: 1896 or any later ed.
191	George Gamow. Mr. Tompkins in paperback. Cambridge: 1967.
187	Physica C.: Superconductivity (Serial).
186	Zentralblatt für Mathematik und ihre Grenzgebiete (Serial).
165	Y.G. Evtushenko. Numerical optimization techniques. Optimization Software: 1985.
161	A.C. Rose-Innes. Low temperature laboratory techniques: The use of liquid helium in the laboratory. 2nd ed. English Universities Press: 1973.
154	William R. Leo. Techniques for nuclear and particle physics experiments: A how-to approach. Springer-Verlag: 1987.
141	C. A. Truesdell. Continuum mechanics. Gordon and Breach: 1965.
132	J. Hano. Manifolds and Lie groups: Papers in honor of Yozo Matsushima. Birkhauser: 1981.
120	Zeitschrift für Physik D: Atoms, Molecules, and Clusters (Serial).
97	Soviet Journal of Particles and Nuclei (Serial).
84	David Halliday et al. Fundamentals of physics. 2nd ed. Wiley: 1986.
75	Physics Briefs (Physikalische Berichte) (Serial).
67	W. Ledermann. Introduction to group theory. Barnes and Noble: 1973.
57	I. M. James, ed. The mathematical works of J. H. C. Whitehead. Macmillan: 1963.
22	Teresa Rickards; R.C. Denney, and Stephen Foster, eds. Cambridge illustrated thesaurus of physics. Cambridge University Press: 1984. (Also published as Barnes and Noble thesaurus of physics)

17   Carl Clifton Faith. Algebra (Vol.1: Rings, modules and categories; Vol. 2: Ring theory). Springer-Verlag: 1973 or later ed.

16   Siegfried Flhugge. Handbuch der Physik: Encyclopedia of physics. Springer: 1955. (English, French, or German)

11   American Mathematical Society Translations (Serial).

Policy Studies

Selector: *Policy Studies 1*

Ellen Isenstein, Associate Librarian for Reference and
    Collection Development
John F. Kennedy School of Government
Harvard University
Cambridge, MA

Policy Studies 2

Peter Malanchuk, Africana and Political Science Bibliographer
University Libraries
University of Florida
Gainesvelle, FL

Minimal Level

2759   John Naisbitt. Megatrends: Ten new directions transforming our lives.
       Warner: 1982.
2732   Statistical Abstract of the United States. GPO; annual.
1618   Michael Barone et al. Almanac of American politics. (1972-)
1587   Congressional Quarterly Weekly Report. (Serial).
1542   William J. Wilson. The truly disadvantaged: The inner city, the under-class
       and public policy. University of Chicago: 1987.
1492   Robert Reich. The next American frontier. Times Books: 1983.
1484   John Eatwell, Murray Milgate, Peter Newman, eds. The new Palgrave: A
       dictionary of economics 4 vols. Stockton Press: 1987.
1388   World Development Report. Oxford ; annual.
1368   Who's who in American politics. Bowker; annual.
1217   Kevin Phillips. The politics of rich and poor: Wealth and the American
       electorate in the Reagan aftermath. Random House: 1990.
1189   William W. Lammers. Public policy and the aging. CQ Press: 1983.
1077   Public Administration Review. (Serial).
969   George Will. Statecraft as soulcraft: What government does. Simon and
       Schuster: 1983.
961   Public Affairs Information Service. PAIS Bulletin. (Serial).
681   F. Stevens Redburn and Terry F. Buss. Responding to America's homeless:
       Public policy alternatives. Praeger: 1986.
676   Steven Kelman. Making public policy: A hopeful view of American gov-
       ernment. Basic Books: 1987.
600   Raymond A. Bauer and Kenneth J. Gergen, eds. The study of policy for-
       mation. Macmillan, Free Press: 1968.
594   Edith Stokey and Richard Zeckhauser. A primer for policy analysis. Norton:
       1978.
540   Arnold J. Meltsner. Policy analysts in the bureaucracy. University of
       California Press: 1976.

Basic Level

465   Jacques S. Gansler. Affording defense. MIT Press: 1989.
454   Martin Linsky. How the press affects federal policymaking: Six case stud-
        ies. Norton: 1986.
449   David P. Farrington, Lloyd E. Ohlin, James Q. Wilson. Understanding and
        controlling crime: Toward a new research strategy. Springer-Verlag: 1986.
448   Earl R. Kruschke and Byron M. Jackson. The public policy dictionary.
        ABC-CLIO: 1987.
431   CIS. Index to Publications of the United States Congress (Serial).
419   Paul T. Menzel. Strong medicine: The ethical rationing of health care.
        Oxford: 1989.
409   John W. Sloan. Public policy in Latin America: A compararive survey.
        University of Pittsburgh Press: 1984.
387   David Runkel, ed. Campaign for president: The managers look at '88.
        Auburn House: 1989.
380   Craig Liske, William Loehr, John McCamant, eds. Comparative public
        policy: Issues, theories, and methods.   Sage Publications/Halsted Press,
        Wiley: 1975.
369   William E. James. Asian development: Economic success and policy
        lessons. Wisconsin: 1989.
366   Davis B. Bobrow and John S. Dryzek. Policy analysis by design.
        University of Pittsburgh Press: 1987.
342   Merilee S. Grindle, ed. Politics and policy implementation in the Third
        World. Princeton University Press: 1980.
328   Daniel B. Baker, ed. Political quotations: A collection of notable sayings
        on politics from antiquity through 1989. Gale: 1990.
323   Jack M. Treadway. Public policymaking in the American states. Praeger:
        1985.
318   Policy Sciences (Serial).
311   Peter William House and Roger D. Shyull. Rush to policy: Using analytic
        techniques in public sector decision making. Transaction Books: 1988.
293   Marguerite Ross Barnett and James A. Hefner, eds. Public policy for the
        Black community: Strategies and perspectives. Alfred: 1976.
276   Paul S. Goodman and Lee S. Sproull. Technology and organizations.
        Jossey-Bass: 1990.
272   William N. Dunn. Public policy analysis: An introduction. Prentice-Hall:
        1981.
270   William B. Farley and Frederick Mosteller, eds. Statistics and public policy.
        Addison-Wesley: 1977.

Instructional Level

254   Brian W. Hogwood and B. Guy Peters. The pathology of public policy.
        Oxford Clarendon/Oxford University Press: 1985.
244   American Review of Public Administration (Serial).
242   Peter H. Merkel. The Federal Republic of Germany at forty. New York
        University Press: 1989.
241   Stuart S. Nagel. Contemporary public policy analysis. University of
        Alabama Press: 1984.

233   Duncan MacRae, Jr. and James A. Wilde. Policy analysis for public decisions. Duxbury Press: 1979.

227   Selig Harrison and K. Subrahmanyam, eds.. Superpower rivalry in the Indian Ocean: Indian and American perspectives. Oxford University Press: 1989.

218   Foundation for Public Affairs. Public Interest Profiles (Serial).

218   The Indian Journal of Public Administration (Serial).

216   Estelle James and Gail Benjamin. Public policy and private education in Japan. St. Martin's Press: 1988.

213   Richard L. Siegel. Comparing public policies: United States, Soviet Union, and Europe. Dorsey Press: 1977.

208   James E. Anderson, David W. Brady, and Charles Bullock III. Public policy and politics in America. Duxbury Press: 1978.

198   Arlene Zarembka. The urban housing crisis: Social, economic, and legal issues and proposals. Greenwood Press: 1990.

191   Alan R. Anderson and Seymour Sudman, eds. Public policy and marketing thought: Proceedings for the ninth Paul D. Converse Symposium. American Marketing Association: 1976.

185   Mark Bennett. Public policy and industrial development: The case of the Mexican auto parts industry. Westview Press: 1986.

181   Opinion Research Service. American Public Opinion Data (Microform).

181   Edward Miles, Robert Pealy, and Robert Stokes, eds. Natural resources economics and policy applications essays in honor of James A. Crutchfield. Institute for Marine Studies, University of Washington Press: 1986.

162   Steven Gendel, ed. Agricultural bioethics: Implications of agricultural biotechnology. Iowa State University: 1990.

155   M.L. Truu, ed. Public policy and the South African economy: Essays in memory of Desmond Hobart Houghton. Oxford University Press: 1976.

139   Dennis J. Palumbo and Donald J. Calista, eds. Implementation and the policy process: Opening up the black box. Greenwood Press: 1990.

134   University Publications of America. Major studies and issue briefs of the Congressional Research Service (Microform).

Research Level

123   Lucius J. Barker, ed. New perspectives in American politics. National Political Science Review, vol.1. Transaction Publications: 1989.

123   W.J. Conroy. Challenging the boundaries of reform: Socialism in Burlington. Temple: 1990.

112   Michael J. Dover and Brain Croft. Getting tough: Public policy and the management of pesticide resistance. World Resources Institute: 1984.

108   Stuart S. Nagel. Basic literature in policy studies: A comprehensive bibliography. JAI Press: 1984.

105   Andrew Graham and Anthony Seldon, eds. Government and economies in the postwar world: Economic policies and comparative performance, 1945–85. Routledge: 1990.

105   David Brian Robertson and Dennis R. Judd. The development of American public policy: The structure of policy restraint. Scott, Foresman: 1989.

95   George M. Guess and Paul G. Farnham. Cases in public policy analysis. Longman: 1989.

94   A. Evers et al, eds. Healthy policy at the local level. Westview Press: 1990.

85   National Newspaper Index (Serial).

79   Baron Dennis Lloyd of Hampstead. Public policy: A comparative study in English and French law. University of London, Athlone Press: 1953.

72   Marsha A. Chandler and William M. Chandler. Public policy and provincial politics. McGraw-Hill Ryerson: 1979.

64   Martin Burch and Bruce Wood. Public policy in Britain. Oxford/Blackwell: 1989.

37   Summary of World Broadcasts. 4 parts. Monitoring Service of the British Broadcasting Corporation.

35   Canada. Parliament. House of Commons. House of Commons Debates. 1951- .

16   Congressional Information Service. U.S. Congressional Committee Prints [from 1830 through 91st Congress, 1st session, 1969]. Greenwood Press: 1976 (Microform).

11   France. Ministère de l'environnement. L'État de l'environnement.

8   ABC News Transcripts Research Publications (Microform).

8   Censo General de Poblacion y Vivienda. Mexico, Secretaria de Programacion y Presupuesto, Coordinacion General de los Servicios Nacionales de Estadistica, Geografia e Informatica: 1981.

2   Tayo Fashoyin. Public policy and labour markets in the Ecowas: A case study of the alien expulsion order by Nigeria, 1983. (Working Paper Series no. 2) Department of Industrial Relationsand Personnel Management, University of Lagos: 1985)

1   El Salvador: The making of a U.S. policy, 1977–1984. National Security Archives: 1989 (Microform).

APPENDIX B

Additional Brief Tests

These are tests not reproduced in the present volume. Selectors have been credited. This does not necessarily imply their endorsement of the brief-test methodology in general or the particular uses to which their selections have been put.

Titles	Selectors
African-American Studies 1	Marie V. Jackson
African-American Studies 2	Marta Dragalin
American Women's History	Lisa J. Bachelder
Anarchism in the United States	Ali Munif Seden
Archeology of American Southwest	Ruth Baker
Architectural History (American Emphasis)	John Manton
Art Photography	Michael Rhodes
Arthurian Literature	Christine Le
Astronomy	Deborah G. Lovett
Biblical Studies	Sandra L. Stump
Biochemisty	Meg E. Spencer
Byzantine Studies	Lauris Olson
Chinese History	Erin Coldren
Christian Religion	M. Judith Bonenberger
Classical Music (Scores)	William Ghezzi
Computer Science	Susan Keller
Contemporary Mexican Literature	Barbara Duno
Criminology	Modest Iwasiw
Developmental Psychology	Victoria M. McGlone
Ecology	Robin N. Sinn
Economics 1	Dr. Roger M. McCain
Economics 2	Mary Comerford
Eighteenth-Century English Fiction	Kathleen H. Turner
Ethics	Brian Simboli
Feminist Theology	Debra B. Rill
German Colonial Africa	Tim McCarthy

Titles *(continued)*

Titles	Selectors
German Literature (Age of Goethe)	Fianna Holt
Herbs and Herbal Medicine	Karen R. Foster
History of Technology	Ed Deegan
Intellectual Property 1	Victoria A. Brown
Intellectual Property 2	Linda Herko Onorato
Interior Design	Drew Alfgren
International Business Law	Connie Smith
Jewish Holocaust, 1939-1945	Susan A. Ottignon
Jewish Law	Wendie H. Gabay
Jewish Women's Studies	Jan Dickler
Library and Information Science	Kenneth Garson
Linguistics	Ellen Landsburg
Manufacturing Planning and Production Control	Howard Friedman
Medical Ethics	Allie Fraser
Medieval History	Van Edwards
Medieval Literature	Janet Lindenmuth
Middle Eastern Studies	Dr. J. Dennis Hyde
Modern American Literature	Minda Hart
Modern Cinema (Films)	Jennifer Teefy
Modern European Jewish History	Roger S. Kohn
Modernist and Postmodern American Poetry	Rudy Meixell
Musicology (Books)	Patrick Setzer
Native American Literature	Gisele Stout
Nigerian Literature	Annette DeFuso
Nineteenth-Century Russian Literature	Sergei Archipov
Oncology	Jill A. Spector
Opera (Books and Scores)	Nancy Adams
Philosophy 1	Martin Mills
Philosophy 2	Dr. Richard Stichler
Philosophy of Science	George R. Lezenby
Policy Studies 3	Rosemary McAndrew
Policy Studies 4	Mary Lynn Morris
Popular Music: Rock Era (Books)	Vito Shimkus
Post-Impressionism in Art	Janet E. Panzer
Postmodern American Novel	Haihua Chang
Primatology	Janet E. Taylor
Psychohistory	Afshin Nili
Roman Law	Stephanie Edwards
Social Theory	C. Suzanne Cole
Sociology of the Deaf	Judith Finestone
The Reformation	Paula Hering
Toxicology	Jamie Alexander
Twentieth-Century British History	John Culshaw
Twentieth-Century Russian History	Sandra Naydock
U.S. Constitutional History	Thomas Fasching
U.S. Constitutional Law	MacFarlane Hoffman
Victorian Literature	Christopher Clifford
Women's Studies	Helen Bauer
Workplace Democracy	Tim Siftar

Bibliography

Abell, Millicent D. (1987). The Conspectus: Issues and questions. *In* Association of Research Libraries, Minutes of the 109th Meeting. *NCIP: Means to an End.* Washington, DC: ARL. 26–30.

Atkinson, Ross. (1986). The language of the levels: Reflections on the communication of collection development policy. *College and Research Libraries* 47: 140–149.

Baker, Sharon L., and F. Wilfrid Lancaster. (1991). Collection evaluation: Materials-centered approaches. In *The Measurement and Evaluation of Library Services.* Washington, DC: Information Resources Press. 39–78.

Benaud, Claire-Lise, and Sever Bordeianu. (1992). Evaluating the humanities collections in an academic library using the RLG Conspectus. *Acquisitions Librarian* 7: 125–136.

Bensman, Stephen J. (1982). Bibliometric laws and library usage as social phenomena. *Library Research* 4: 279–312.

Bushing, Mary. (1992). The Conspectus: Possible process and useful product for the ordinary library. *Acquisitions Librarian* 7: 81–95.

Christiansen, Dorothy E., C. Roger Davis, and Jutta Reed-Scott. (1983). Guide to collection evaluation through use and user studies. *Library Resources and Technical Services* 28: 432–440.

Coale, Robert P. (1965). Evaluation of a research library collection: Latin American colonial history. *Library Quarterly* 35: 173–184.

Coffey, Jim. (1992). The RLG Conspectus: What's in the numbers. *Acquisitions Librarian* 7: 65–80.

Coleman, Jim. (1985). Verification studies: Design and implementation. *College and Research Libraries News* 46: 338–340.

_____. (1992). The RLG Conspectus: A history of its development and influence and a prognosis for its future. *Acquisitions Librarian* 7: 25–43.

Crandlemire, Debbie, and Paul Otto. (1988). The development of Canadian Conspectus online. *Canadian Journal of Information Science [Revue Canadienne des Sciences de l'Information]* 13: 110–119.

Farrell, David, and Jutta Reed-Scott. (1989). The North American Collections Inventory Project—Implications for the future of coordinated management of research collections. *Library Resources and Technical Services* 33: 15–28.

Ferguson, Anthony W. (1992). The Conspectus and cooperative collection development: What it can and cannot do. *Acquisitions Librarian* 7: 105–14.

Ferguson, Anthony W., Joan Grant, and Joel S. Rutstein. (1988). The RLG Conspecutus—Its uses and benefits. *College and Research Libraries* 49: 197–206.

Forcier, Peggy. (1988). Building collections together—The Pacific Northwest Conspectus. *Library Journal* 113: 43–45.

Futas, Elizabeth and Sheila S. Intner, eds. (1985). Collection evaluation. *Library Trends* 33:3.

Gaughan, Thomas M. (1991a). AL Asides—Challenge: Personal litmuses. *American Libraries* 22: 15.

_____, (1991b). AL Asides—Challenge: Your personal litmuses. *American Libraries* 22: 474–475.

Gorden, Raymond L. (1977). *Unidimensional scaling of social variables: concepts and procedures.* New York: Free Press.

Grant, Joan. (1992). The Conspectus: An important component of a comprehensive collection management program. *Acquisitions Librarian* 7: 97–103.

Gwinn, Nancy E., and Paul H. Mosher. (1983). Coordinating collection development: The RLG Conspectus. *College and Research Libraries* 44: 128–140.

Hall, Blaine H. (1985). *Collection assessment manual for college and university libraries.* Phoenix, AZ: Oryx.

Hanger, Stephen. (1987). Collection development in the British Library—The role of the RLG Conspectus. *Journal of Librarianship* 19: 89–107.

Heaney, Henry. (1990). Western European interest in Conspectus. *Libri* 40: 28–32.

Henige, David. (1987). Epistemological dead end and ergonomic disaster? The North American Collections Inventory Project. *Journal of Academic Librarianship* 13: 209–213.

Henri, James. (1989). The RLG Conspectus Down Under—Report on an Australian seminar, the RLG Conspectus and Collection Evaluation. *Library Acquisitions: Practice and Theory* 13: 73–80.

Jakubs, Deborah L., ed. (1989). *Qualitative collection analysis: The Conspectus methodology.* SPEC Kit 151. Office of Management Services, Association of Research Libraries.

Johnson, Susan W. (1991). The WLN Conspectus service and collection assessment. *Information Retrieval and Library Automation* 26(11): 1–4.

Kaag, Cynthia Stewart. (1991). *Collection evaluation techniques; A short, selective, practical, current annotated bibliography 1980–1990.* Chicago: American Library Association.

Kreyche, Michael. (1989). BCL3 and NOTIS: An automated collection analysis project. *Library Acquisitions: Practice and Theory* 13: 323–328.

Larson, Jeffry. (1984). The RLG French Literature Collection Assessment Project. *Collection Management* 6: 97–114.

Lucas, Thomas A. (1990). Verifying the Conspectus: Problems and progress. *College and Research Library News* 51: 199–201.

MacEwan, Bonnie. (1993). An overview of collection assessment and evaluation. In *Collection management for the 1990s,* ed. Joseph J. Branin. Chicago: American Library Association. 95–105.

McGrath, William E., and Nancy B. Nuzzo. (1991). Existing collection strength and shelflist count correlations in RLG's Conspectus for Music. *College and Research Libraries* 52: 194–203.

McIver, John P., and Edward G. Carmines. (1981). *Unidimensional scaling.* Beverly Hills, CA: Sage Publications (Sage University Paper 24).

Machlup, Fritz. (1978). Our libraries: Can we measure their holdings and acquisitions? *In* Fritz Machlup, Kenneth Leeson et al. *Information through the printed word: The dissemination of scholarly, scientific, and intellectual knowledge.*, vol. 3: *Libraries.* New York: Praeger. 192–196.

Marshall, Jessica. (1994). Inside publishing (Hard copy). *Lingua Franca* 5(1): 17–18.

Matheson, Ann. (1987). The planning and implementation of Conspectus in Scotland. *Journal of Librarianship* 19: 141–151.

_____. (1990). The Conspectus experience. *Journal of Librarianship* 22: 171–182.

Metz, Paul. (1983). *The landscape of literatures: Use of subject collections in a university library.* Chicago: American Library Association.

_____. (1990). Bibliometrics: Library use and citation studies. In *Academic libraries; Research perspectives,* ed. Mary Jo Lynch and Arthur Young. Chicago: American Library Association. 143–164.

Miller, Robert C. (1987). NCIP in the United States. *In* Association of Research Libraries, Minutes of the 109th Meeting. *NCIP: Means to an End.* Washington, DC: ARL. 11–13.

Mosher, Paul H. (1984). Quality and library collections: New directions in research and practice in collection evaluation. In *Advances in Librarianship,* v. 13. Orlando, FL: Academic Press. 211–238.

_____. (1985). The nature and uses of the RLG verification studies. *College and Research Library News* 46: 338–340.

_____. (1990). Collaborative interdependence—The human dimensions of the Conspectus. *IFLA Journal* 16: 327–331.

Newby, Jill, and Patricia Promis. (1990). Collection assessment using the RLG Conspectus. *Collection Management* 13: 1–14.

Nisonger, Thomas E. (1992). *Collection evaulation in academic libraries; a literature guide and annotated bibliography.* Englewood, CO: Libraries Unlimited.

Oberg, Larry R. (1988). Evaluating the Conspectus approach for smaller library collections. *College and Research Libraries* 49: 187–196.

OCLC [Online Computer Library Center]. (1989). *OCLC/AMIGOS Collection Analysis CD User Guide.* Dublin, OH: OCLC.

_____. (1994). *OCLC Annual Report 1993/94.* Dublin, OH: OCLC.

Powell, Nancy, and Mary Bushing. (1992). *WLN collection assessment manual.* 4th ed. Lacy, WA: WLN.

Pratt, Allan D. (1975). The analysis of library statistics. *Library Quarterly* 45: 275–286.

RLG [Research Libraries Group]. (1987). The most-cataloged books in RLIN: A mid-1987 sampling. *Operations update* 43: 23–24.

_____. (n.d) Expanded collection intensity indicators for assessing non-research collections. Mountain View, CA: RLG.

Sanders, Nancy P., Edward T. O'Neill, and Stuart L. Weibel. (1988). Automated collection analysis using the OCLC and RLG bibliographic databases. *College and Reserach Libraries* 49: 305–314.

Schenck, William. (1990). The year's work in acquisitions and collection development, 1988. *Library Resources and Technical Services* 34: 326–337.

Seay, Jerry. (1992). The Conspectus: A selected annotated bibliography. *Acquisitions Librarian* 7: 177–189.

Siverson, Scott E. (1992). Fine-tuning the dull roar of Conspectors: Using scaled bibliographies to assess collection level. *Acquisitions Librarian* 7: 45–64.

Stephens, Dennis. (1992). Multi-type library collection planning in Alaska: A Conspectus-based approach. *Acquisitions Librarian* 7: 137–56.

Stielow, Frederick J., and Helen R. Tibbo. (1989). Collection analysis in modern librarianship: A stratified, multidimensional model. *Collection Management* 11(3/4): 73–91.

Strauch, Katina, and Richard J. Wood. (1992). Conclusions. *Acquisitions Librarian* 7: 191–192.

Thatcher, Sanford G. (1995). The crisis in scholarly communication. *Chronicle of Higher Education* 41(25, March 3): B1–B2.

Treadwell, Jane, and Charles Spornick. (1991). Translating the Conspectus: Presenting collection evaluation results to administrators. *Collection Management* 6: 45–59.

Underwood, Kent. (1992). Developing supplemental guidelines for music: A case report. *Acquisitions Librarian* 7: 157–168.

Wallace, Danny P., and Bert R. Boyce. (1989). Holdings as a measure of journal value. *Library and Information Science Research* 11: 59–71.

White, Howard D. (1987). Computer techniques for studying coverage, overlap, and gaps in collections. *Journal of Academic Librarianship* 12: 365–371.

_____. (1988). Evaluating subject collections. *Annual Review of OCLC Research July 1987–June 1988*. Dublin, OH: OCLC. 46–48.

_____. (1992a). The impact of cooperative automation on three college libraries: Levels of monograph collecting. Philadelphia, PA: College of Information Studies, Drexel University.

_____. (1992b). Reference works, databases, and the repertoire. *In* Howard D. White, Marcia J. Bates, and Patrick Wilson. *For information specialists: Interpretations of reference and bibliographic work*. Norwood, NJ: Ablex. 27–78.

Wiemers, Eugene et. al. (1984). Collection evaluation: A practical guide to the literature. *Library Acquisitions: Practice and Theory* 8: 65-76.

Wood, Richard J. (1992). A conspectus of the Conspectus. *Acquisitions Librarian* 7: 5–23.

Wood, Richard J., and Katina Strauch, eds. (1993). *Collection assessment: A look at the RLG Conspectus*. New York: Haworth Press. (Also published in 1992 as *Acquisitions Librarian* 7: 1–192.)

Index

Association of Research Libraries, 4

Bibliometrics, 13, 120
Brief tests
  administration of, 50–51, 55–56, 91, 111–13
  automation of, 13, 147–49
  bias in, 41
  blocks of titles in, 40, 46
  Byzantine studies test, 44–45
  calibration with RLG scale, 46, 123–24
  cheating in, 41
  checklists and, 31, 35, 49–50, 107–18
  client–centered measures and, 7, 116
  collection–centered measure, 7, 116
  combining, 40, 90–91
  consortia, use in, 6, 89–105
    pooling effect, 91–94, 97, 103, 105
  construction of, 34, 36, 40–41, 42–43, 73–74, 126–32
  criticisms of, 48–49, 81–82
  cumulativeness and, 12, 37–38, 39–40, 56, 58–59, 118
  cutpoints in, 124, 126–29, 131, 134–35, 151
  difficulty effect, 9–12, 36
  difficulty of, 46–47, 93, 94–95, 123, 131
    controlling, 47, 123, 126–30

discrepant results, 74–75, 86–87
distinguishing levels with, 34–35, 38, 90–91, 113–14
efficiency of, 38, 56, 82, 117–18
electronic access and, 44
errors of measurement in, 57
50 percent threshold in, 37–38, 51, 149
French literature test, 91, 107–20
grading of students and, 34–35, 75, 80–81
Guttman scales and, 37, 38–40, 58
holdings counts and, 11–13, 36
interpretation of, 56–58, 61–62
interviews and, 35–36
inverse relationships, 11, 36, 125–26
language codes and, 87
librarians' behavior and, 59–61
librarians' judgments and, 3, 6, 50, 74–75, 77–78, 84–87, 114–16
libraries, types of, and, 6–7, 57–58, 60–61, 144–45
logic of, 33–36
mechanical assignment of titles, 44–47, 132–35
nature of, 3, 6, 13, 30–31, 34–38, 42–43, 47–49, 59–62, 150–51
nonconforming results, 61–62
nonprint materials and, 44
online searching for, 43–44
origin of, 8–11

overlapping test items, 63
power tests and, 36, 42, 45, 50, 58,
   114
PRISM and, 43–44
ranking titles in, 44
RLG scale and, 47–48, 145–49
scoring procedures for, 37, 51, 79–
   81, 91
selectors for, 34, 41, 42–43, 44–46,
   47, 55–56
setting levels with, 3–4, 34, 55–71
"single work" tests and, 33, 36
size of, 6, 34–35, 36, 40–41, 49, 61,
   117
sources of items for, 42–43, 55
specialization and, 36, 48, 51, 136
titles and, 6, 12–13, 49
   intuitions about titles, 45–46, 51,
      138–39
trials, 55–56, 82
validating, 49–50, 58, 62–63, 70–71
verifying levels with, 3–4, 34, 73–
   87, 114–15
WLN scale and, 4, 78–87

Collections
"long, thin collections," 61, 101,
   148
"strata" as metaphor for, 118–19
strength of, 7, 20
Conspectus
collection evaluation with, 4, 7, 39,
   73
lines, 4, 73–74, 147–48
RLG, 4
WLN, 4, 78–79, 82
Coverage of literatures, 15–17, 31, 35,
   147, 148–49

Discriminant analysis, 132–35, 151–52

Expected demand, 139, 141

Holdings counts, 12–13, 44, 48–49,
   124–26, 149
distribution of, 124–26, 131
dynamism of, 44, 149
midpoint of, 135–36
range of, 43, 124
Holdings–count scale, 123–36

cutpoints, 124, 126–29
hierarchy of values and, 49
in–print status of titles and, 142–43
perceived audience appeal and, 49
qualitative differences in levels and,
   129–30, 136–45
qualitative differences in titles and,
   145–47
RLG scale and, 123–49

Internet, 50, 111–12

National Shelflist Count, 7
North American Collections Inventory
   Project, 4

OCLC (Online Computer Library
   Center), 3, 12–13, 146–47
collection management information
   system, 13
online union catalog, 12–13, 43–44,
   50–51, 128
OCLC/AMIGOS Collection Analysis
   Compact Disk, 13, 14, 152

Pacific Northwest Conspectus, 4

RLG (Research Libraries Group), 3–4
RLG scale, 4–5, 7, 15–24, 40, 137–39,
   142–45
Basic level, 5, 21, 129
categorization and, 143
collection sizes and, 23
Comprehensive level, 5, 21–22, 34,
   129–30
cumulativeness and, 4, 14, 35, 39
distinguishing levels in, 22, 34–35,
   113–14
holdings counts and, 123–49
Instructional support level, 5, 21
language codes in, 5
levels, 5, 129–32, 136–39, 142–45
librarians' judgments and, 15
Minimal level, 5, 21, 22–24, 40–
   41, 129, 137
Minimal–level "superworks," 11,
   124, 126
multidimensionality of, 47–48
names of levels in, 20–21, 23–24,
   146

Out–of–Scope level, 5, 21, 34
politics and, 15, 20
qualitative differences in levels and,
  129–30, 136–45
qualitative differences in titles and,
  145–47
Research level, 5, 11, 21, 129, 137

Tri–College Research Project, 89–105,
  109–10

Verification studies, 15–22, 25–31
checking lists in, 18–19
compiling checklists for, 17
content of, 17, 119–20
conversion problem in, 20–22, 29
  "curve" scheme, 22
  "Gwinn–Mosher" scheme, 22
  quartile scheme, 21, 120, 129
  quintile scheme, 21–22
cumulativeness and, 18

French literature study, 10, 16–17,
  91, 107–9, 116–18, 120
laboriousness of, 25–30
length of, 17, 25–30
levels in, 17
national needs and, 30
number completed, 18, 19, 56
problems with, 15–31
resistance to, 19
sample sizes in, 19–20
Supplemental Guidelines and, 29, 30

WLN, 13–14
WLN Collection Assessment Manual,
  4, 24–25, 30, 78–79
WLN scale, 77, 78–82, 115
collection sizes and, 24–25
cumulativeness and, 14
levels, interpretation of, 79, 80–81
Minimal level and, 24–25

About the Author

HOWARD D. WHITE is a Professor in the College of Information Science and Technology at Drexel University. He has presented numerous papers and workshops, and his work has been published in journals such as *Library Quarterly, Journal of the American Society for Information Science, Library Journal*, and the *Journal of Academic Librarianship*. In 1993 he received the Research Award from the American Society for Information Science.

ISBN 0-313-29753-3

90000>

EAN

9 780313 297533

HARDCOVER BAR CODE